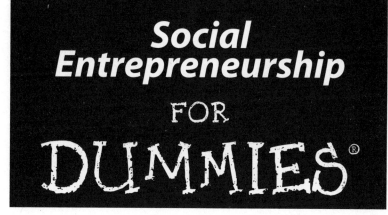

Social Entrepreneurship FOR DUMMIES®

by Mark B. Durieux, PhD,
and Robert A. Stebbins, PhD

WILEY

Wiley Publishing, Inc.

Social Entrepreneurship For Dummies®

Published by
Wiley Publishing, Inc.
111 River St.
Hoboken, NJ 07030-5774
www.wiley.com

WILEY

About the Authors

Mark B. Durieux, PhD: Mark is an applied and clinical sociologist who teaches and consults widely with community groups and the public concerning the contemporary study and practice of compassion and social entrepreneurship. He also teaches a comprehensive range of sociology courses at the university level — everything from social statistics and research methods to social psychology and leisure. But his courses in the areas of the sociology of compassion, social entrepreneurship, and grounded theory methodology are well known for their innovative content and delivery. Mark is currently collaborating with a number of extremely supportive and well-respected academic and frontline colleagues in developing and creatively extending the last three areas.

Robert A. Stebbins, PhD: Robert is faculty professor in the Department of Sociology at the University of Calgary. He has also taught at the University of Texas at Arlington and Memorial University of Newfoundland. Robert received his doctorate in sociology in 1964 from the University of Minnesota. Among his 35 books are *A Dictionary of Nonprofit Terms and Concepts* (with David H. Smith and Michael Dover) and *Serious Leisure: A Perspective for Our Time*. Robert was elected Fellow of the Academy of Leisure Sciences in 1996 and, in 1999, elected Fellow of the Royal Society of Canada. His own serious leisure includes volunteering in Calgary's French-language community. He has helped establish two social enterprises and served on the boards of directors of several others.

Dedication

To Friedel (mom); Barney (dad); Sherry (wife and very best friend); Meghan, Matthew, and Emma (fantastic children, really!); Bob Stebbins and Jaber Gubrium (super-supportive colleagues); and the truly compassionate and social entrepreneurial friends and folk I encounter daily.

—Mark Durieux

To Karin.

—Robert Stebbins

Authors' Acknowledgments

Books as complicated as this one always have a supporting cast who work behind the scenes to bring them to fruition. This book has been no different. Stacy Kennedy was our first contact with Wiley Publishing; she patiently and efficiently worked out the many details of the writing schedule and the publisher's contract. She also put us in contact with Corbin Collins, who was responsible for reworking our manuscript to fit the distinctive style of the *For Dummies* series; this book would not have been published without his extensive knowledge and experience in this area. Finally, we want to thank Elizabeth Kuball, who edited the entire text, bringing it to the polished level of publication that you're about to read, as well as Eric Corey Freed who worked behind the scenes to ensure technical accuracy and made a variety of most helpful suggestions.

Publisher's Acknowledgments

We're proud of this book; please send us your comments at http://dummies.custhelp.com. For other comments, please contact our Customer Care Department within the U.S. at 877-762-2974, outside the U.S. at 317-572-3993, or fax 317-572-4002.

Some of the people who helped bring this book to market include the following:

Acquisitions, Editorial, and Media Development

Project Editor: Elizabeth Kuball

Contributor: Corbin Collins

Acquisitions Editor: Stacy Kennedy

Copy Editor: Elizabeth Kuball

Assistant Editor: Erin Calligan Mooney

Editorial Program Coordinator: Joe Niesen

Technical Editor: Eric Corey Freed

Senior Editorial Manager: Jennifer Ehrlich

Editorial Supervisor and Reprint Editor: Carmen Krikorian

Senior Editorial Assistant: David Lutton

Editorial Assistants: Jennette ElNaggar, Rachelle Amick

Cover Photos: © iStock

Cartoons: Rich Tennant (www.the5thwave.com)

Composition Services

Project Coordinator: Katie Crocker

Layout and Graphics: Ashley Chamberlain, Yovonne Grego

Proofreaders: ConText Editorial Services, Inc.

Indexer: Cheryl Duksta

Publishing and Editorial for Consumer Dummies

Diane Graves Steele, Vice President and Publisher, Consumer Dummies

Kristin Ferguson-Wagstaffe, Product Development Director, Consumer Dummies

Ensley Eikenburg, Associate Publisher, Travel

Kelly Regan, Editorial Director, Travel

Publishing for Technology Dummies

Andy Cummings, Vice President and Publisher, Dummies Technology/General User

Composition Services

Debbie Stailey, Director of Composition Services

Contents at a Glance

Table of Contents

Part II: Establishing Your Organization 93

Introduction

. . . .

*W*elcome to *Social Entrepreneurship For Dummies!*

If you're browsing through this book, chances are good that you're more than a little worried, anxious, or frustrated about a world that is absolutely bristling with problems. Maybe you're not exactly mad as hell — yet — but on some days you feel like you're getting close. It's a good bet that you're also feeling that it's about time you stepped up to the plate and tried to make a positive difference.

Maybe you've already dipped a toe in these waters. Maybe you've volunteered, but didn't feel quite fulfilled. Volunteers tend to work on already recognized issues, whereas you, on the other hand, may be dismayed by problems that not enough others see. Or maybe the problems you see *have* been recognized, but reaction times in addressing them seem *soooo slooow* that you just have to shake your head.

Things needed to be done yesterday! *You* sense the urgency. Doesn't anybody else? Is it that others just haven't got around to it yet? Is there a lack of know-how or available resources? At this point, it doesn't much matter. Somebody's got to do something. And you have a feeling that somebody is *you*.

About This Book

If we've just sketched a portrait of you, in however rough an outline, this book is intended for you. You may not know it yet, but you're a social entrepreneur in the making.

Very simply put, a *social entrepreneur* is someone who uses business principles to address social or environmental problems. Social entrepreneurs become experts on the problems they fight — whether those are local, regional, national, or global — and, as often as not, they're visionaries. Social entrepreneurs see that we're *all* our brothers' and sisters' keepers, and they form effective organizations to carry out missions to demonstrate that in one form or another. This book walks you through what it takes to become one of these visionaries and lays out many of the principles and strategies social entrepreneurs employ, both practical and philosophical.

Conventions Used in This Book

To make this book as easy to use as we can, we try to define each new term as it comes up. We also use the following conventions:

- *Italics* are used when we introduce new terms (which we define shortly thereafter, often in parentheses).

- **Boldface** words and phrases in bulleted lists and numbered steps help you pick out the keywords at a glance.

- Web addresses, or URLs, are in a special `monofont` typeface. The link may be only one page of a larger, interesting Web site, so take advantage and explore the rest of the sites we mention in this book.

When this book was printed, some Web addresses may have needed to break across two lines of text. If that happened, rest assured that we haven't put in any extra characters (such as hyphens) to indicate the break. So, when using one of these Web addresses, just type in exactly what you see in this book, pretending as though the line break doesn't exist.

What You're Not to Read

You're busy — we know that. So if you need to skip over sections of the book, you can safely skip the sidebars and any chapters that just don't seem relevant. You can also skip anything marked by a Technical Stuff icon (for more on icons, see "Icons Used in This Book," later in this Introduction).

Foolish Assumptions

If you've read even this far, we assume the following:

- **You want to become a social entrepreneur, or at least want to know enough about it to make a decision.** You may be moving in this direction because you're concerned about the state of the environment or because you recognize that creating an organization is the best way to battle poverty, for example, or homelessness, or the issues of hunger or drinking water availability in some far-off land.

- **You don't have a lot of experience running an organization.** That's why we slow down and address many fundamental concepts that go into the effective operation of organizations.

✔ **You want to look for ways to give your existing business a social entrepreneurial slant.** You have a for-profit business and you're thinking about your corporate social responsibility and how to implement it.

✔ **You're committed to making a difference, and you're not attached to the status quo.** You're ready for change and willing to take risks to get it.

✔ **You're curious.** You want to discover more about what you don't know. You're reading this book to expand your thinking about the various ways of tackling your chosen issue.

✔ **You're willing to put some real effort into this.** You're not an armchair quarterback anymore. You realize we can't give you your social enterprise or run it for you, and we can't even cover everything you need to know in the limited space we have here. You're ready to continue your research after reading this book.

How This Book Is Organized

We've organized this book in five parts. Each part builds on the one before, but don't feel like you have to read the chapters in order. Each chapter stands on its own as an examination of a piece of the social entrepreneurial puzzle.

Part 1: An Introduction to Social Entrepreneurship

In Part I, we introduce the fundamental concepts of social entrepreneurship and the social context within which it takes place. Compassion is at the heart of social enterprises, and it's the main theme of Chapter 2. Motivation is another important component, and Chapter 3 presents a set of ideas and concepts aimed at helping you understand what motivates people to become social entrepreneurs.

Social entrepreneurship is almost always a group effort, and in Chapter 4 we cover the vital issue of communication within an enterprise. The final chapter in this part, Chapter 5, examines the multitude of trends that currently bear on social entrepreneurship. They can subtly influence how your own enterprise will evolve and whether it's likely to fail or succeed.

Part II: Establishing Your Organization

In Chapter 6, we set out a smorgasbord of areas in which social entrepreneurship has succeeded over the years, while pointing out that more work of this kind remains to be done. The intent is to help you zero in on the specific area of life where you'd like to generate significant social change. We get down to discussing the initial planning of your enterprise, including setting your mission and goals, in Chapter 7 and help you answer the question of whether to organize as a nonprofit group or one that seeks a profit in Chapter 8.

Finding the money necessary to run your enterprise is invariably an early concern, especially if you choose to be a nonprofit organization; various ways of obtaining money are the subject of Chapter 9. In Chapter 10, we look at the importance of establishing the identity of your new enterprise and creating your own unique brand; we also explore ways of achieving these things effectively.

Part III: Growing Your Organization

Getting something up and running is one step, but keeping it alive and growing requires more knowledge and skills. The main theme of the chapters in Part III is finding out how you can make your organization into a continuing success. Networking is an important strategy for reaching this goal (Chapter 11), and so is working effectively with the media — newspapers, radio, television, magazines, the Internet, and other public outlets (Chapter 12).

The dreaded concept of bureaucracy is often a necessary part of a social enterprise, and keeping it under control can sometimes be difficult, as we explain in Chapter 13. Bureaucracy is usually part of a formalized social enterprise — one that is incorporated, has a constitution, and perhaps has governmental charity status — which we discuss in Chapter 14.

Part IV: Keeping Your Organization Running for the Long Haul

It takes leadership and good management to keep an organization on course for the long haul. Chapter 15 takes a close look at the entrepreneur side of social entrepreneurship, including the fundamentals of capitalism, the need for innovation, and the development of relevant knowledge.

All strong organizations have, or should have, a good set of leaders. In Chapter 16 we explore the principles of leadership and the power of charisma, and we address problems stemming from overusing power. We give broader consideration in Chapter 17 to the management of social enterprises — of recruiting and managing paid staff and volunteers, whipping up morale, and looking after your organization's expenses. The final chapter in this part, Chapter 18, centers on teamwork and the roles of passion and compassion in motivating effective coordinated group efforts.

Part V: The Part of Tens

If you're inspired to start a social enterprise, but you haven't yet found a social problem around which to organize it, look at Chapter 19 for a list of ten great areas for social entrepreneurial action. And always steer clear of common mistakes in this field, a helpful list of which appears in Chapter 20. Finally, the appendix lists many useful further resources for starting and running a social enterprise.

Icons Used in This Book

Throughout this book, you'll see little pictures in the margins, called *icons*. Icons are there to grab your attention. Here's what each of the icons means:

Ideas next to this icon help you move your social enterprise forward or highlight especially relevant information that can save you time.

Paying attention to the tidbits next to this icon saves you time, money, and perhaps even some heartache. This icon warns you about possible problems or glitches you may encounter on the way to becoming a social entrepreneur.

This icon flags information that you should keep in mind in the long term, if not memorize, as you explore social entrepreneurship.

This icon indicates more advanced, arcane, or difficult stuff, such as deeper details or background, which may or may not interest you. You can safely skip this material.

Throughout the book, we use concrete or hypothetical examples to illustrate important concepts. Seeing the idea in action often gives you a better idea how to apply it.

Where to Go from Here

Are you ready to get started? Although you can start with any chapter, here are a few suggestions to get you off to a good start.

If you're new to the whole concept of social entrepreneurship, we suggest starting with the chapters in Part I. Heck, start with Chapter 1, if you like, and don't look back.

If you have a fairly good idea what social entrepreneurs do and what you care about in particular, you might start with the chapters in Part II to wade straight into ideas on forming your own organization.

Feel free to use the book's handy Table of Contents or Index to look up your specific areas of interest and dive straight in that way.

However you use this book, and wherever you start your exploration, we hope you become as enamored and inspired as we are about the possibilities of social entrepreneurship. And we wish you the best in your future success.

Now, read on!

Part I

An Introduction to Social Entrepreneurship

"I always thought my wife was cut out to be a social entrepreneur. She's smart, imaginative, inspiring, and you should see the incredible meals she makes out of leftovers."

In this part . . .

We believe that laying some groundwork for the foundations of social entrepreneurship before building your organization is a good idea. And that's what this part is all about.

Chapter 1 is an overview of what social entrepreneurship is and how it works. Chapter 2 wades — gently — into some important aspects of social entrepreneurship theory that we believe can be crucial to your success. Chapter 3 takes on the issue of motivation, because knowing why people do what they do in the field of social entrepreneurship can have untold long-term benefits. Chapter 4 explores the currency of any enterprise: communication. And Chapter 5 gives you some insight into the larger forces currently at work that affect all social entrepreneurs.

Chapter 1

Social Entrepreneurship: A Calling for You

In This Chapter

▶ Discovering what social entrepreneurship is all about

▶ Seeing where you fit in and how to get started

▶ Being inspired by examples of social entrepreneurs

▶ Preparing to move forward with your passion and ideas

A t the most basic level, social entrepreneurs want to fix problems. What kinds of problems? Well, what kinds of problems might you be concerned with? Some problems are nuisances or pet peeves, like overcrowded roads, outrageous dress, rude drivers, barking dogs, and telephone solicitors. Other problems threaten or degrade our way of life: environmental pollution, crime, corruption in business and government, economic crises, and so on. And then there are the problems that threaten life itself: climate change, war, famine, genocide, disease, and natural disasters — a grisly list for sure.

It's probably true that the world today is plagued with more problems of all three types than at any other time in history. We face challenges like never before. The world's "to do" list is enormous and growing. For social entrepreneurs, that means take your pick — please! You can start small, focusing on a narrow, local issue, and work your way up to bigger and broader goals, building on your successes. The good news — and the bad news, of course — is that there is no shortage of problems around, waiting to be tackled.

What Is Social Entrepreneurship?

Social entrepreneurship and its methods, borrowed from the world of business, are becoming more and more popular among morally conscious people itching to solve a particular social problem and possibly make money in the process. Social entrepreneurs execute innovative solutions to what they define as social problems — be they local, regional, national, or international.

In social entrepreneurship, people use the principles of *enterprise* — business principles and even capitalism itself — to create social change by establishing and managing a venture. Some are altruists. They set up small, medium, or large nonprofit groups designed to ameliorate a difficult situation threatening certain people, flora, fauna, or the environment — or sometimes a combination of these. Others are profit seekers with a heart, who manage to establish a money-making enterprise that improves a situation in one of these four areas.

Whether starting and running a nonprofit or for-profit social enterprise, these entrepreneurs are usually practical. Each entrepreneur has a mission, typically one that is powerfully felt with urgency and compassion, and each takes concrete action leading to solution of the problem targeted in that mission.

We've just described the *scope* of social entrepreneurship, or what social entrepreneurs do. But what is the nature, or essence, of social entrepreneurship? One way to answer that question is to look at its three essential elements: motivation, organization, and society.

Social entrepreneurship is motivation

Any discussion of social entrepreneurship and its entrepreneurs must include why people get involved in it in the first place. Sure, they're trying to solve a pressing problem, one that bothers them and probably other people. But look at the desire to be a social entrepreneur in still broader terms.

Some entrepreneurs hope to develop a for-profit social enterprise — they're seeking a livelihood of some sort. It may not be much at first, but they hope it brings reasonable success in the long run.

For other entrepreneurs, eventually becoming a for-profit social enterprise may be a side effect, even an unexpected one, of their first efforts. And some are only interested in working toward building a successful nonprofit enterprise.

These possibilities of for-profit and nonprofit organizations raise the question of what the entrepreneur gets out of all this, besides solving a problem and changing the world as a result of the solution. What is that person's motivation? Motivation has long-term effects. Why you do something often determines how and how well you end up doing it.

We discuss this matter of motivation in several ways throughout this book. It comes up when we consider the feelings or urgency and compassion that inspire social entrepreneurs. It comes up when we explain social entrepreneurship as either a special form of *leisure* (the nonprofit form) or a special form of *work* (the for-profit form). And it comes up when we look at commitment and obligation.

Social entrepreneurship is organization

A social enterprise is an *organization,* often one that is legally incorporated (see Chapter 14 for more on that). As in all successful organizations, leaders of social enterprises must engage in careful planning, organizing, and building their group's identity. They have to decide on the structure of the enterprise, the nature of its constitution, and the elements of its bureaucracy. Sooner or later, they have to decide whether to be a for-profit or nonprofit entity — a decision that has implications for the organization's status as a tax-deductible charity. The organization needs a mission statement, which sets out its vision, and a clear set of goals toward which to work. Those are the minimal things that must be done in order to have much of a chance at success.

The nature of organizations requires that there be leaders and followers. The principles of good leadership apply as much to social enterprises as to any other kind of organization. The same may be said for managing the people who participate in them. In for-profits, these people, or *staff,* are paid; whereas in nonprofits, they're either paid or serve as volunteers. Some nonprofits rely on both paid staff and volunteers.

Social entrepreneurship is society

Social entrepreneurship doesn't take place in a vacuum — far from it. Working with others is the whole idea, and not just internally within the organization itself. As with other organizations, social-enterprise leaders must adapt to and take advantage of the organization's external environment. In practice, this means publicizing the enterprise and establishing networks of communication and influence with like-minded groups and with private and governmental sources of power, all of which can help or hinder the enterprise's goals.

A multitude of large-scale trends currently bear on social entrepreneurship. They include the international movement of national populations, decline in amount and sources of money, and patterns of communicable disease, among others. Trends can subtly or not so subtly influence how your own enterprise evolves, and even whether it eventually fails or succeeds.

Note that for-profit social enterprises are, at bottom, capitalistic entities. Their leaders must necessarily be familiar with the fundamentals of capitalism, the need for innovation, and the need to remain abreast of relevant information about and knowledge of the world of business. The biggest difference is that whereas normal businesses exist to serve one bottom line — profit — social businesses add two more: social and environmental impact. (We discuss the three bottom lines at length in Chapter 8.)

Social Entrepreneurship: How Do You Get Started?

Don't get us wrong. We're not asking you to do the Clark Kent thing and transform yourself into a superhero — or become a saint. Not at all. We *are* asking you to free yourself enough, to be deviant enough, to find the suffering of others, and the state of our world, objectionable. After you do that, what you plan to do about it is up to you. People all over the world are claiming this responsibility and inalienable right to address social and other problems — a right that comes simply from being a person on this precious planet. If you feel like it's time for you to step up to the plate, then you've come to the right place. Stepping up starts here. Object to the crummy, miserable things going on. You have that right and responsibility. No one else is going to do it for you — or at least, not the way you'd do it. Refusing to rely on governments and other organizations to take care of your objection is a big part of the decision to become a social entrepreneur.

As a social entrepreneur, you'll challenge the status quo, to be sure. Some people may even object to you, and that's probably a good sign. The important thing is that your journey as a social entrepreneur will have begun. You're not simply bothered about something and leaving it at that. You *object*. That objection is a precondition for your commitment to positive change.

But how do you change things? Wow. That's where the rubber hits the road. That's where, for you, the plot thickens. If your "deviance" takes you to the threshold of a strange land, you'll cross over into that land when you try to change things for the better. You won't be alone, though. We'll be here with you, in this book, at your shoulder.

You may already have an idea of which problem you want to address, change, or fix. Coming to grips with how to tackle that problem is basically a three-phase process: recognizing and stating your objections to the problem, taking action to try to solve the problem, and starting a social enterprise.

Recognizing and stating objections

First, you have to see the problem clearly enough to determine what action to try to take. That means finding out everything you can about it. In complex problems, such as those motivating the International Red Cross or Ryan's Well Foundation (both profiled later in this chapter), getting a clear view of the problem may take considerable research.

You aren't going to be able to effectively fight against something until you have a decent idea of what you're fighting against. Doing your homework also focuses your sense of urgency and compassion. And it helps you define what you object to about the problem. Write down as clearly and completely as possible what the problem is and why you feel so passionately about it.

Here's an example of what we're talking about.

Project Laundry List (www.laundrylist.org) is a nonprofit social enterprise incorporated in the United States, with official charitable status. Its mission is to make hanging out laundry to dry in the open air a respectable and environmentally friendly practice in America. Project Laundry List further recommends using cold water to wash clothes, which it sees as an easy but effective way to save energy.

One of the conditions inciting the founders of Project Laundry List was the enactment of local rules that prohibited drying laundry in the open air. The arguments for such regulations included the belief that laundry openly exposed results in a decline in property values, is unsightly, and is unnecessary given the widespread availability of mechanical, indoor clothes dryers.

The local rules opposed by Project Laundry List are mainly community covenants, landlord prohibitions, and zoning laws. Though it operates only in the United States, the leaders of this social enterprise also point to the existence of similar restrictions in Canada and elsewhere in the world. It's time, they say, to enact "right to dry" legislation. Project Laundry List also operates as an advocacy group for this cause. The best dryer of clothes, claims the organization, is the solar dryer — hanging out clothing in the sun. By the end of 2009, clothesline legislation had been debated in at least nine states. Project Laundry has also established a National Hanging Out Day in both the United States and Canada.

How did such an unusual and interesting venture get started? Project Laundry List was born when students at Middlebury College in New Hampshire reacted to plans by Hydro-Quebec to build some major dams in Canada and U.S. plans for expanding use of nuclear power. The students protested by hanging political messages on clotheslines.

The following is another fairly typical, hypothetical example of how a social enterprise might get its start.

Say you've noticed that homeless people tend to congregate around the entrance to your local library. For everyone, trips to the library involve negotiating some half-dozen panhandling requests and perhaps some closer-than-comfortable, close-range scrutiny from strangers. You find that you object to the fact that these folks have nowhere else to go and nothing else to do. And maybe you object to having to interact with strangers who place continual demands on passersby, or even see the situation as a safety hazard. Maybe you start limiting your trips to the library, and maybe other people do too. What can you do about this? Read on for one potential way to address it.

Taking action

Once your objection is clarified and galvanized by urgency and compassion, you then enter phase 2 — making some initial attempts to solve the problem. You ask yourself, and probably other people, two questions: What *should* be done, and what *can* be done?

In practice, answering these questions means first trying to solve the problem through existing arrangements. It may mean that you, as an objector, learn that appropriate governmental, private-sector, or nonprofit organizations for solving the problem either don't exist or are inadequate for the job. In our hypothetical example, maybe the library says its property is open to the public, and perhaps you find that there's no effective law against panhandling in your town. Moreover, the only homeless shelter nearby has closed, and no community center is currently open. Maybe you even ask the homeless people why they gather there, and they tell you that they were kicked out of the park a few blocks away, and there's nowhere else for them to go.

Trying to solve the problem by taking action through ordinary, existing channels is an important step. But it's because of this step that most people bothered by a particular problem fail to get beyond objecting to it. One reason for doing little other than objecting to the problem is that, often, the objector is unable to answer the questions about what should and can be done about it. Put another way, objectors may see no action in which they're both willing and able to engage.

In our homeless-at-the-library example, if the library is no help, and neither is city hall or the police, and nothing else exists that could easily replace the activity, what should be done? Maybe you think there *should* be a safe place for homeless people to get together, but maybe you go further and think there should be a way to prevent your fellow community members from being homeless in the first place. What can be done about that? If there's no shelter, community center, or job-training program, as a social entrepreneur that should set some bells ringing.

Why *aren't* there those resources? And you finally realize: *You* can be the one to get them started. At that point, it occurs to you that if you really want to fix the problem, you'll have to organize a more coherent and effective approach to solving it. You will, in fact, need to establish a social enterprise. The time has come to engage in some social entrepreneurship and move on to phase 3. If you succeed, you will have helped the homeless people and achieved your goal of taking action to address a perceived problem in your community.

Starting a social enterprise

Social entrepreneurship is, says Muhammad Yunus, winner of the Nobel Peace Prize and pioneer of the idea of microcredit, "any innovative initiative to help people." Let's look at another very simple example to see this definition in action. As you'll see, what qualifies as a "social enterprise" can be quite informal.

A neighbor's dog spends most days outside, often with no apparent food or water. The poor creature barks out of sheer despair and boredom. It's driving you nuts — both the animal's sad, pleading noise and its lonesome lot in life. With your objection clarified, you enter the second phase: action. First, you speak about the problem with the dog's owner, but he tells you to get lost, that he works all day, that the dog would chew his furniture if he left him inside, and that he can't afford to hire someone to watch the dog. You call animal control, but they say they can't do anything. You even consider moving away from the neighborhood, but that's not a realistic option. Kidnapping the dog and letting him loose in the country flicks briefly through your mind, and now you're horrified at yourself. Perhaps there is a municipal bylaw about cruelty to animals in your town? But your search reveals that there is nothing that applies to this situation. You're at the end of your rope, right? Wrong. You aren't a hapless, wilting objector — you refuse to let the dog's problem go unsolved. What you need is help. Problems often begin to be solved when you reach out to others.

You talk to other neighbors and learn that they're as irritated with the neighbor as you are. You get organized and hold a meeting to map out some strategies. It turns out that several of you have some free time at least one day a week. What if you got together and provided some free doggie day care for your community? You have a garage you could convert into a place where dogs could congregate. And one of the concerned neighbors knows someone on the city council who may be able to provide some funding. She'll talk to this person to see what can be done. Another woman is a lawyer who suggests a bylaw on dog neglect be written and submitted to the city council in order to add some leverage to the idea that's forming. You volunteer to write a letter to the editor of the local newspaper, explaining the need for this municipal bylaw pertaining to neglected animals — and announcing your plan for you and other neighbors to help take care of animals during the day. Someone else says he's starting a local blog on the matter, as a way of swaying public opinion toward enacting the suggested bylaw.

Let's give this a happy ending: These measures are sufficient to pressure the city council member for your district to propose an amendment to the municipal noise bylaw pertaining to dogs left alone outside during the day. This measure passes. The city council agrees to help offset your costs in converting your garage, and you and the other neighbors work out a schedule whereby one of you is there every weekday to take care of animals whose owners work and would otherwise leave their dogs alone.

You may not realize it, but what you've done is use social entrepreneurship to solve a problem. You didn't make any money doing it, but maybe that's the next step. Maybe you could begin charging a small fee after you run through the city's stipend. (We talk about earning money from social entrepreneurship throughout this book.)

The Beginnings of Social Enterprises

Why do some people devote huge amounts of time and sometimes personal funds to solving a social problem? You could argue that, in the case of for-profit entrepreneurs, the answer is obvious: They want to make money. But, if profit is the motive, keep in mind that nearly all social enterprises are substantially risky ventures. If you want to be sure to make even a modest amount of money, there are far more secure businesses than ones that try to solve social problems, too.

Social entrepreneurship becomes necessary when objectors find that appropriate governmental, private-sector, or nonprofit organizations for solving the problem don't exist or are inadequate for the job. Objectors discover these weaknesses during phase 2, the action phase.

In the illustration about the neglected dog, government help was inadequate. The objectors, forced by these circumstances, decided to try the entrepreneurial route, or phase 3. It's this basic impulse that spurs social entrepreneurial action. Making money may be a nice bonus, but it's not what motivates social entrepreneurs in the first place.

The homeless and animal-neglect examples were local issues used to illustrate typical small-time social entrepreneurial action. Of course, many of the opportunities for social entrepreneurship are broader than that and of much greater import for humanity.

The founding of the Light Up the World Foundation (www.lutw.org) is an example. It's a nonprofit humanitarian organization dedicated to providing lighting to poor people in remote areas who currently rely on kerosene lamps or even wood fires. In addition to improved nighttime lighting, this utility brings physical, educational, and financial benefits.

As you're probably beginning to see, social entrepreneurship is, in some ways, limited only by your imagination and determination. We round out this chapter with four more examples of how some of today's social enterprises first sprang into being. These examples show how broad and consequential — and inspiring — social entrepreneurship can be.

The International Red Cross

It wasn't until the mid-19th century that an attempt was made to develop a system for nursing casualties among combatants in war. What existed prior to this time were sporadic nursing stations, which were unprotected from enemy action. Swiss businessman Jean-Henri Dunant set out to ameliorate this situation for men wounded on the battlefield. He was inspired, or more accurately, horrified, by the carnage he observed in June 1859 during the Battle of Solferino, a particularly ugly part of the Austro-Sardinian War.

Dunant had been on his way to Algeria to tend to his business interests. But now he saw that approximately 40,000 soldiers on both sides died in this engagement or were left wounded on the field. Yet there was next to no medical service or even basic care for these men. Dunant abandoned his plans to go to Algeria. Instead, he spent several days helping to treat and care for the wounded.

Subsequently, Dunant managed to organize a massive system of relief assistance. This he accomplished by persuading local people to aid the wounded and to do this for soldiers on both sides. Upon returning to his home in Geneva, he wrote *A Memory of Solferino,* a book he published in 1862 with his own money. He sent copies of it to main political and military figures everywhere in Europe. In his book, he argued for the establishment of national voluntary relief organizations whose mission would be to help nurse wounded soldiers. He also pointed to the need for international treaties that would protect neutral medics and establish field hospitals for soldiers wounded in battle.

Then, in 1863 in Geneva, Dunant set up the Committee of the Five, which also consisted of him and four other leading members of well-known Genevese families. The committee's goal was to study the feasibility of Dunant's ideas and then to hold an international conference to consider the possibility of implementing them. To better communicate its mission, the committee renamed itself the International Committee for Relief to the Wounded.

The committee submitted resolutions to a diplomatic conference sponsored by the Swiss government, to which national governments throughout Europe and those of the United States, Mexico, and Brazil were invited. The conference resulted in the signing of the first Geneva Convention by 12 governments and kingdoms. Now, for the first time, legally binding rules would be enforced during armed conflict involving neutrality and protection of wounded soldiers, field medical personnel, and certain humanitarian institutions.

Soon, the signing countries established their own national societies devoted to implementing the Geneva Convention and to using what had become their common symbol — a red cross. In 1876, the international body became the International Committee of the Red Cross (ICRC), which is the name still used to this day. Today the ICRC (`www.icrc.org`) also provides relief assistance in response to emergency situations not caused by war, including disasters caused by human and natural forces.

Ryan's Well Foundation

Ryan Hreljac claims he's just a "regular, average kid." And he is. And he isn't. When Ryan was a mere 6 years old, he learned from his elementary school teacher that people were dying because they didn't have clean water to drink. All it would cost, Ryan figured, was $70 to drill one well that could make a huge difference. So Ryan did tons of chores, and soon enough he had his money. Unfortunately, he learned that $70 wasn't nearly enough. He actually needed about $2,500 to make his dream come true. No problem, Ryan declared. He'd just do more chores.

Well, it wasn't quite that easy, but where there's an indomitable child's will to do good, it seems people are quick to follow. Soon, with the steadfast support of his family, friends, neighbors, and folks from afar, Ryan's Well began. Ryan garnered attention for his cause early on, beginning with a friend of the family who starting e-mailing her friends about it.

The rest, as they say, is history. Today, at age 18, Ryan is recognized by UNICEF as a Global Youth Leader. He has twice been a guest on *Oprah* and has appeared frequently in many other forms of media. More important, of course, is the good that Ryan's vision continues to do. Believing that every person on this planet deserves clean water, Ryan's Well Foundation (`www.ryanswell.ca`), founded in 2001, has now contributed to building 461 wells in 16 countries, bringing clean water and sanitation services to more than 600,000 people so far.

My Life My Soul

Ivette Attaud-Jones, a former Army wife, is a survivor of 20 years of domestic violence. Sadly, Ivette lost a daughter during this unpleasant period of her life. Now Ivette speaks out against this social epidemic to raise awareness. She is also the founder of and program director for My Life My Soul, The Unspoken Journey of Life after Domestic Abuse, an empowering nonprofit support group for women, established as a program of the Church of the Resurrection and incorporated in 1970.

After abused women leave their abusers, what happens? Attaud-Jones believes that before turning to the police, they look to faith-based communities. So she established a training program to help those communities address domestic violence in their services. She also wrote a book about this situation entitled *Silent No More*.

Ivette is, not surprisingly, deeply committed to women's justice issues, involving herself in many ways. My Life My Soul (`www.mylifemysoul.com`), whose headquarters are in New York, is also committed to raising sensitivity to domestic violence through public education and community awareness projects.

The Lost Boys and Girls of Sudan

The previous examples — and many more that you'll encounter in this book — document the cases of individual social entrepreneurs. However, one of the most fascinating and historically important examples of social entrepreneurship involves a large and impressive cohort of young men and women, some 15,000 strong. These are the Lost Boys and Girls of Sudan.

They're refugees and, too often, orphans of the Second Sudanese Civil War — in many ways, the precursor to the current round of mass killings in Darfur — which claimed more than 2 million lives and displaced an estimated 4 to 5 million civilians. As victims of this civil war, almost 26,000 little boys and girls between the ages of 4 and 12 years of age fled for their lives, heading east toward a hoped-for safe haven. But along the way, almost 10,000 of these children died. Only little friends were there to bury those lost.

Few Westerners growing up today can imagine the atrocious — let's say hellish — conditions faced by these children. And yet virtually all the Lost Boys and Girls of Sudan share one mission, one purpose, one dream: to keep the promise they made as children to the refugee-camp elders and return home to take part in the redevelopment of their beloved homeland. That, in itself, is a magnificent phase 1 rebuttal of the powers that would eradicate them and their people.

From there, the Lost Boys and Girls of Sudan moved into phase 2: collaborating with each other and Westerners and mobilizing their resources in an effort to prosper in their new homes, primarily the United States, Australia, and Canada. The Chicago Association for the Lost Boys of Sudan (`www.lost boyschicago.com`) is a striking case in point.

With a firmer foundation in place, these heroes are now entering phase 3: the social entrepreneurial phase. From fundraising to building schools, churches, roads, wells, and much more, the Lost Boys and Girls of Sudan are taking every opportunity to rebuild Southern Sudan under the tenuously protective umbrella of the Comprehensive Peace Agreement signed in 2005. The Valentino Achak Deng Foundation (www.valentinoachakdeng.org) is today one of the better-known examples of these efforts.

Moving Forward with Your Ideas and Passion

If you already have one or more social problems in mind to solve through social entrepreneurship, the process of expanding and moving forward is simple: Read those parts of this book that best fit your needs. But, assuming that you've read this chapter because you were curious about social entrepreneurship without having a particular social problem in mind, what's your next step?

Well, you should read the rest of this book, or as much as interests you. But overall, here's what you're going to be doing, in five broad steps, all of which are covered in detail in this book:

1. **Identify a social problem for which you have substantial passion and a sense of urgency.**

   The chapters in Part I address this issue. If you need to further stimulate your imagination, turn to Chapter 19 for a list of ten great areas for social entrepreneurial action.

2. **Develop a plan for solving the problem you've identified.**

   Your plan will be rough and preliminary, sure, but you have to start somewhere. You may want to consult with someone else as you prepare this plan. The idea in general is to put something on paper sufficient to show others in an initial meeting.

   Chapters 7 through 9 in this book are designed to help you plan. Additionally, Chapters 1 through 6 give you different kinds of useful background information that can help you sell your ideas to others whose assistance you may need, to family and friends whose opinion of your project you value, and last, but not least, to yourself.

3. **Decide whether to try to solve this problem alone or with the help of some other people.**

   If you're going to need help, then who might want to help? Whom do you know who shares your passion and sense of urgency about the problem? Do they have some time to commit to helping you solve it? Will they bring some critical expertise to the table? Will they be team players? Are they able to work well with others?

   Several chapters in this book can help you reach out and lead others, including Chapters 4 and 11 and the chapters in Part IV.

4. **Call a meeting to discuss your preliminary plan.**

   The idea here is to find sufficient agreement on a more final plan among those who want be involved in your evolving social enterprise. In other words, your draft plan, initially conceived alone or mostly alone, is your starting point in this step. Bear in mind that it may change. It's possible that not everyone will like it. Some may drop out right there because the project isn't what they thought it was going to be. But others will stay on longer. It's among this latter group that you must find agreement on a draft of the plan. All this may take a series of meetings.

5. **Execute your plan.**

   With your plan and team in hand, you've developed a significant consensus among a group of people ready to work with you on setting up a social enterprise. Now it's time take action. At this point, it would be good to reread Chapters 7 through 9 in light of the new plan.

Chapter 2

Building Public Compassion

*B*efore getting into the nuts and bolts of building your social enterprise, we want to step back and consider the lay of the land. And by *land,* we mean the social environment in which your social entrepreneurship takes place. After all, you'll be setting up and running your enterprise within the surrounding culture, and the more you understand the interaction between your enterprise and the attitudes that are all around it, the better you can focus and direct your efforts.

But we know, we know. . . . Lots of people, including, no doubt, a few social entrepreneurs, despise anything that smacks of "theory." Why? Well, theory is seen by many as over-the-top, abstract, and irrelevant. As one young social entrepreneur we know put it recently: "It's hard for me because, as I have commonly seen it, theory has been something that professors in school ask you to use in papers, but never truly expect you to apply to everyday situations, or to really use ever again."

We understand. We hear it all the time. But think about what Kurt Lewin, the pioneering social psychologist once said: "There is nothing so practical as a good theory." Lots of people, for example, try to help chronically homeless youth. In our experience, Marilyn Dyck, executive director of The Doorway (www.thedoorway.ca), succeeds admirably in doing that. That agency, now in its 20th year of operation and boasting a 70 percent success rate, delivers the goods because she understands and applies many of the theoretical strands we discuss in this chapter to almost every aspect of her agency's workflow.

The stuff we cover in this chapter is meant to be practical, meant to help you put your social enterprise in context. The social theorist Charles Lemert once said that "Social theory is a survival skill," precisely because it can orient us to the world in useful ways. What we cover in this chapter will enhance the survivability of your social enterprise. Theoretical insights can set the bar, giving you important information about where you need to go and how you can get there. It's true that the abstractness of theory can make it difficult to achieve, but that doesn't take away from the fact that it's often still worth striving for. We do our best to make this tour as painless as possible.

If you ignore all the research and findings that abound with regard to the *social* half of social entrepreneurship, you may find that, before too long, the wheels start falling off your wagon. You'll wonder why your months or years of well-intentioned efforts came crashing to the ground. That may be because you missed some crucial truth about the way social culture affects social enterprises. We invite you to at least browse through this chapter as soon as you can. We think it's that important.

Public Compassion as the Groundwork for Success

Social entrepreneurship is often about pulling off a complex and challenging social project or program. A big part of the challenge and complexity lies in the context of the work, especially the *social* context regarding the public capacity for compassion.

Your success rests in part on tapping into the public capacity for compassion — and strategically contributing to that capacity.

Like it or not, we've entered a new era in human history, one in which traditional "saintly" compassion has lost its exalted place within the concept of "doing good." That's not to say that we deny the importance of special people. We agree with Margaret Mead's advice: "Never doubt that a small group of thoughtful, committed citizens can change the world. . . ." But we might challenge what Mead next went on to say: "Indeed, it is the only thing that ever has."

That may have been true back in the day, but it doesn't hold as much water now. The sheer variety and enormity of the problems that the world is facing today demand that compassion become *publicly participatory* — in other words, today's problems are so widespread and pervasive that they require public participation in their solutions.

What compassion is

Most people have a pretty good sense of what *compassion* means. But just to set the record a little straighter, for the purposes of this book we define compassion as follows:

Compassion is a deep awareness of and feeling for another's suffering, combined with an active, engaged desire to alleviate it. Compassion is about more than acknowledgment — it's about *action*.

Compassion begins with a generous promise made from one party to another. The promise is generally that the caring party will *be there* for the care recipients.

Compassionate engagement can be as large as Al Gore's attempts to promote global climate-change policy and innovations. It can be a nation's apology and assurance of assistance to its wronged indigenous peoples. Or it can be as small as helping an elderly person in the last stages of Alzheimer's — rubbing her back, holding her hand, or stroking her hair, just to let her know that someone is close by.

Note that immediate success or failure is not part of the compassion equation. You can be compassionate and fall short in your bid to help others (although we hope you don't, and that's why we're here). The deep desire to do something truly positive for others and the promise and willingness to get out into the world and actually do just that are what compassion is about. Compassion tests character and integrity — but it also builds them up.

Why compassion is everybody's responsibility

We believe it's time to move beyond the traditional dependence on the isolated efforts of saintly folk. And in many ways, as a society, we've begun that process — one of the great accomplishments of our times has been to insist that receiving compassion, in the face of violating and unwarranted suffering, is everyone's birthright, and that such a right should be institutionalized and formalized (as in the United Nations Declaration of Human Rights). As a result, vast international cooperatives like the United Nations, mammoth governmental bureaucracies, and many professions have tried to marshal their resources in order to guarantee that birthright.

But two things have happened with that goal:

- ✔ **We, the public, have become dependent on these institutional responses, which has made us complacent about divesting ourselves of our own compassionate responsibilities.**

- ✔ **We're now regretting that complacency as we realize that those same institutional responses are proving, for any number of reasons, to be quite limited in terms of what they can achieve.**

There's a serious incongruity to all of this. In its saintly version, delivering compassion was reserved for only the most reverent and dutiful. Today, compassion is often "ghettoized" into enclaves, and the public, which should be the linchpin of the whole process, is still not seriously involved.

The result has been a move *away* from public compassion, not *toward* it. With these developments, grassroots movements face enormous challenges in energizing themselves for compassion. But beyond that, every corner of society must begin to contribute to an ongoing productive social dialogue on the practice of compassion.

You, the social entrepreneur, are one of the most important keys to invigorating grassroots action and enabling dialogue on the widest possible scale. Lead the way! If enough people do so, policymakers will be forced to pay attention and lend a hand.

How social entrepreneurs fit in

If you're the social entrepreneurial type, don't think of yourself as just another "subcontractor" in the ghettoizing of compassion. Instead, you're more like the organizer and catalyst of a unifying, synergistic, and creative public compassion. We can't overstate your importance.

As a social entrepreneur, you must always pursue two interlocking goals:

- ✔ **Succeed at your social enterprise.** This goal is first and foremost, of course.

- ✔ **Get others to share your compassion.** A secondary goal is to advance, directly or indirectly, everyone else's capacity for compassion.

Achieving that second goal is more than the right thing to do — it actually helps you reach the first goal. Practically speaking, you need the broad-based support and resources of a compassionate public if you're going to sustain and succeed in your efforts.

You also have to broaden your own compassion beyond your pet issues. Social entrepreneurs can't help but compete as they pursue scarce resources, but it would be a contradiction if someone claiming to promote compassion cared about only one particular cause. That doesn't wash — compassion isn't narrow.

A brief history of social compassion

Almost 400 years ago, philosopher Thomas Hobbes claimed that man's life is filled with "continual fear and danger of violent death." Famously, he described human existence as "solitary, poor, nasty, brutish, and short." There continues to be some truth to this. Nevertheless, the historical record also shows that humans, and even their predecessors, have always been compassionate. Simple, brutish self-interest is not the whole story here.

Archaeologist Terisa Green relates the story of a *Homo erectus* woman identified as KNM-ER 1808. Apparently, this individual suffered and died from lesions and growths on her limbs. The condition was probably caused by vitamin A overdosing — the result of eating the livers of carnivores. Green notes that the condition leads to nausea, dizziness, and cramps, followed slowly by bone swelling and great pain. Poor KNM-ER 1808 wouldn't have been able to care for herself. Yet, despite her advanced condition, she still survived to a relatively advanced age and quite a distance away from water, where the carnivores would have hung out. How? She had to have had at least one caregiver. We're talking between 1 and 2 million years ago.

Then there's the case of "Nandy" the Neanderthal. The Neanderthals never had it easy. As hunters of large, fierce game, they led dangerous lives and suffered the traumatic injuries to prove it. Nandy had it doubly hard. He was born with a useless right arm, which was amputated below the elbow, and was likely blind in one eye (he suffered an earlier nasty blow to the head), so it's hard to imagine how he would have been able to fend for himself. Nevertheless, Nandy lived to be a ripe old 40-something, which in today's terms would be like pushing 80. How was that possible? Archeologists believe that Nandy must have been accepted and supported by his people up to the day he died from a rock fall in the communal cave. The discovery of Nandy radically changed our appreciation of the complexity of Neanderthal social behavior.

Then there are the examples from well-loved sacred texts. Judaism promotes the concept of *tikun olam,* or "repairing the world," and the Torah conveys God's commandment to "be kind to the stranger in your midst for you were strangers in the land of Egypt." Christianity has the story of the Good Samaritan. Islam has the prophet inquiring about the well-being of one who had tormented him daily. Buddhism has Prince Siddhartha Gautama teaching a simple truth: "A generous heart, kind speech, and a life of service and compassion are the things which renew humanity."

What are the historical lessons here for the social entrepreneur? One is to take heart, knowing that you're carrying on one of humanity's noblest traditions. Another is to realize that voluntarily taking on the mantle of compassion can be fulfilling in its own right. Cynics point to the shackle of obligation created by compassion, but compassion is voluntary. You don't have to fear that the "real you" will be swallowed whole and vanish. The real you has already willingly embraced compassion, and compassion brings out the best in all of us.

Breaking Down Exclusionary Social Distance

Some people practice compassion all right — but only for people they believe are like them. They don't mind helping out someone from their hometown, say, who shares their ethnicity and goes to their church. But others — those who are "different" — are on their own. This tendency is called *exclusionary social distance,* or just *social distance* for short. We're talking about the very old habit of circling the wagons against outsiders.

Understanding the reality of social distance

For you as a social entrepreneur to exercise compassion, you may well need to breach or violate the reality of exclusionary social distance. The Good Samaritan, after all, crossed the road in order to help someone who wasn't his "kind."

Social distance operates vividly everywhere you look. As of this writing, the world is in a protracted economic crisis, the likes of which haven't been seen since the early part of the 20th century. In Europe and elsewhere, masses of people have marched in the streets, outraged at the greed and lack of moral compass demonstrated by modern financial elites and governments. We heard of bailouts, stimulus packages, and big bonuses for upper-echelon jobs poorly done. Along with that came job losses for millions. Is this the world we want our children to inherit, many ask, in which the rich get richer and the poor get table scraps, misery, and shorter lives?

The problem of social distance and a related phenomenon called the *politics of exclusion* (the systematic sidelining or elimination of certain groups or points of view) continue to define and divide social life. Back in the 1930s, the American sociologist Emory Bogardus showed that it was a culture's promotion of social distance — not twisted, individual psychologies — that lay behind widespread prejudice, discrimination, and racism. Since then, hundreds of studies have shown that social distance is firmly fixed in the way people live, from the way people tip in restaurants (with minority servers earning smaller gratuities) all the way up to "old boy" networks and international relations.

To put it mildly, many refuse to "get it." Why? It may be as simple as the fact that they have a vested interest in *not* getting it. Certainly, once upon a time, stockpiling scarce resources for family, kin, and tribe against the marauding hordes just over the mountains or across the water made sense. From there, it may have been just a short hop to the creation of social hierarchies, stratification, and structured inequality — all of which, over time, came to seem both natural and real. Old habits do die hard.

Tearing down social distance through social entrepreneurship

Some signs of hope do exist. More and more people, especially younger people, are finding social distance less attractive. And regardless of your political leanings, it's hard to deny the notion that the election of Barack Obama was part of an attempt on the part of the American people to break down the barriers of social distance, both within the United States and between the United States and the rest of the world.

We believe that, given the amplified problems of today, exclusionary social distance may have run its course. As a social entrepreneur, you get to be on the vanguard of helping it along toward its demise.

Start decreasing social distance by thinking and acting *inclusively.* By that we mean including more and more kinds of people in your endeavors, of course, but also keeping social distance in mind and including it in your calculations about where and how to focus your efforts.

In the following list, we take a look at a few people who are committed to battling social distance:

- ✔ **James Nachtwey** is one of the greatest war and social-conflict photojournalists of our time, having worked in more than 30 countries. He says that he is privy to "unmitigated pain, injustice, and misery." Why, then, does he do what he does? Because, he says, he wants to "shake" people out of their indifference — in other words, out of their exclusionary social distance. That is the function of a war photographer, as Nachtwey sees it — to allow people to "be there just once to see for themselves what white phosphorus does to the face of a child, or what unspeakable pain is cause by a single bullet, or how a jagged piece of shrapnel can rip someone's leg off."

- ✔ **Brian Steidle** served as an unarmed military observer in Darfur before his photographs of the atrocities there broke the story open, in *The New York Times,* to the United States and the world. Ryan Spencer Reed has powerfully documented the genocidal civil wars and tremendous suffering in both southern Sudan and Darfur. Ryan notes that "images are powerful statements by witnesses who were present as these events unfolded. . . . Yet an image becomes powerful only after it is given an audience."

- ✔ Internationally known video-journalist and social entrepreneur **Rick Castiglione** left a lucrative career as a broadcast journalist to found Cielo Pictures. His passion is to tell stories about prospering social entrepreneurs. One of his most important messages is that social entrepreneurs should model social inclusiveness to the rest of the world. When Castiglione is invited to speak publicly, he makes a point of challenging his audience. "If there were 100 people living next to you, or just down the street, in extremely dire circumstances, would you help them out?" His audiences always reply yes, of course. "Well," he replies, "Most of those in dire need are only about 10 to 20 hours away. You'd drive that to visit your relatives and friends, right? Why not make an equivalent trip to help the two-thirds of the world who have so little and who are also your neighbors?"

✔ **Dr. Gopa Kothari** is a Mumbai baby doctor who has devoted her life to bettering the lives of India's poorest and most unfortunate. The caste system in India has to be one of the most extreme examples of social distance in the world. But being born into the high Hindu Brahman caste has not kept Dr. Kothari from working to dismantle negative social distance against seemingly insurmountable odds. In 1982, Dr. Kothari founded the Child Eye Care Charitable Trust, which brings family health, nutrition, treatment, and education programs to India's urban and rural poor. As a result of Kothari's efforts, 68,000 children have been protected from preventable blindness, more than 1.3 million women have received health education to protect their children, and more than 5,000 Indian children have received informal school education. Dr. Kothari is a perfect example of what fighting social distance can do.

✔ In 1998, 6-year-old **Ryan Hreljac** was appalled and saddened when he learned in school that many African children had to walk great distances every day just to get water, and that the water they fetched wasn't even fit for drinking. In fact, the water was the cause of tremendous suffering. It brought numerous illnesses, blindness, and death to many, many Africans. Ryan decided to build a well for a village in Africa. By earning enough money doing household chores and doing some public speaking on clean-water issues, Ryan's first well was built in 1999 at the Angolo Primary School in a northern Ugandan village.

Now a young man, Ryan has torn down the idea of the so-called "distant" needy. Ryan's Well Foundation has helped dig a total of 502 wells in 16 developing countries and brought clean-water services to more than 600,000 people.

The work of the foundation continues to inspire young and old everywhere. As Ryan puts it: "Youth today want to be more involved in society. . . . [They] are working to support positive change in their communities and in the world. Adults now recognize that kids and teenagers can and do add value. And young people recognize that they will benefit from the advice and support of the world's leaders and change makers."

✔ **Patricia Erb-Delfin,** a former Argentinean activist and one of only two people to have survived being one of the "disappeared," now coordinates an AIDS prevention Project in Bolivia. The purpose of the project is to teach local youth how to work as HIV/AIDS prevention trainers. These youth conduct workshops for peers and other teens in and around the city of Cochabamba, which has the highest HIV/AIDS infection rate in the country.

Attachment: Emotional Bonds and Public Compassion

There is a flip side to exclusionary distance. The fact is that exclusion runs counter to one of the most basic human tendencies: our deep-rooted need and desire to *attach* to each other. As a social entrepreneur, you can use attachment as a powerful tool in your enterprise.

The emergence of attachment theory

Harry Harlow, the controversial American psychologist, tested the biblical aphorism "Man does not live by bread alone" on infant rhesus monkeys. What Harlow did was separate the babies from their mothers 6 to 12 hours after birth. He then reared them in the company of two types of artificial replacement or surrogate mothers — one of which was made of wire, and the other of soft terry cloth. The monkeys in the experiment preferred the soft terry-cloth mother, even if only the wire mother provided milk.

The experiment showed that the monkeys needed what he called *contact comfort,* even at the expense of nutrition. And so do humans, of course. Seeking out and satisfying a need for contact comfort is essential to primate survival. Beyond that, contact comfort is vital to establishing thriving, properly functioning, fully integrated members of families and communities.

The incredibly important lesson in this was not lost on John Bowlby, Mary Ainsworth, and many other eminent scholars who have gone on to develop and refine what they call *attachment theory*. From cradle to grave, humans need *attachments* — the emotional bonds that have their origins in contact comfort. From the infant's cries to the dying person's desire for loved ones to gather 'round, attachments are the heartstrings that link our lives together.

When attachments don't form properly

The importance and value of early, successful emotional bonds simply can't be exaggerated. These bonds are central to a child's emotional, cognitive, and behavioral development. Emotionally, attachments are the basis of positive and respectful close adult relations, including those that become the foundation of the intimate partnerships that later lead to a new generation of parent-child relations.

Cognitively, successful attachments are closely linked to developing the confidence needed to engage, creatively explore, gain knowledge from, and innovatively adapt to the world. In fact, the desire and ability to push limits often arises out of knowing that there is a fallback position — the safe haven of a secure base — to retreat to if needed before striking out again. Behaviorally, impaired attachments put trust at risk. When that happens, participation in the family unit and in communities of all sizes is compromised.

Because the effects of infant attachments are so far-reaching, they're necessary to individual and collective social functioning and to the ultimate health of every society. This claim is corroborated by a massive amount of clinical and observational literature. In fact, the cross-cultural and international study of human attachments is by now, after 50 years of inquiry, so widespread that a child's universal primordial needs for parental or caregiver love and protection, known as *affectional bonds,* are now globally recognized.

Suffice it to say that children who are deprived of secure bases or who grow up feeling unsure about the integrity of the affectional bonds with caregivers end up exhibiting very important deficits. These deficits make it much harder for them to establish positive, mutually supportive, and long-lasting relationships with others. And these deficits have immense implications for a person's health, social behavior, and participation in organizational and community life.

Applying attachment theory to social entrepreneurship

So, what does all this information on attachments have to do with social entrepreneurship? When something goes wrong with attachments, it usually leads to trouble for the individual, and that often ends up meaning trouble for society. Many social ills are either rooted in attachment difficulties or are often unaddressed because of attachment difficulties. On the other hand, as you foster or work with individuals who are well attached, you'll find that those individuals are more likely to help you push social limits in a positive and confident manner.

This leads to the important idea of a *politics of attachment,* a blend of politics, psychology, social sciences, and moral philosophy. In this arena, social entrepreneurs and others are applying attachment theory to communities in need and promoting much more satisfying fixes between individuals and their societies.

In his wide-ranging *New York Times* bestseller, *Social Intelligence,* Daniel Goleman discusses human attachments in great detail and draws connections from the theory to everyday life for business people, parents, educators, health professionals, and community leaders. Check out this book to further your understanding of social intelligence.

Andrea Pound, in an article titled "Hope in the Inner-city: Towards a New Deal," looks at three broad groups of children living in urban centers. The three groups are the children of depressed mothers, children whose parents have divorced, and children living in poverty. Pound describes a number of parent support schemes that have grown out of attachment research. These schemes are successful enough that they should be informing policy and helping to prevent the accelerating cycle of disadvantage for society's children and youth.

If such children are your target, we highly recommend exploring Pound's article for ideas. You can find it as Chapter 4 in *The Politics of Attachment: Towards a Secure Society,* edited by Sebastian Kraemer and Jane Roberts (Free Association Books).

The sociologist Ray Pahl notes that the simple idea of friendship is an expression of community that, in turn, is deeply rooted in attachments. Pahl proposes that putting friendships on the political agenda would presumably lead to something sorely needed: greater social cohesion. Friendships and other attachments serve as a life-sustaining remedy to the absolute dominance of states over individuals. Whereas state and other kinds of bureaucracies tend to strip people of *social capital* — the connections within and between social networks — friendships and attachments do just the opposite.

Some visionary philanthropists believe so strongly in attachment theory that they put their money where their mouths are. Case in point: The very much theory-based FHL Foundation of New Mexico explicitly promotes "attachment theory as a guiding principle toward understanding and solving societal problems." Named for Frederick H. Leonhardt, an organic chemist and former president and chairman of the board of Fritzsche Brothers (purveyors of essential oils, flavors, and fragrances), the foundation extends the Fritzsche Brothers' original corporate philosophy: Ensure that technological advances support people's striving for home and belongingness. Today, the foundation works to alter the basic ways in which Western societies tend to function. It wants to see sweeping changes in our current social arrangements and institutions so that human attachments can acquire the safety, security, and nurturing they need and deserve. The foundation's funding activities cover everything from infant and child development research and programs to youth transition programs, from community art initiatives to the YWCA to Habitat for Humanity. You can visit the FHL Foundation online at http://128.121.62.12.

Some organizations choose their targets based on what will grab and yank at folks' heartstrings — and human attachments certainly qualify in that regard. Hence, attachment issues are quite marketable. But as we argue through the rest of this chapter, as a social entrepreneur you need to draw on more than heartstrings to really make a difference.

Supercharging Public Compassion: The Secret's in the Culture

As you know by now, forming healthy attachments is essential to lessening social distance and ultimately building more successful social relationships and communities. But despite the fact that we're driven to form attachments from the very beginnings of our lives, attachments still don't happen automatically. What we know from studying feral children and children who have faced prolonged social isolation confirms that attachments need the right kinds of social and cultural contexts to survive and flourish. It turns out it really does take a certain kind of village to raise a well-attached child. And when villages are culturally flying apart at the seams, children — and future generations — are in trouble.

Why culture matters

So, enshrining the practice of forming and sustaining attachments within families or neighborhoods and communities doesn't just happen. It only happens through the trigger of culture. In other words, without the nourishing water of an appropriate cultural context, the full potential of attachments only wither and die on the vine.

Although ballet, professional wrestling, and stamp collecting are technically examples of culture, generally speaking we talk about culture in the broader anthropological sense. By *culture* we mean the things people in communities do and feel and think — the ways of living that are socially shared, transmitted, and learned by *members* of communities.

If all this seems obvious to you, that's fantastic! But in our experience, not nearly enough people, including social entrepreneurs, fully appreciate the power of culture. Beyond the link to healthy attachments, culture can be reshaped, sometimes in a hurry, to produce rapid and breath-taking shifts in historical direction. This quality is something that every social entrepreneur should be trying to tap into. More than anything else, how you "do culture" can make or break you.

"Doing" culture

How do you "do" culture? The first principle is that you take advantage of humans' innate ability to imitate and learn from others by imaginatively putting themselves in other people's shoes — something called *role taking*. Even very young children can do this. They can empathetically infer the intentions behind the actions and words of others. With that, they can imitate in uncanny ways. So, be a good role model! People are always watching and learning from you.

Next, be explicit — but not heavy handed — in your socialization toward others. *Socialization* simply means teaching or conveying to others what is socially expected. Given our innate propensity to imitate, the job of learning social norms is already half done by genetics. All you need to do is learn how to help imitative learning along, avoiding punitive sanctions as much as possible while encouraging successful role taking with appropriate rewards.

If you're wondering what such socialization might look like, it could involve a creative combination of leadership (see Chapter 17) and leisure (see Chapter 3). Walk ahead. But if you take the time to stop and invite others to join you on a journey worth sharing, you may find that they'll do more than simply follow — they'll race to catch up and walk at your shoulder.

How do you ensure that your journey is invitational? This is where leisure — especially serious, project-based leisure — comes in. Consider, for example, the fact that much of what nongovernmental organizations (NGOs) do with their supporters involves leisure principles and practices. Sure, there are the usual fundraising galas. But there's much more, and the possibilities are really mushrooming. Some NGOs take their supporters spelunking or rappelling down the side of an office building, on weeklong retreats, on excursions to build affordable housing, and so on. You're limited only by your imagination!

It's in your efforts toward cultural and social change that the hidden compassionate potential of humanity can be unlocked. As a social entrepreneur, the key to spreading the truths of attachments and healthy societies, inclusivity, and compassion lies in your ability, as a social change agent, to shape culture.

Jeroo Billimoria, founder of Childline, India's phone emergency outreach service for children in need of care and protection, has repeatedly used culture and socialization to advance awareness. For example, when it became evident that police, health, and other officials in communities were doing little to assist Childline efforts, despite administrative promises of support, Billimoria went on the cultural offensive.

Childline designed a series of training workshops for frontline workers at police stations, hospitals, schools, and train stations. The workshops were designed to encourage a more sympathetic response to the plight of children in distress. During training, children were brought in to tell their moving personal stories — which brought out the role-taking abilities of the workers. Childline further developed the role taking through role-playing with the youngsters. Discussion about children's rights under Indian law, which strengthened the idea of social norms, followed. Finally, after some 700 training sessions dramatically transformed these public sites into safe havens for India's troubled children, awards were presented to those deemed most "child friendly." See? Cultural change isn't easy, but it can be done and it can bring impressive results in relatively short periods of time.

The ever-changing *forms* of culture have to do with agreed-upon conventions, socialization processes, and empathetic and imitative learning. Culture is incredibly plastic and open to change. This turn-on-a-dime quality is useful to social change agents like you. For example, a decade ago, who was talking about sustainability? No one, really, except a few intellectuals. Nowadays, sustainability is all the buzz. That's another example of changing culture.

The point here is that social entrepreneurs like you should be first in line to identify and shape those aspects of culture that influence attachments. Social and traditional media, for example, are practically tailor made to do this. (Chapter 11 includes discussion on using social media, and Chapter 12 is all about using the media to advance your goals.)

Spreading Public Compassion: The Clarity of Social Insight

Having promoted the notion of culture as a tool you need to use, we'd like to qualify that a little bit: You can almost always take culture — and for our purposes we mean culture promoting attachment, inclusion, and public compassion — to a higher level. As a matter of principle that's consistent with compassion, try to be more effective and more efficient in your attempts to keep your generous promises and make a positive difference in the world, even though you may still fall short in the attempt. This area is where the considerable muscle of human intelligence comes into play.

Discovering social insight

Consider the words of Dr. Martin Luther King, Jr.: "True compassion is more than flinging a coin to a beggar; it comes to see that an edifice which produces beggars needs restructuring." In other words, culture may teach you that certain actions, such as flinging a coin to a beggar, are compassionate. But if you use intelligence to think critically about these things, you may develop the *social insight* to realize that, in flinging the coin, you may be helping to pay for lunch but you're also perpetuating social problems and not dealing with the real and often hidden issues.

The Dr. King quote challenges you to think your compassion through and be more fully generous by understanding that you *must* consider the realities of social institutions and social structures in your compassionate response. Because this kind of thinking and practice is rarely straightforward — typically involving social research and analysis — resource costs are involved. Even more frustrating, the need for social insight often comes at a time when people need your help immediately — and the last thing you want is to get caught up in "analysis paralysis."

Still, we caution you not to scrimp on achieving social insight. Doing so will only come back to haunt you because your understanding of the situation won't *fit* or *work* as well as it could — and you could end up wasting people's time or even hurting them. Ignoring social insight produces only irrelevant or contradictory efforts. Communicating for social change (see Chapter 3), however, helps enormously in developing social insight because, done properly, it puts your finger on the pulse of people's real-life experiences. That focus provides your organization with a powerful value proposition, and knowing what the *real* problems are enables you to set out to fix things.

Seeing social insight in action (and inaction)

A classic example of what happens when good intentions lack social insight comes from Lake Victoria, Africa's largest lake and the third largest lake in the world. Back in the 1950s, British colonial officers thought it would be a good idea to stock the lake with Nile perch. These predatory perch multiplied dramatically and killed off many indigenous species in the lake.

The increasing numbers of perch encouraged the development of a large commercial-fishing industry for Uganda, Tanzania, and Kenya, the countries bordering the lake. In fact, this industry eventually grew to encompass 35 fish-processing plants to meet the growing demands of local and European Union markets. Somewhere along the way, as at least a partial reaction to these market dynamics, the Lake Victoria Fisheries Organisation (LVFO) was formed in 1994 in order to manage Victoria's fish stock.

But that wasn't good enough. Planners and officials didn't fully grasp the demand for the perch and the rising numbers of Lake Victoria fishermen who would rush to supply that demand. So, the numbers of boats on the lake shot up, and uncontrolled fishing, often with illegal gear, was soon rampant. Is this fiasco an unintended consequence as well? Not at all. We argue that critical social insight was missing.

Today, Lake Victoria's fish stocks are seriously depleted. Ten factories have closed, and the remaining 25 are operating at between 30 percent and 50 percent capacities. With rising freight charges and fuel costs, and the opening of new export markets in the Democratic Republic of Congo, Central Africa Republic, and Southern Sudan, even the price of perch fish heads is now beyond the reach of most locals. The livelihoods of some 40 million East Africans are threatened. Tensions and conflicts are growing. These developments could have been predicted and, perhaps, avoided.

A compelling, positive example of the importance of working with culture and doing so in a socially insightful way can be found in Jürgen Griesbeck's social entrepreneurial efforts. Griesbeck was called to change the world for the better in 1994, when his good friend, Andres Escobar, a Colombian national soccer player, was murdered. Escobar had accidentally scored on his own goal in a World Cup first round loss to the United States and, with that loss, his team was eliminated from the tournament. Many Colombians, including gambling syndicates that had bet large amounts of money on Colombia to qualify for the second round, blamed Andres for the team's quick exit from play. On arriving back home in the city of Medellín, Escobar was shot 12 times outside of a bar.

Medellín is known as a violent, crime-plagued city. Griesbeck knew that he couldn't take on the whole crime establishment, but he also recognized that a big part of the problem behind Escobar's death was the general culture of sport surrounding soccer. This, he thought, he might be able to change. Griesbeck started Football for Peace, a soccer program that emphasized breaking down gender barriers, promoting fair and nonviolent play, and keeping children out of gangs. With 10,000 children involved and local leaders trained to continue the program, Griesbeck eventually moved on to spread his version of soccer culture worldwide, using it to battle social exclusiveness, xenophobia, and racism.

Griesbeck realized that children's positive experiences playing soccer around the world were not being shared and celebrated across ethnic and geographic boundaries. He created Streetfootballworld (`www.streefoot ballworld.com`), a Web-based platform for spreading the good news of kids' participation in soccer around the worldToday, Streetfootballworld has achieved a cultural coup. It is now partnered with FIFA — a French acronym for International Federation of Football Association, which organizes the World Cup. FIFA's corporate social responsibility strategy now focuses explicitly on social development. In many ways, Jürgen Griesbeck has managed to transform the cultural institution of soccer at the highest levels and on a global scale, demonstrating remarkable social insight. Andres Escobar, still known as "The Immortal Number 2" and "The Gentleman of Football," would certainly be proud of his good friend's efforts.

There are many other examples of social entrepreneurs who have used social insight to great advantage, but we'd like to mention just one more: Mahatma Gandhi. Gandhi was the trailblazing architect of *satyagraha* (resistance to tyranny through mass civil and nonviolent disobedience).

Gandhi thought long and hard about the nature and dynamics of Britain's institutionalized colonial oppression of India's people. He determined that Britain could justify its treatment of Indians only on the basis of a Eurocentric, elitist, objectifying, and socially distanced conception of the Indian population. To the British, the Indians were uncivilized, lesser humans. This cultural lens justified British rule by force.

Gandhi's nonviolent methods were designed not simply to protest British rule but also to resist it through non-cooperation that was carried out from the highest moral ground of nonviolent love and compassion. This meant that when British authorities physically beat protesting — but completely nonviolent — Indians, they betrayed their own high cultural self-esteem. In an earlier campaign in South Africa, which Gandhi had used to experiment with his initial ideas on nonviolence, Jan Smuts, then South Africa's interior minister, summed up the power of Gandhi's approach when he privately admitted to Gandhi: "You reduce me to helplessness. How can we lay hands on you without looking like villains?"

Developing your own social insight

Social insight is definitely out-of-the-box thinking. It's innovative and creative and difficult to do properly. It does, however, relate directly to what it means to be "entrepreneurial" and it does model leadership, subjects we consider in later chapters.

Where does social insight come from? It's not crystal ball magic. It's the reasoned ability to connect the dots from specific facts on the ground — what's happening to real people — to the social realities they're caught up in as *cultural members* of a complex number of groups embedded in institutional realities. In a nutshell, you start by answering these basic questions:

- Who's doing what to whom, when, and where?
- How and why are these things happening?

By the time you get to the *why,* you'll have achieved a bird's-eye or big-picture understanding — which is, trust us, far too rare.

You need to *work* toward achieving social insight. If you fail to truly consider the *why* of social problems, you'll be stuck in providing band-aid solutions and handouts when hand-up interventions are what people need. Without social insight, you're relegated to just doing charity work — treading water.

Fostering social insight decreases social distance and increases social inclusion by improving your appreciation of what others are going through. It also enhances your ability to make the most appropriate plans and take the most appropriate actions in the name of compassion. As such, you can think of it as the capstone test for compassion.

Chapter 3

Motivation and the Volunteer Spirit

· ·

In This Chapter

▶ Discovering the elements of motivation for social entrepreneurs

▶ Seeing social entrepreneurship as serious leisure

▶ Finding rewards and costs in serious leisure

▶ Working as a devotee in for-profit entrepreneurship

▶ Becoming a social entrepreneurial volunteer

· ·

Knowing what motivates social entrepreneurs and volunteers can pay untold dividends down the road. If you're reading this book, you're probably already motivated to some extent by the passion you have for your chosen issue or project. But to actually put your passion into practice requires a lot more than a desire to fix something. To begin with, other people you may hire or work with may have different motivations, along with different ideas about what they're willing to do. Getting a handle on the kinds of motivation in the social enterprise is key to your success.

In this chapter, we go over many of the elements of motivation and the will to volunteer. Here you find information that can help you understand what it takes to succeed in social entrepreneurship. Some questions we consider are

  ✔ What impels people to take on the different roles that make up a social enterprise?

  ✔ What makes some people want to devote their lives to it, and others to devote a few leisure hours per week to it?

  ✔ How can you use knowledge about the different types and levels of motivation to maximize success in your social enterprise?

What Motivates Social Entrepreneurs?

Would-be social entrepreneurs have a vision of what the world would be like if they succeeded in effecting the change they want. That vision drives them onward to see that change put in place. In this sense, it's simple: They want to solve the problem that's bothering them and help their target of benefits get what is currently lacking. (The *target of benefits* is the group or cause you're trying to serve — we discuss this concept in detail in Chapter 7.)

But that's not the end of the story. Social entrepreneurs also have a very human desire for something interesting and fulfilling to do in their free and/or work time. Social entrepreneurs may be driven by one or more of the following motives:

- ✔ Altruism
- ✔ Community engagement
- ✔ Generosity
- ✔ Compassion/sympathy
- ✔ Leisure
- ✔ Volunteerism

The first three motives in this list invariably inspire social entrepreneurs. The fourth — compassion/sympathy — although exceedingly common, is not a universal motive in the world of entrepreneurship. We cover these four motives in this section. The final two — leisure and volunteerism — are complex; we cover those motivations later in this chapter.

Altruism

Altruism is the selfless pursuit of the well-being and interests of others.

Altruism in the natural world has been a difficult topic in biology and zoology: Some scientists have said that it contradicts Darwin's notion of the survival of the fittest, whereas others have described ways in which altruism is compatible with Darwin.

All altruism consists of a mix of humane caring and sharing of oneself and one's resources with others exclusively for their benefit. Altruism rests on a deep sensitivity to certain needs and wants of a target of benefits. In social entrepreneurship, we see two main forms of altruism: pure altruism and relative altruism.

The desire to help

Abraham Maslow, one of the world's best-known psychologists, said that human needs are ranked by their priority, such that basic needs like food and shelter must be met before meeting advanced needs like self-esteem and achievement. These last two needs can be satisfied by participating in serious leisure, including nonprofit social enterprises, and devotee work, which includes for-profit social enterprise. Moreover, altruism can be expressed in these two kinds of work and leisure, both of which we discuss in later sections of this chapter.

Pure altruism

Pure altruism is the ideal form of altruism, which is only rarely achieved in human beings. The purely altruistic person is totally focused on helping and satisfying another person, group, or other target of benefits, with no sense whatsoever of personal satisfaction that might flow from the altruistic act.

Mohandas Gandhi might be the most famous example of someone displaying pure altruism. (By the way, Gandhi was an extremely active social entrepreneur.) True, he gained considerable acclaim, even power, as a national leader in India, but for him, this status was coincidental. It was not something he sought for its own sake, though he must have subsequently found power to be useful for reaching certain social goals.

Relative altruism

In *relative altruism*, by contrast, the altruist gains a degree of personal satisfaction through the altruistic act. For example, through relative altruism a person may feel good about being altruistic; acquire valued skills, knowledge, or experience; or enjoy the satisfaction of the people who have been helped. The relative altruist gains these benefits while helping the target of benefits experience some satisfaction of their own.

In practice, most altruism is relative. Usually, it's a reciprocal process offering a level of satisfaction for both the altruists and the targets of their benefits.

Community engagement

The social entrepreneur working with a target of benefits wants to change the community in a particular way. This is true even if the entrepreneurial efforts are directed toward the environment. *Community engagement* means performing a civic duty, responsibility, or obligation by working toward amelioration of a community concern.

The motivational platform of community engagement is built from one or more of the following three planks:

- ✔ A desire to solve a community problem
- ✔ A desire to give back to the community, often in the sense of wanting to return what the entrepreneur feels she has gained from it
- ✔ A desire to be part of the community by becoming involved in it and interacting with its members

By the way, the *community* in which one becomes engaged doesn't necessarily have to be your local community. It could be located elsewhere — in a different city, state, region, or country.

All three community engagement planks rest on the vision of working through the community to make it a better place to live. However, different people sometimes have different notions of whether something makes the community *better*. For example, some people oppose the fluoridation of municipal water; they consider it to be poisoning (whereas other people, including many dentists, believe it's an important strategy for reducing tooth decay). Coming to terms with the different points of view in a community is an important aspect of community engagement.

Generosity

People who give liberally of their time, money, or other possessions are *generous*. All generosity is altruistic, though the reverse is not true — that is, a person may altruistically give money or time, but in amounts that may appear to others as ungenerous. Yes, even stingy people can be altruistic, provided they give *something*.

If you want your enterprise to succeed, you'd better be prepared to be generous with *all* the resources you have. Others in the enterprise may well be required to do the same, but you, as the founder, usually have the biggest stake in its success, so you need to be the most generous. People tend to notice outsized contributions. Your success may well rest on especially notable expenditures of time, if not money and, depending on the target of benefits, other resources.

Compassion and sympathy

Compassion means "to suffer with," and *sympathy* means "to feel with." Compassion and sympathy are generated by sensing another person's suffering, leading to an inclination to show mercy for, give aid to, or care for that person — in other words, they lead to altruistic action. We discuss compassion in detail in Chapter 2. Here we focus on its motivational properties as they bear on starting a social enterprise.

We use the term *sympathy* to refer to the compassion toward animals, birds, and other living creatures, reserving *compassion* for inter-human feelings.

Compassion is expressed in response to one or more of three human core values. *Human core values* revolve around humane caring, sharing, and social support. They help motivate social entrepreneurs to act and establish goals in line with their missions. We divide human core values into the following categories:

- **Social religiosity:** Compassionate people may, through religious teachings, become concerned about the suffering of others.

- **Sociability:** Compassionate people may want to interact directly with the objects of their feelings. This, they feel, is the most rewarding and effective way of expressing these sentiments.

- **Personal social service:** Compassionate people may want to satisfy the needs and wishes of others.

Some social entrepreneurs have no need to be compassionate. For example, some aspire to better the environment for aesthetic reasons — maybe they're running a campaign to remove signboards along highways or organizing a club to pick up the litter found on public beaches.

Take some time to examine your own motivations for wanting to engage in social entrepreneurship. Write down what you come up with. You may be surprised by what you find. You may even discover that you can use the information to refocus your goals, change your direction or target of benefits, or seek a different career path that fits better with what you want. If you're running a social enterprise, encourage your volunteers and other hires to write down their own motivations. Doing so could help you make your enterprise more efficient.

The Fresh Air Fund: The compassion of Reverend Willard Parsons

The Fresh Air Fund came into being in 1877 as an independent nonprofit organization. Its mission was simple: to give children living in the poorer urban communities a chance to escape the heat and noise of the street by enjoying free summer vacations in the countryside.

At the time the fund was established, New York City had large numbers of poor children living in overpopulated apartment buildings. Among other miseries, they were susceptible to the tuberculosis epidemic of the day, the cure for which was believed to lie in getting some "fresh air."

Around 1875, the Reverend Willard Parsons was serving as minister of a small, rural parish in Sherman, Pennsylvania. Reverend Parsons encouraged members of his congregation to volunteer as host families, and in this manner provide the neediest of the children of New York with a country vacation. From this altruism, the Fresh Air Fund was born. Its success was almost immediate. By 1881, the fund was growing so rapidly that Parsons appealed for financial help from *The New York Tribune*. With its largesse, the fund was incorporated in 1888 as "The *Tribune* Fresh Air Fund Aid Society."

Today the Fresh Air Fund provides thousands of inner-city young people with escape from the mean streets in which they live. Volunteer host families still help with this project, along with five camps that the fund now operates in upstate New York.

Serious Leisure: Social Entrepreneurship as a Career Choice

As a social entrepreneur, just what are you doing? Sure, you're trying to solve a pressing problem — one that bothers you and perhaps others who are important to you. And yes, you're trying to change the world or a small part of it. But in a career sense, what are you doing?

If you hope to develop a for-profit social enterprise, then the answer to your question might be *work,* or at least something that's work-related. But if you're not sure you're building a for-profit social enterprise — if you don't know whether that's even conceivable, or you don't need or want money from it — then is it really work? How do you place your proposed nonprofit activity in the context of your community? These are important questions to answer because *why* you're doing something can affect every aspect of *how* and *how well* you do it.

If you don't know the answers to these questions, you're not alone. From our own observations on social entrepreneurship, we know that many entrepreneurs never even inquire into the nature of what they're doing. But we believe that having a deeper understanding of what you're doing and why you're doing it can be most clarifying and helpful in your attempt to reach your goals, for three main reasons:

- ✓ It can tell you more about your own motivation for doing what you do.
- ✓ It can show how your efforts fit with other parts of community life.
- ✓ It can help justify your entrepreneurial mission and your zeal for pursuing it.

If what you're doing isn't exactly work, what is it? Well, in a way it's leisure. *Leisure* is uncoerced activity engaged in during free time. In other words, leisure is what you *want* to do, using your abilities and resources in a way that fulfills you. Unlike work, most leisure is free of *obligation* — that's where the uncoerced part comes in. You're obligated to work for a living, unless you're independently wealthy. But you're not obligated to help humanity.

Now, we're not talking about vegging out in front of the boob tube. We define *serious leisure* as the systematic pursuit of an amateur, hobbyist, or volunteer activity that people find so interesting and fulfilling that they launch themselves on a (leisure) career. Staying with an activity such as developing a social enterprise takes considerable effort because you have to stick with it long enough to acquire the special skills, knowledge, and experience you need to succeed.

Serious leisure — what social entrepreneurs engage in — requires the following six traits:

- ✓ You need to have the drive and the commitment to persevere at the activity.
- ✓ You need to have or be aiming at a career that you can pursue.
- ✓ You need to be willing to put in effort in order to gain skill and knowledge.
- ✓ You need to be able to realize special benefits, such as self-fulfillment, self-expression, and group accomplishment.
- ✓ You need to be cultivating an attractive personal and social identity.
- ✓ You need to maintain a unique ethos and be involved in your social world.

By *social world* we mean an internally recognizable set of participants, organizations, events, and practices that have coalesced into a shared sphere of interest and involvement. The social world of a social enterprise might include its funding contacts, suppliers, repair people, service partners, relevant governmental connections, and, of course, the target of benefits (beneficiaries of the work of the enterprise).

To find serious leisure through social entrepreneurship, you must have a sense of commitment and a moral obligation to your enterprise and its target of benefits. These two attributes are key in motivating you to serve as a volunteer in your own social enterprise.

A strong sense of commitment

Many social entrepreneurs have a strong commitment to their enterprise and to their mission. They most certainly *want* to do it, so they *choose* to do it. Yet, it's something they *could* deny themselves, perhaps because they decide they lack the time, energy, money, knowledge, or other resources needed for such an undertaking.

Commitment and leisure may sound like an odd couple, but in serious leisure, commitment is a central condition.

A sense of moral obligation

A strong sense of *moral obligation* drives some people to develop social enterprises. To the extent that they feel "coerced" by their own conscience into social entrepreneurship, they aren't doing it as leisure. Entrepreneurs may be fired up by strong religious convictions, beliefs about social injustice, or a sense of imminent environmental disaster, for example. They feel they have no choice but to act, so they become determined to get a social enterprise up and running. They'd rather be doing something else in their free time. So, it's not really leisure in these cases, but neither is it work exactly because very few of these advocates (dare we say crusaders?) will earn a livelihood through their cause. Still, their compulsive drive can be said to be a kind of personal obligation — one they're powerfully committed to.

Volunteering: Working for something other than money

As you acquire the skills, knowledge, and experience necessary to build a social enterprise, a sense of *career* emerges. And this career — the career of serious leisure that nonprofit social entrepreneurs pursue — is often that of the volunteer. A *volunteer* is someone who offers uncoerced altruistic help, either formally or informally and with little or no pay, for the benefit of both the target of benefits and the volunteer. We discuss volunteers in more detail later in this chapter, but here we want to fit them into our picture of social entrepreneurial careers.

Remember: Volunteering social entrepreneurs are not volunteers for someone else's group or organization. They're volunteering their time and expertise in their *own* enterprises.

But I thought leisure meant relaxation and fun?

Remember the qualifier *serious*. Serious leisure is one of three forms of leisure — the other two are casual leisure and project-based leisure. People "volunteer" in all three forms, but their volunteering is most complex and substantial in the serious form. Serious leisure is a systematic pursuit that can lead to a career.

Casual leisure is short lived, immediate, pleasant activity (think naps, gossiping, or watching TV). It requires little or no skill or knowledge to enjoy. Casual volunteering includes stuffing envelopes, distributing leaflets on a street corner, or taking tickets at a charity event.

Project-based leisure is a short-term, moderately complicated, occasional creative undertaking carried out in free time. It requires some planning, effort, and sometimes skill or knowledge, but it's not intended to become serious leisure. Common projects include throwing a surprise birthday party, working on a home improvement project, learning an instrument, or volunteering at festivals and sporting events.

It's Not All Altruism: Rewards and Costs of Serious Leisure

Why do social entrepreneurs — yourself included — engage in serious leisure? Never fear — people have actually looked into this. Years of research have identified ten rewards of serious leisure. When you engage in serious leisure, you get the following:

- ✔ **Personal enrichment** from cherished experiences
- ✔ **Self-actualization** through the development of skills, abilities, and knowledge
- ✔ **Self-expression** by using the skills, abilities, and knowledge that you've already developed
- ✔ **Enhanced self-image** by becoming known to others as a particular kind of serious leisure participant
- ✔ **Self-gratification** via a combination of enjoyment and satisfaction — also known as fun or, for the slightly more hip, flow
- ✔ **Re-creation or regeneration** of oneself, often especially gratifying after an obligatory workday
- ✔ **Financial return**, often a minor payment for a serious leisure activity
- ✔ **Social attraction** by associating with other serious leisure participants and in the social world of the activity

✔ **Group accomplishment** derived from a sense of helping with a group effort in accomplishing a serious leisure project

✔ **Contribution to the maintenance and development of the community,** including senses of helping, being needed, and being altruistic in making the contribution

Note that the first seven rewards are personal and the last three are social. *Social* rewards are enormously important for volunteer social entrepreneurs. When asked about their own motivations, most social entrepreneurs place the last two items at the top of the list, though for-profit entrepreneurs also stress the importance of financial return. By comparison, amateurs and hobbyists tend to place the first three items at or near the top.

The drive to find fulfillment in serious leisure is the drive to experience the rewards of a given leisure activity. Get enough rewards, and the cost of achieving them become worth it. These rewards are nothing to sneeze at, either. The desires to realize talents and develop oneself — to find personal fulfillment — are powerful interests, described by psychologists as being among our basic needs.

Some costs also come from engaging in serious leisure in general, and social entrepreneurship in particular. For example, many social entrepreneurs have had to face the disappointment of failing to receive funding from a foundation or other granting agency. Moreover, entrepreneurs find some aspects of their serious leisure disagreeable, among them: filling in reports for government to justify charitable status, having to dismiss incompetent paid staff or volunteers, and dealing with community opposition to their social goals. There may be tensions, too. For example, some members of the enterprise can be difficult to get along with and there may be tense relations at times with the targets of your group's benefits.

In short, you *will* also face various costs and you need to consider whether experiencing the rewards and pursuing the social goals is worth it. It probably will be, but examining your social enterprise from this negative angle of costs is a good idea.

The costs of leisure may also be seen as one kind of leisure constraint. *Leisure constraints* are those things that limit your participation in leisure activities, your use of services (for example, limits of bank financing, accounting fees, costs of utilities), and your satisfaction or enjoyment (such as sense of achievement, personal enrichment, and group accomplishment). In volunteering, for example, money, transportation, scheduling, and even your gender can be constraining. (All cultures promote beliefs about what is considered appropriate activity for men and women. So, a woman whose social enterprise revolves around promoting certain religious views would probably not be taken seriously in societies where religious interpretation has always been done by men.) Costs, constraints included, dilute the enjoyment and fulfillment that you experience in pursuing certain leisure activities. This is true even if such costs are overridden by the powerful rewards you get.

For-Profits: The Entrepreneur as Occupational Devotee

The distinction between a serious leisure pursuit and really, really loving your paycheck-generating job is not always clear.

Occupational devotion is a strong, positive attachment to a form of self-enhancing work, where achievement and fulfillment are high, and the core activity has such intense appeal that the line between work and leisure is virtually erased. An *occupational devotee* is someone inspired by this kind of occupational devotion. *Devotee work* — the core activity of the occupation — is work that's capable of inspiring occupational devotion.

Work and leisure are not so easily separated. Although casual leisure and nondevotee work can be seen as separate "coins," serious leisure and devotee work are really two sides of a single, separate coin (see Figure 3-1).

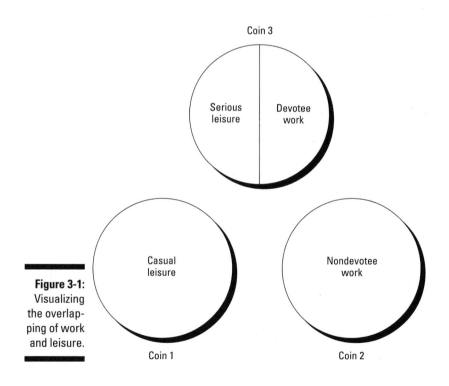

Coin 3

Serious leisure | Devotee work

Casual leisure

Nondevotee work

Coin 1

Coin 2

Figure 3-1: Visualizing the overlapping of work and leisure.

Occupational devotees turn up chiefly, though not exclusively, in four areas of the economy, as long as their work there is not too bureaucratized (see Chapter 13 for more on bureaucracy):

- Certain small businesses
- Skilled trades
- Consulting and counseling occupations
- Public- and client-centered professions

Occupational devotees are, by definition, people who have a passion for their work. Unfortunately, most people work at jobs that they aren't particularly passionate about. But as someone who's interested in starting or running a socially conscious business, you may be one of the lucky ones — you've found work that meets the following six criteria:

- **The valued core activity is profound.** A *core activity* is the set of inter-related actions or steps that you must follow in order to achieve the outcome or product you find attractive (that is, enjoyable, satisfying, and fulfilling). In order to perform the core activity well, you need substantial skill, knowledge, or experience — or a combination of these.

- **The activity offers significant variety.** You're not stuck at a desk doing the same thing day after day. Instead, your job involves many different activities. One day is never the same as the next.

- **The activity gives you the chance to be creative or innovative in your work — your work becomes an expression of your individual personality.** What you're doing on a daily basis results in something new or different that you can shape. You're using your imagination to carry out daily routines. As an added bonus, you're not likely to be bored as a socially conscious entrepreneur.

- **You have control over the time you invest in your job, which means it never becomes a burden.** Medium and large bureaucracies tend to not provide this criterion. In the interest of the survival and development of their organization, managers often feel they must deny their employees this freedom and force them to accept stiff deadlines and heavy workloads. No activity, be it leisure or work, is so appealing that it invites unlimited participation during all waking hours.

- **You're good at the work you're doing — and you *like* it.** One man's meat is another's poison. John finds great fulfillment in being a physician, for example — an occupation that holds little appeal for Jane who, instead, adores her for-profit social enterprise (work that John finds unappealing).

- **You work in a physical and social environment that encourages you to focus on the job at hand.** This criterion refers to the working conditions in your enterprise, to its lighting, temperature, level of noise and the like, and to the people with whom you work, including their personalities, behavior, and commitment to their roles in your enterprise.

A number of things can happen that transform what was a devotee job into one that becomes largely disagreeable. There may be a reduction in the variety or level of inventiveness the job once offered, for example. A lawyer in a firm may be assigned only one kind of case, whereas before she was handling a variety. Or the lawyer is told to follow a certain model of legal procedures that eliminates the inventiveness of being able to choose her own. Someone may have to work significantly longer hours — even serious leisure can't be pursued indefinitely without rest and rejuvenation. Or the physical and social environment can change for the worse, such as increased ambient noise or heat or reduced quality of air. Or maybe a new colleague comes to work in your enterprise who turns out to be unlikeable or uncooperative.

If any of these changes happen, and you nevertheless stay with the enterprise and its mission, you become an entrepreneur driven by *disagreeable obligation*. In other words, it becomes just a regular job like so many others. Keep this in mind as you pursue a career in social entrepreneurship: The devotee and leisure qualities of the activity can become undermined by uncontrollable external forces. (We examine many of these potentially damaging external forces in Chapters 13 and 18.)

But this is a two-way street. You may currently be employed in a nondevotee job — whether it's one that was formerly highly attractive to you or one that never was. Starting and running a social enterprise can become one way of escaping this unpleasant situation. At first, this is likely to be serious leisure, carried out after stints of disagreeable employment. Later, it may become devotee work, as the enterprise becomes more profitable.

Leisurely Volunteering

So far, this chapter has mentioned three kinds of social entrepreneur: volunteer, obligated, and for-profit. Whichever kind you are, it is highly probable that, at least in the early stages of development of your enterprise, you'll also seek volunteers to help realize your mission.

To the extent that your enterprise becomes driven by profit motives, reliance on volunteers tends to decrease and may even disappear. In fact, volunteer workers of the casual and project-based variety are almost exclusively found in the nonprofit sector of the economy. And this only makes sense, as the altruistic motive of selflessly giving your time to an endeavor squares poorly with the business ethic of labor compensation.

Defining what a volunteer is

Volunteers are people who feel that they're engaging in enjoyable serious, casual, or project-based leisure for an activity that they can accept or reject on their own terms. (We're *not* talking about social entrepreneurs here, but about people who give some of their time to help the social entrepreneur.)

A key element in the leisure conception of volunteering is the absence of coercion, moral or otherwise, to undertake a particular activity.

The preceding paragraph is sometimes called the *volitional* definition of volunteering. (The more common *economic* conception of the volunteer just means people who don't get paid, avoiding the messy, though critical, question of motive that we're examining in this chapter.)

A volunteer performs, for a period of time, a valued service or benefit in either an informal or formal setting. It's through *volunteer work* that the volunteer provides a service or benefit to a target of benefits. He usually receives no pay (though people serving in volunteer programs are sometimes compensated for out-of-pocket expenses), and it must be actual work. Giving, say, blood, money, or clothing may be altruistic and even generous, but it's not volunteering.

Identifying what volunteers get out of the deal

As a social entrepreneur, you as a volunteer and the people you engage as volunteers are, in both instances, altruistically providing a service or benefit to others who are also benefiting from the rewards mentioned earlier in this chapter (pleasant social interaction, self-enriching experiences, a sense of contributing to nonprofit group success, and the like).

Volunteering is motivated by both altruism *and* self-interest.

The self-interested component of volunteering is important because personal interest is a main explanatory element in leisure motivation. To prove this, you only have to consider that many people want to help others, but they tend to gravitate toward "interesting" altruistic opportunities, from which they believe they'll reap some positive, personal, nonmaterial rewards — such as experiencing pleasure, developing themselves by acquiring a new and valued skill, or expressing their skills and knowledge in satisfying ways.

Volunteer activities in the world of social entrepreneurship can be divided into six types of interest. Volunteers develop an interest in activities focused on one or more of the following:

- ✔ People
- ✔ Ideas
- ✔ Things

✔ Flora (trees and other plants)

✔ Fauna (fish, birds, mammals, and other animals)

✔ The natural environment

Each type offers its volunteers an opportunity to pursue, through altruistic action, a particular area of personal interest. Thus, volunteers who like working with certain ideas are attracted to idea-based volunteering (such as spreading a religion or teaching a language), whereas those who like certain kinds of animals are naturally attracted to faunal volunteering (saving the seals, the whales, the polar bears, or the whooping crane).

Any one of these six kinds of interest may be pursued by following any of the three kinds of volunteering: casual, project-based, or serious.

Searching for volunteers

Volunteers are not all the same. They differ in their reasons for volunteering — they may be pursuing serious, casual, or project-based leisure through their volunteer activity. And, depending on which of these three they're pursuing, their contributions to your enterprise will vary.

Serious leisure volunteers

Social entrepreneurs, as we've mentioned, are volunteers of the serious leisure variety. They may also need to engage other, similar types of serious leisure volunteers to serve as lobbyists, legal advisors, publicity specialists, secretaries, or treasurers on a board of directors, to give just a few examples. The social entrepreneur usually recognizes such people as kindred spirits, who find the same kinds of rewards and levels of commitment in their leisure.

Consider environmental volunteering, which entails either monitoring or changing a particular set of external conditions that affect people, flora, or fauna. Serious leisure volunteering in this case might include maintaining hiking trails and trout streams as well as organizing and conducting environmentally related publicity campaigns. These campaigns might include anti-smoking, clean air, clean water, anti-logging, or anti-mining campaigns; or promoting access to natural recreational resources such as lakes, forests, and ocean frontage. Any of these could also be pursued as leisure projects. The casual volunteer finds plenty of opportunities in these examples, seen in door-to-door distribution of leaflets promoting a clean air campaign, for example, or picking up litter in a park or along a highway.

If you don't bump into these kindred spirits in the course of establishing your social enterprise, you may want to turn to organizations that train serious leisure volunteers. One such organization — Social Entrepreneur Corps — was established to train such volunteers for work in *development,* a fancy term for assisting less developed countries. The company was founded as a worldwide organization for social entrepreneurs. The founders, former Guatemala Peace Corps volunteers, worked for many years to create intelligent entrepreneurial and educational solutions for long-standing developmental challenges. Social Entrepreneur Corps provides university students, recent graduates, and young professionals with the means to experience and participate in innovative developmental work. The organization has been able to assemble highly effective teams in which all members — interns, volunteers, travelers, and locals — gain from their participation in the common project. You can find out more about Social Entrepreneur Corps at www.socialentrepreneur corps.com. You may also want to consider VolunteerMatch (www.volunteer match.org) or One Brick (www.onebrick.org), two organizations that try to match the needs of nonprofit organizations with volunteers who can help meet those needs.

You can also try local volunteer centers. Such groups often offer training or steer you to sources of training for volunteers serving in certain positions, particularly those on boards of directors. Usually, though, you train your own volunteers (see Chapter 18).

Casual and project-based leisure volunteers

Nonprofit social entrepreneurs often need one or both of the other two types of volunteers — those serving in casual roles and those serving in projects. True, the serious volunteers could also conceivably act in these ways, but as you see in Chapter 18, if you rely too heavily on your serious volunteers, you risk overusing these valuable people. So the wise entrepreneur searches for other helpers to meet casual needs and those associated with projects.

Casual and project-based volunteers are all looking for their own leisure experiences, of the sort described earlier.

Building things is one activity with a lot of project-based volunteering. Some *material volunteers* organize their work for Habitat for Humanity as a project, as do those who donate their trade skills to fix plumbing or electrical problems at their church or help construct the set for a high school theater production. More examples of material volunteering as serious leisure include regular volunteers who repair and restore furniture and clothing donated to the Salvation Army, prepare meals for the indigent, and perform secretarial or bookkeeping services for nonprofit groups.

Volunteers providing water filters and electrical lighting to developing countries are engaging in serious leisure material volunteering, as are volunteer firefighters (when they're not rescuing people or cats up trees). Casual material volunteering refers to such activities as regularly stuffing envelopes for a nonprofit group mailing, picking up trash along beaches or roadsides (which could also be classified as environmental volunteering), and helping keep score at youth sporting matches.

Casual and project-based volunteers are looking for their own leisure experiences — not careers. Casual and project volunteers can certainly become committed to the tasks they've agreed to perform, but in order for this to happen the tasks must be short term. If these volunteers were looking for long-term altruistic involvement, they would seek opportunities to volunteer for serious leisure positions. (See Chapter 18 for a lot more on managing volunteers in your enterprise.)

Mixed-interest volunteering

Many volunteer activities bridge two or more of the types described in this chapter. One example would be pro bono legal service, which deals with both ideas and people. Volunteer consultants also work with ideas and people, as do zoo and museum guides and volunteer teachers and instructors.

Missionary work invariably centers on both ideas and people and may also involve material work, such as building a school, church, or hospital. Conceivably, missionary work could extend across *four* kinds of interest: people,

ideas, things, and the natural environment. In this situation a missionary would work with local people to establish safe water practices and resources, which would require cleaning up the surrounding environment.

Membership in certain nonprofit groups brings with it many different types of activities. Examples include Boy Scouts and Girl Scouts, in which youth are instructed in such diverse endeavors as knot tying, leadership skills, outdoor survival, and identifying plants and animals.

Chapter 4

Communicating for Social Change

In This Chapter

▶ Being your own muse by talking to yourself

▶ Communicating with small groups and hierarchies

▶ Breaking down barriers to communication

▶ Communicating for the common good

ommunication has a central place in achieving social change. Initially, many might react skeptically to that statement. Talk and things get better? Aren't we supposed to walk the walk, not just talk the talk? Isn't talk cheap — and don't actions matter more? "Sticks and stones may break my bones," we're told as kids, "but names will never hurt me."

Well, as we hope to show in this chapter, even the very naming of things in the world does have a transforming power. In many respects, the world changes — rapidly — as a direct result of human communication.

As a social entrepreneur it behooves you to master the world-changing power of language, so that your communication is powerful and effective. This chapter aims to show you some ways of harnessing your communication capabilities in the field of social entrepreneurship.

We think a good place to start is close to home. That is, with you.

Talking to Yourself Helps More Than You'd Think

Before you can communicate effectively with others about changing the world, you need to figure out how to communicate effectively with yourself. After all, if you don't know what you're talking about, how will anybody else? You have to develop a healthy and productive internal dialogue with yourself.

Sometimes this internal conversation happens automatically — you may not even mean for it to happen. Depending on your worldview, the welling-up origins of unexpected internal conversations might be found in your deepest spirituality, your unconscious mind, your evolutionary programming, your innate capacities for creativity, a chance remark made by someone — or whatever. The ancients used to call this internal voice the *muse*.

Your muse may strike in profoundly emotional ways that shake you up and demand your attention. You might then go on to debate with yourself, for example, a flash of insight about your enterprise — or not. You might turn it over in your mind before deciding what to do about it. Or you might simply trust it implicitly and wholeheartedly from the beginning.

Maybe you have a little voice in you that tells you to do something (similar to Leymah Gbowee — see the nearby sidebar, "The market women of Liberia"). Great! But take that as a starting point, not the end of the discussion. Psychological research shows that your success in such matters depends to an important degree not so much on your optimism — though pessimism can certainly have a negative impact! — but on your keeping your mental nose to the grindstone and maintaining self-regulation. According to social cognition psychologist Alain Morin, it's through sustained self-observation, setting clear and reasonable goals, avoiding distractions (such as the desire for immediate gratification), and avoiding *self-control depletion* (through, for example, fatigue) that you achieve the self-regulation you need to succeed.

And the key to self-regulating is your *self-talk* — your internal conversation. Simply put, self-talk enables you to keep focused on what you need to pay attention to. By exercising an active and controlled internal conversation with yourself, you engage your *working memory capacity,* a fancy term for your capacity to keep vital information in an agile, rapidly recoverable form. Communication begins with you. By routinely accessing your internal communication guidance system, you maintain focus and keep yourself on task.

What's the most effective way to talk to yourself? Don't leave the process to chance or whimsy; keep track of it. Start journaling. As a social entrepreneur, you need to continually make sense of your efforts and their context. To do that, you'll need to routinely tap into the knowledge embedded in the practice and know-how of your own experience and the experience of others.

Stay with it. The groundwork knowledge that you draw on will only grow and develop to its fullest potential when you systematically record what you're experiencing and learning. What you're finding must be kept available to your agile working memory capacity throughout your journey. Journaling as self-talk allows for that to happen. Socrates claimed that, "The unexamined life is not worth living." So keep examining yours — and talking to yourself about it.

The market women of Liberia

Social entrepreneur, Leymah Gbowee had a dream a few years ago. Her people — the people of Liberia — had suffered enormously during the 1990s and early 2000s in a civil war between the corrupt and ruthless government of Charles Taylor and warlords battling to overthrow him. Untold tens of thousands were killed during those years, and Liberia under Taylor was a country in ruins. The women of Liberia, led by the likes of Etweda "Sugars" Cooper, Vaiba Flomo, Asatu Bah Kenneth, and Leymah, were desperate for their families and the welfare of the country and weary of a life that had become a living nightmare. That's when Leymah had her vision.

"It was like a crazy dream," she remembers in the internationally acclaimed, award-winning documentary film *Pray the Devil Back to Hell.* "It was somebody telling me to get the women of the church together to pray for peace." That dream became a rallying call for one of the most inspiring women's movements in history — the "market women" of Liberia.

Every day for 2½ years, these women organized close by the fish market where they earned their meager livelihoods and sustained their families. They prayed and talked about peace, networked to get their word out, and rallied to pressure Taylor to negotiate a peace agreement. Ultimately, the women would play a major role in ousting Taylor and replacing him, in 2006, with Ellen Johnson-Sirleaf, the first woman president of any African country. Whether divinely inspired or not, the point is that a fundamental social change in African and Liberian history was aided by a social entrepreneur's unexpected internal conversation — a "crazy" dream.

Communicating in the Social Enterprise

As a social entrepreneur — heck, as a human being functioning within almost any social context — you're constantly sending and receiving information through talking, gesturing, writing, signing, singing, taking videos and photos, touching, making eye contact, and, yes, even ignoring someone. There really can't be any meaningful communication unless there is a sender and a receiver. They work together in a commonality. To show that such a commonality exists, the receiver of communication generally provides feedback.

There also needs to be some sort of medium or channel through which the communication takes place. At one end — let's say it's your end — you need to have an idea that you want to share, for whatever reasons. You deliver your message as clearly as possible in a format that's understandable. At the other end, it helps if the receiver of your communication is ready for your communication. For example, let's hope they're not distracted by a hungry baby or a radio blaring in the kitchen.

You'd think that would be enough to constitute communication. However, even if your message has been delivered well and the receiver is ready to accept it, it still has to be decoded correctly. As you know, interpreting a poem, a work of art or architecture, or even a simple conversation isn't always easy. Finally, your message has to be responded to — that feedback thing. Knowing whether the receiver "got" your message is vital, and feedback usually conveys whether accurate understanding took place.

You may think this stuff is simple and obvious. But we see many social entrepreneurs who never even get this far into practicing effective communication. And they wonder why dealing and working with others is such a struggle.

The etiquette of communication

According to linguists, a large part of communication has to do with etiquette. A listener will go to almost any length to give a speaker the benefit of the doubt regarding whether something said actually makes sense — but the listener will often take offense at the smallest perceived slight, which is of course almost always unintentional on the part of the speaker. That's why communication is filled with elements like "please" and "if you don't mind" and "I hope I'm not bothering you, but . . ." and so on. It's also why people use smiley faces in e-mail messages.

To make communication in your enterprise flow more easily, everyone needs to follow a few basic rules:

- ✔ **Operate under the assumption that all incoming and outgoing messages have value.** No message should be regarded as pointless or boring. When you're sending a message, keep in mind what your audience wants to hear — what's going to seem most important to them. And when you're receiving a message, try to grasp why the sender thinks that what he's saying is important enough to communicate with you.

- ✔ **Always clarify things when they seem muddled, and confirm things when you think you've got things right.** Nip any potential for misunderstanding in the bud, or it can snowball into misunderstanding. That may be all right for a sitcom plot, but you've got an enterprise to run.

- ✔ **If you're going to be critical, be positive first.** Finding the value in the other person's messages and building on that is a good idea.

- ✔ **Communicate to gain trust.** Remember that no social entrepreneur will succeed without strong collaboration — and collaboration won't happen without *trust*, a basic building block in all human relationships and, therefore, societies. So, be sure that your communication with others is always honest and transparent. Anything veiled or two-faced will not only quickly dismantle the collaborative bridges you need to be building but also destroy your credibility as an entrepreneurial leader and community role model.

Communicating in small groups

Working day in, day out with small groups of 3 to 15 people is the lifeblood of social entrepreneurship. Basically, there are two kinds of small groups: those with leaders and those without.

Groups without leaders

Leaderless groups, such as those you might find in a circular configuration where you tend to communicate only with your neighbor, tend to be pretty slow in getting things done. With everyone working as equals, there is little need for a coordinator of information, making it hard for a leader to emerge. On the other hand, the team spirit of leaderless groups tends to be high and these groups show flexibility when it comes to solving problems.

Groups with leaders

On the other hand, *leadership* in small groups tends to arise where there is a need for an information hub or coordinator of communications. The presence of a leader certainly speeds up the communication process and produces good results when confronting relatively straightforward problems, but it doesn't necessarily work well when problems are very complex. Group members who find themselves farthest away from the group leader (in terms of communicating over physical distance or across cultures) may feel alienated. When convoluted, unforeseen problems demand large amounts of information sharing, the "leadership-as-hub" structure tends to bog down, bringing the system back to a more or less leaderless type.

Communicating in hierarchies: Directions and grapevines

As you move into more elaborate organizational structures or hierarchies, formal and informal communication takes on *direction*. In hierarchies, the direction of formal communication is typically downward, with order givers issuing directives to order takers. Understandably, regardless of the content, downward communication doesn't usually make for close relations among organizational members.

A common feature of hierarchies is that communication, whether formal or informal, is documented. Hierarchies are the home of the paper trail — or nowadays, the e-mail trail. Rarely is there ambiguity in a hierarchy regarding who said what to whom.

But formal communication can also be upward and sideways. More progressive managers these days encourage solicited and unsolicited, informal, upward communication. Tasks and decisions are often merely delegated rather than micromanaged, for example. This situation is a kind of empowerment, and it's motivating and satisfying to organizational members. Knowing that a decision or suggestion is treated appreciatively as that information makes its way up the hierarchy is highly rewarding. Needless to say, you want to create an organizational culture that values and provides genuine opportunities for upward communication.

Sideways, or lateral, communication occurs as bureaucratic levels and departments becoming increasingly interdependent. In these situations, you find more personal conversations, small-group get-togethers, troubleshooting sessions, and so on.

Hierarchies can also exhibit more informal "diagonal" communication that bridges people and departments on different levels. The flow is multidirectional and requires trading lots of information. Working on a major project that pulls together many organizational resources and calls for speedy exchanges is a natural fit for diagonal communication.

Grapevines, on the other hand, are nearly impossible to control and can spread all over the place, including outside the organization, regardless of chains of command. Information often flows much faster through grapevines than it does through formal channels for a couple reasons:

- ✔ **In grapevines there is no documentation, which means that information is easy to create and modify — and is open to ridiculous variations in interpretation.** There's a natural tendency to fill in the gaps in information that is often fragmented and incomplete.

- ✔ **Grapevines grow through chained small clusters of people.** When information quickly works its way along the chain and hits a cluster, *boom!* — it's off in a whole bunch of new directions.

Naturally, grapevines can be dangerous and can create massive headaches for managers, especially those who tend to be control freaks. But grapevines do have an upside: They can be very useful in supplementing more formal channels of communication. They can tap into people's imaginations, satisfy people's most basic curiosities about what's really going on, and provide a safe place to vent fears and frustrations.

If grapevines get out of hand, it's generally because of misinformation or ambiguity surrounding an issue. So, work hard to be clear about what's really going on. And if things aren't so clear, if things are still being worked out, then admit to that, clear the grapevine air by telling the truth, and make a commitment to filling people in regularly.

Overcoming barriers to communication

Despite the importance and power of communication, successful communication doesn't necessarily come easily. In fact, many, many barriers to successful communication can spring up unannounced at any time. You should always make every effort to anticipate these barriers before they appear or manage them when they do. Broadly speaking, communication barriers come in two forms, which we call noise and bias.

Noise barriers tend to be physical, biological, or social system issues such as loud undesirable sounds, speech difficulties, poor eyesight, time constraints, physical distance, organizational complexity, language differences, and so forth. Noise barriers are often easily remedied, but because not everyone reports such problems, they can go unnoticed.

Bias barriers, on the other hand, are quite complex. They're rooted in culture and tend to manifest in terms of individual choices — for example, using jargon, awkward sentence structure, poorly organized ideas, emotional barriers born of aggression or fear; selectively filtering or distorting information (as in hearing what one wants to hear); making false assumptions about motives; paying attention to communications from managers but not underlings; and communicating in gendered or culturally specific ways. All these problems can degrade the operation of your enterprise, so watch out for them.

How can you anticipate or overcome noise- and bias-related communication barriers? Well, as trite as the advice may sound, there are three important and very basic principles to observe. The first relates to noise, the second to bias, and the third to both:

- ✔ **Know and control your setting as much as possible.** If, for example, you're getting ready to speak to seniors in an auxiliary hospital or facility for transitional care, you may want to be sure that you're in close proximity to your audience and emphasize a friendly, audible, physical presence. Take a moment to assess the physical surroundings or communication technology you're using and make adjustments as necessary.

- ✔ **Know your audience.** To continue with the seniors' example, double-check to be sure that your communication is not demeaning or in any way threatening to your audience's sense of capability. Elders often strongly resist being treated as incompetent, so you need to temper your concerns with tact — especially when dealing with sensitive subjects.

- ✔ **Ask for and give frequent feedback.** View every communicative attempt as a pilot project, tentatively made and always subject to revision. And keep the big picture visible. As the writer Antoine de Saint-Exupery put it: "If you want to build a ship, don't herd people together to collect wood and don't assign them tasks and work, but rather teach them to long for the endless immensity of the sea."

Communication in Social Development

No discussion of communication and how it relates to social entrepreneurship can be complete without looking at the place of communication in *social development* — the fancy name for the process of transforming social structures to improve the capacity of societies to reach their potential.

Development communication versus communication for social change

Over the years, some interesting differences in terminology have developed. Academics, planners, and other "experts" tend to talk about the discipline of *development communication.* More grassroots-oriented communication specialists, such as Alfonso Gumucio-Dagron, tend to refer to *communication for social change.*

Although both approaches respect culture and tradition, local knowledge, and dialogue between development specialists and communities, *development communication,* according to Gumucio-Dagron, has become institutionalized and often implies a static, inflexible "blueprint" for social development. *Communication for social change,* however, "does not attempt to anticipate which media, messages, or techniques are better, because it relies on the process itself, rooted in the community from which the proposed action must emerge." We prefer to go with the more grassroots approach of communication for social change, which features many elements of participatory informal or popular education, while respecting any contributions that can also be made by the academics and planners.

As the recent documentary film *What Are We Doing Here?* (directed by Brandon, Daniel, Nick, and Tim Klein) demonstrates in frustrating detail, when social entrepreneurs , nongovernmental organizations (NGOs), philanthropic foundations, and others attempt to deal with serious health and poverty issues in Africa, the lines of communication — and related policy-making — typically run from the top down. In other words, the Western "experts" end up dictating terms to the local peoples on the ground. This is often a recipe for disaster, and we have the failed development aid initiatives, spanning several decades now, to prove it.

But when local voices prevail — when local interventions are coordinated by local, truly democratic, participatory, and emerging policies and lines of communication — social development efforts have a tendency to "fit" and work much, much better.

Homemaker's Union and Foundation

A superb example of how communication for social change models can work comes to us through the efforts of a group of Taiwanese homemakers. Homemakers? Yes, as we've seen elsewhere in this book, women, especially mothers, are often on the forefront of social and environmental change. Many grassroots social and environmental change initiatives organize around the compassionate undercurrents of what's sometimes called *motherwork*, which centers on family, children, and future generations. (We expand on this topic, among others, in Chapter 5.)

Four decades of oppressed homemaker social energy was unleashed with the lifting of martial law in 1987. Formerly socially marginalized, a group of Taiwanese women became a force to be reckoned with as they founded the Homemaker's Union and Foundation (HUF), a potent organization responsible for developing an environmental, consumer, and educational reform movement.

HUF's tremendous success was a direct result of the way in which members communicated with each other and their public. The group initiated contact with academics, planners, and other experts in order to learn as much as they could about their many pressing issues. They then brought what they learned back to their communities, educated their neighbors, and communicated for social change through demonstrating, petitioning, distributing pamphlets, being interviewed on radio and television, meeting with local politicians to influence policy — and much more. It was their communication strategy that enabled them to achieve reforms.

HUF also pursued other, more action-oriented avenues. "Talking the talk" — called *advocacy,* the pursuit of influencing outcomes — can lead to action. But starting out with action can also end up reaping huge returns. In 1993, HUF initiated cooperative buying of two products: rice and grapes. Within seven years, the group had expanded its buying to 300 items and, through local word of mouth, had attracted 6,000 members to its co-op.

This, by the way, was also the method of Jim Grant, former CEO of UNICEF. Millions of children's lives were saved as the result of simply going out and making vaccinations cheaply and widely available. Prior to Grant's tenure, all the advocacy in the world wasn't having the needed impact. With Grant, however, advocacy arose in waves, spontaneously, often through sheer word of mouth, *after* the good work was done.

Participatory democracy: The foundation

Communication dynamics work much better with the context of *participatory democracy* firmly in place — and people the world over are waking up to that reality. That is, if communication has a central place in effecting social change, that communication will happen more effectively and efficiently within participatory democratic structures. Whether you're working at home or abroad, this means that in a globalized and highly interconnected world, you can expect that a participatory ethos will be framing much of your communications.

As Kumi Naidoo, Secretary General and CEO of CIVICUS, South Africa, put it recently: "Although faith in traditional political institutions is waning, this should not be taken as a sign of citizen apathy. On the contrary, people are finding new and more direct ways to get involved in public life and decision-making — marking a shift from representative democracy to what is often called participatory democracy." CIVICUS (www.civicus.org) is an international alliance of organizations that works to strengthen citizen action and civil society throughout the world, especially in countries where democracy is weak.

Establishing just such a context, then, is a high priority. That's why the United Nations' Economic and Social Commission for Asia and the Pacific (ESCAP) currently promotes the Urban Forums movement, which aims to help cities and countries achieve sustainable and effective development around social, economic, and environmental issues. (Visit the commission's Web site at www.unescap.org.) Another example is the Korat Forum. (Korat is the nickname for the Thai city of Nakhon Ratchasima.) Through its activities, designed to enhance public awareness of the principles of participatory democracy, Korat is today a healthier, friendlier, more livable city than it was in the past.

Communicating trends and tipping points

The next chapter, Chapter 5, discusses the use of trends in social entrepreneurship. Here we want to look briefly at communication's place in promoting social trends. One of the most hoped-for developments among social entrepreneurs is that their message will be propagated and listened to, and that their efforts will be supported or replicated by many others over time. Using communication to start and contribute to a noticeable cultural shift is probably the secret wish of most social entrepreneurs.

You know you're really promoting social change when the average Jane and Joe accept and celebrate what you do. Although achieving such status isn't the sole or even most important criterion for success, given the scale of problems today it is entirely natural to want to feel that your efforts amount to more than a drop in the ocean.

The publication of Malcolm Gladwell's book *The Tipping Point* (Back Bay Books) increased the popularization of social trends. Now, it seems, people are keener than ever before to spot the "levels at which the momentum for change becomes unstoppable," as Gladwell puts it — the points at which one more straw will break the camel's back. One of the book's themes is that the communication dynamics between people can be compared to an epidemic, or a viral outbreak. An idea takes on a life of its own and replicates itself through communication networks. As a social entrepreneur, you should try to capitalize on and promote your ideas via this phenomenon whenever you can.

Another point Gladwell makes is that three types of people — "Mavens" (information experts), "Salesmen" (charismatic endorsers), and especially "Connectors" (social relationship hubs) — work together to disseminate information to larger groups. Whereas Gladwell plays up the role of "connectors," Duncan Watts, a network theory sociologist, shows that other, less socially connected members of networks, and perhaps the networks *themselves,* are at least as important in driving emerging trends.

Trends tend to spread to the larger culture out of small groups that adopt and encourage early versions of trends. Our advice for you, the social entrepreneur, is this: Get thee into trendsetting groups and tell your story there. If you're successful, your story will spread outward.

The Lost Boys and Girls of Sudan have been able to garner increasing recognition and support for their cause by taking their message to university campuses, coffee houses, and bistros all over Europe, North America, and Australia. These remarkable social entrepreneurs, intent on redeveloping a homeland catastrophically decimated by decades of civil war (more than 2 million dead and 5 million displaced), have become widely recognizable and are the subject of a good deal of media buzz. Couple that trend-seeking communication strategy with the capacity building that the Lost Boys and Girls are doing in Southern Sudan, and you have the makings of an authentic and significant emerging social trend.

Chapter 5

Using Trends to Harness the Next Big Things

*W*hen you're starting or running a social enterprise, your objective should be to ensure, to the best of your ability, that your efforts today fit the needs of tomorrow. A correct reading of future trends makes it much more likely that you'll remain in a position to cooperate with others in making the world a better place. It also helps you maximize the resources that are available to you. Appropriately plan for the future, and your enterprise will profit in many, many ways.

Paying close attention to trends will make a big difference in the success of your enterprise. Trends paint a picture of what's happening today. They indicate broad patterns of regularity and changes in direction or movement, including revisions to human needs and behaviors. The earlier you can identify, participate in, and respond to these changes, the more proactive, instead of reactive, you can be in effectively developing and maximizing new social entrepreneurial opportunities for yourself.

Identifying Major Trends Facing the World Today

In this section, we cover the kinds of trends that you can count on, not the "here today, gone tomorrow" garden variety. Many prognostications come and go, and their authors often seem to have simply generated them in order to bring attention to themselves. But the trends we cover here are large-scale, global trends that have shaped our world for some time and will continue to do so for the next decade or more. In other words, we consider these particular predictions about trends to be relatively solid. You can probably bank on them being around for some time and return to them as you envision the future contexts of your social ventures.

Get together regularly with other social entrepreneurs to discuss these and other trends. You just may find that you achieve a sophisticated view of major trends that rivals that of the experts, so don't sell yourself short. Discussing trends enables you to work smarter (not harder), steer clear of nasty surprises, minimize your weaknesses, and play your strengths to the hilt.

Before we look at specific trends, we need to preface those vistas with a few disclaimers:

- ✔ **We don't claim to accurately anticipate specific future events here — that's why they're called *trends*.** What we do hope to do is provide you with reasonably plausible — good enough — scenarios that will allow you to align and influence your future:

  - Alignment: Alignment has to do with understanding that perhaps more often than not, you can only know how things are developing and go with the flow.

  - Influence: Influence recognizes that, if you know the course of history, you may, especially with the right allies, be able to change that course somewhat, at least as it pertains to you.

- ✔ **What we're up to is not technically *forecasting*, which relies on quantitative, statistical modeling.** Though we do draw somewhat on these methods, in this chapter we're essentially trying to provide some intuitive foresight into the conditions that may well impact you and other social entrepreneurs over the next few years.

- ✔ **When it comes to predicting the future, definitions and methods are imprecise, right across the board.** In principle, this is because we're extrapolating beyond any available data, which is always a dangerous and iffy practice. Indeed, some may claim that, given that reality, it's not worth the bother. We disagree, simply because although trend watching is far from certain, the alternative — not paying attention to trends — can be deadly to your efforts.

Globalization of science and technology

The term *globalization* is one of the greatest buzzwords of our times. Different people define the term differently. Here's how we define it: the increasing integration and interdependency of human culture.

Thanks to advancing communications technology — especially sophisticated cellphones, cable television, and the Internet — economic, political, social, and environmental cultures are all able to spread rapidly all over the globe. Perhaps the most permeating culture sweeping the world is the globalization of science and technology itself.

By *science* we mean the systematic study of the natural world through experimental observation. By *technology*, we mean the practical application of scientific knowledge to understanding our environment and developing and producing artifacts.

Understanding how science and technology affect everything else

Of course, the spread of technical knowledge has been going on for much of the history of our species. Even our earliest ancestors were very likely capable of observation, categorization, pattern recognition, prediction (hypothesis testing), and causal reasoning — in other words, all the hallmarks of scientific thinking. Yet it wasn't until relatively recently, with the advent of the Industrial Revolution from the 18th to the early 19th century, that things really began to take off. With the Industrial Revolution, major changes in agriculture, manufacturing, mining, and transport had a profound effect on the socioeconomic and cultural conditions in the United Kingdom, Europe, North America, and eventually the world. As a result, our daily lives have never been the same.

Today, continual and accelerating innovation in technology is almost universally seen as a basic determinant of globalization. And, of course, science and technology also play an important role in the spread of other cultural forms such as politics, economics, the arts, and so on.

Compare the possibilities for life today versus those of even 100 years ago. The standard of living that many people enjoy today would've been totally inconceivable back then. In fact, some scholars claim that half the population of the United States is alive today simply because of 20th-century technological improvements to the delivery of public health.

Beyond that, just consider some recent scientific/technological achievements: high-energy subatomic particle physics, sequencing the entire human genome, the Hubble telescope, sending spacecraft out of our solar system, and much more.

Even human intelligence, as measured in IQ tests, seems to have leapt beyond the confines of its genetic limits. IQ gains are shown to increase dramatically from one generation to the next, which isn't supposed to happen. This remarkable phenomenon seems to be very closely tied to the power of human culture and socialization — and at least in part, to the rise of scientific literacy.

Using science and technology in social entrepreneurship

How can you use and further such interesting developments? Be a leader and an innovator and build new enterprises. And do one more thing: Accomplish these goals while retaining your moral compass and leaving a lasting legacy for tomorrow. You'll find all these themes addressed in detail throughout this book, with the moral compass issue covered in the next section. The nearby sidebar "Innovator in rural electricity: Fabio Luiz de Oliveira Rosa" contains a particularly stellar example of what we're talking about.

Science and technology: Neutral tools

For all its marvelous successes, the globalization of science has also become an enormous problem, thanks to the proliferation of powerful knowledge and technologies that can cause untold destruction. This is not science's fault, though. Science is, at its core, just a tool — it simply shows us how to get from A to B. It has nothing to say about *why* we've decided we need to get to B in the first place. The *why* is a matter of our values. In a world of competing value spheres, dishonorable ends can too easily displace honorable ones. The fact that Nazi doctors conducted horrific medical experiments on Jews, for example, shows that even the healing arts can be bent to deadly aims. That's why scientific work is so heavily scrutinized by ethical review committees worldwide.

With a tool, you have to keep the *ends* in mind. But as the classical social thinker Max Weber pointed out, sometimes no explicitly held ends exist. This might be the case now, when rapid competitive innovation and social change create such a sense of flux that we've "lost our way." Or maybe it happens when we lose our ability to socialize each other toward some common end. Regardless, in those situations of an "ends" vacuum, the means can become the ends. It can be argued that scientific means have become their own ends.

As a social entrepreneur, when you embrace science to get things done, you should never forget the honorable ends you're pursuing or allow them to be displaced by scientific means, as enticing and powerful as they may be.

Perhaps one of the best examples of this needed balance coming to life is the growing push to democratize the Internet through social and participatory media and citizen journalism. There's a whole world at stake. The futures of inequality, community, politics, organizations, and even culture itself may well hang in the balance, depending on how the remarkable technology of the Internet continues to develop. For starters on further investigation, you may want to visit the Media Consortium (www.the mediaconsortium.org) or MediaShift Idea Lab (www.pbs.org/idealab), both of which are excellent and frequently updated resources for keeping abreast of these issues.

EXAMPLE
EXAMPLE

Innovator in rural electricity: Fabio Luiz de Oliveira Rosa

Fabio Luiz de Oliveira Rosa is a social entrepreneur of almost legendary proportions in southern Brazil. His story begins when a friend's father, Ney Azevedo, was elected mayor of Palmares do Sul, a rural municipality in Brazil. Azevedo soon invited Rosa to take on the post of secretary of agriculture for the municipality. After accepting his new position, Fabio set out to talk to local farmers and other rural residents. He discovered that where politicians talked of building roads, impoverished rural folk talked of needing to boost local agricultural output, family incomes, and quality of life.

Why was agricultural output so low? The vast majority of arable land in Palmares was lowland, useful only for growing rice. But the water needed for growing rice was held by wealthy landowners who kept it behind dams and in private irrigation channels. They would *sell* their water, but the cost to local farmers was exorbitant. So, no water, no rice production.

Eventually there did prove to be a way around this problem: A college professor in the region, Ennio Amaral, had, some years earlier, developed an electrical amplification technology that could inexpensively deliver electricity from the public grid to rural areas. When Fabio turned up Amaral's solution, modified it, and put it into practice, the beneficiaries were hundreds, then thousands, then more than half a million families who could now afford refrigeration, indoor plumbing, water pumps for irrigation, common household and farm electrical appliances, and so on. Affording the water pumps meant fewer expenses in growing crops, more production, and in some cases increases of more than 400 percent in farm incomes.

This situation not only boosted local consumption, industry, and commerce, but demonstrated that rural life was once again feasible. That reversed the flow of migration from rural to urban areas and also proved to be great for Brazil's cities, because the burden placed on their social services was lightened.

As fate would have it, though, when Brazil's public electricity system was suddenly privatized in the 1990s, rural electrical delivery was immediately viewed as unprofitable. Services were directed toward cities, large industries, and farms. Fabio's initiatives ground to a halt.

But he was undeterred. Now the problem was how to affordably get off-grid electricity to rural areas. The answer was solar panels. In 2003, Rosa's market research established that rural Brazilians spent an average of $11 per month on batteries and other nonrenewable energy sources such as candles and kerosene.

Rural Brazilians weren't interested in buying solar panels, for a number of different reasons, but they *were* ready to rent the technology if it could be made affordable on a monthly basis. So Rosa, through his for-profit The Sun Shines for All (TSSFA) venture, charged customers an initial modest installation fee and then micro-leased (offering low rent over long periods of time) a photovoltaic energy system to rural households for less than $10 per month. The program was a success, overcoming local suspicions about the affordability and reliability of solar electricity.

Urbanization

In learning to collectively and culturally use science to master the world (or at least better survive in it!), it was sensible and efficient, and perhaps inevitable, that humans would continually rethink the division of labor. Along with a whole host of factors, the increasingly sophisticated specialization of interdependent labor created a need for larger and more complex human settlements that enabled closer communication, mutual regulation, and proximity to valuable resources.

Bigger, denser, more problematic

Both developments — more sophisticated divisions of labor and more complex forms of human settlement — have contributed to the continual rise of science by taking advantage of our social and cultural leanings. Throughout human history, people have been living in larger and more dynamically dense settlements — a process called *urbanization.* The world is rapidly becoming a city — and the gargantuan *megalopolis* (an extensive metropolitan area or a long chain of continuous metropolitan areas) is here, springing up all around the world, to prove it.

Current trends indicate that new births and rural *out-migration* (people moving from the country to the city) are boosting urban populations everywhere. The United Nations estimates that more than half of the world's population now lives in urban areas — towns or cities — for the first time in history. This first 100 years of this new millennium is, according to UN-HABITAT (the United Nations agency for human settlements), the "Urban Millennium."

The urbanization trend represents an enormous change from the beginning of the 19th century, when cities of 100,000 or more inhabitants housed less than 2 percent of the world's population. By 2050, the same UN body estimates that more than 6 billion people, or about two-thirds of humanity, will be living in urban settings.

Some experts think those estimates might be high because rapid urbanization can be messy and unsustainable. In worst-case scenarios, though, rapid urbanization outpaces any functionally available supporting infrastructure, resulting in *pseudo-urbanization* (when a large city comes to exist where there's no supporting infrastructure to support it), which only aggravates the usual urban problems of overcrowding, poverty, unemployment, crime, social upheaval, and environmental degradation. Under those conditions, many people who've migrated to cities looking for a better future will end up leaving. Right now, if anyone is leaving cities, it's the affluent and socially mobile. By "counter-migrating" to suburban and satellite areas, they benefit from improvements in rural electrification and Internet service, while at the same time taking advantage of public transit for commuting.

What social entrepreneurship can do about urbanization

Solving the infrastructural problems of urbanization and the basic physical and organizational conditions that cause counter-migration are possible only with the help of various levels of government, which can network scientific and technical expertise on a large-enough scale. In 2006, for example, the Indian government sought a whopping $60 billion to finance, among other things, the water and electrical system installations required for Mumbai's distant suburbs and satellite areas. Projects like that are, of course, beyond the abilities of even the most deeply pocketed social entrepreneur.

Nevertheless, every social entrepreneur and member of the public should keep in mind that government — which is, like science itself, a tool — ought to be the means to ends, not the ends themselves. The urbanization of the world packs with it enormous challenges, and governments are, on their own, relatively powerless to meet those challenges. Governments need moral direction from *all* of us — including you, the compassionate social entrepreneur, listening so closely to community needs. (We continue considering the role of government in the section "Swamping governments," later in this chapter.)

Where governments fail in producing adequate means to achieving honorable ends, you have to hold them accountable — and you should also be ready to pick up the slack until the government gets its act together and helps out. You can see, then, the tremendous responsibility that you shoulder as a social entrepreneur! Often somebody has to get the ball rolling, and countless examples abound of exactly this kind of situation prompting the efforts of some of our most heroic social entrepreneurs. (See the nearby sidebar "Innovator in AIDS treatment: Veronica Khosa" for an example.)

Innovator in AIDS treatment: Veronica Khosa

In 1990, Veronica Khosa, a nurse to those suffering from HIV/AIDS in South Africa's Gauteng province, saw that the needs of those patients were overpowering her own capacities to provide care, not to mention the capacities of a completely ineffective healthcare system. Hospitals, in dealing with what the UN called the "worst infectious disease catastrophe since the Bubonic Plague," were sending HIV/AIDS sufferers home without so much as a dressing or ointment for open sores or aspirin for pain.

Knowing that something had to be done and that government at all levels was ill-equipped to deal with the problems, Khosa decided to completely reinvent fundamental healthcare around a community-, family-, and home-based nursing model. Today, Khosa's Tateni Home Care Nursing Services, in partnership with SOS Social Centre, delivers care to thousands of people living with HIV/AIDS as well as orphaned children. Just as important, Khosa's model is so successful that the Gauteng provincial government has widely adopted it in policy and practice.

Innovator in immigrant education: Judy Koch

Judy Koch, former English teacher turned CEO of RSP Manufacturing Corporation, understood the importance of the urban multicultural reality and its place in social productivity. Eighty percent of her employees were Hispanic, so she concerned herself with helping them and their children improve their language skills.

But when Koch retired after selling RSP in 1997, she took things much further. She founded the Bring Me a Book Foundation, a self-sustaining social enterprise that provides read-aloud workshops and libraries to underserved English, Spanish, Vietnamese, Mandarin, and Cambodian communities. The Bring Me a Book Foundation (www.bring meabook.org) has served more than 480,000 families to date in more than 850 libraries in such diverse settings as preschools, child-care centers, homeless shelters, clinics, hospitals, community centers, Boys & Girls Clubs, and businesses throughout the United States and elsewhere.

Urbanization carries with it other impressive opportunities for social entrepreneurs — which you may well want to tap into. In our current global knowledge economy, prosperity cannot exist without constant innovation. But that innovation depends on social investment in the talent and creativity of a nation's people and its future generations — that means all its people and everyone to come, not just a select and homogenous few. It's the cross-fertilization of ideas spanning cultures and different ways of looking at the world that will drive innovation and prosperity in the future. Societies, therefore, will need to create environments of inclusion in which all citizens can contribute with their particular skills and ideas if they're going to get ahead. (See the nearby sidebar "Innovator in immigrant education: Judy Koch" for an example.)

Population growth

Go forth and multiply? Check. We're at almost 6.8 billion and counting — that's despite China's one-child family planning policy (introduced in 1979).

The rising tide of humanity

Some experts believe that rising population is the number-one trend affecting the world today, but we think current population issues are an unsurprising outcome of the first two major trends we've discussed so far in this chapter.

Over the past few centuries, the global population has been growing. Gradually, life grew less brutish, harsh, and short, and fewer infants and women died in childbirth. For a long time, human populations had grown slowly, and thanks to high rates of disease and violent death, these populations tended to be young. But then science began to turn the tide in our favor. To an extent much greater than ever before, we could affect nature and transform the world in ways that benefitted us. Humanity has adaptively succeeded to such a great extent that the reality in which we live today is very much one that we, as technicians and toolmakers, have fashioned for ourselves.

As a result of our increasing scientific prowess, infant mortality decreased and life expectancy increased. Humans became victims of our own success at survival, and our numbers began to explode. It wasn't all about science, however. Along with that and just as important, women, under the unswerving regulation of pre-modern traditions, continued to bear and raise large numbers of children, doing so over about 70 percent of their adult lives. This potent meeting of new and old culture explains how the Earth's population soared in 150 years from fewer than 1 billion in 1800, to 2.5 billion by 1950 — and then shot through the roof in just 50 years to 6 billion by 2000. If that's not incredible enough, in less than a decade, as of mid-July 2009, we've gained another three-quarters of a billion! According to the Web site Worldometers (`www.world ometers.info`), which provides world statistics updated in real time, the world's population is increasing at a rate of about 150 per minute. That's 9,000 per hour; 216,000 per day; or 78,840,000 per year.

Although we should be clear that most Western countries have achieved virtually zero population growth without immigration (see the upcoming section, "The nuclear family"), this same potent meeting of new and old cultures scenario is now especially at work in developing countries, where the populations are soaring to previously unimagined heights. For example, China's population, by 2050, is expected to reach 1.4 billion. India's, by 2030, will surpass even that — by 2050 it should be about 1.6 billion. All told, our global population is expected to top 9.2 billion by the midpoint of the 21st century.

However, substantial population *decreases* are being seen in certain areas, due to changes in governmental policies; the rising cost of raising children in industrializing, industrialized, or post-industrial societies; and women's desire to work rather than only have babies. Western societies are either not growing or are declining in population. And part of the reason for India's population overtaking China's is because China's population is already in decline. Figure 5-1 graphs these trends.

Social entrepreneurship and population issues

The coming slowdown doesn't mean that the global population is reversing. No, as Figure 5-1 shows, our numbers will continue to increase over the next few generations, just not as rapidly. There will continue to be a huge need for population control measures and sexual and reproductive healthcare — and for innovative solutions to the problems brought on by population increase.

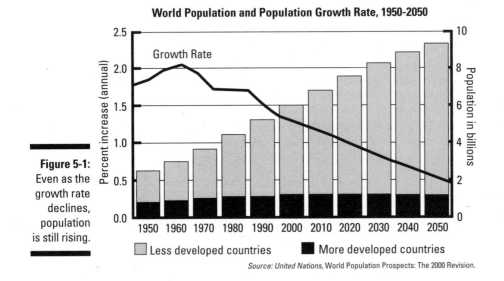

World Population and Population Growth Rate, 1950-2050

Figure 5-1:
Even as the growth rate declines, population is still rising.

☐ Less developed countries   ■ More developed countries

Source: United Nations, World Population Prospects: The 2000 Revision.

This area is one in which social entrepreneurs have made and will continue to make a difference. There will still be a need for efforts like Population Action International (www.populationaction.org) and Population Connection (www.populationconnection.org), both of which seek to bring our numbers into balance with our environment and help reduce global poverty by advocating for women's rights and social justice issues such as providing access to sexual and reproductive health.

EXAMPLE

Innovator in health products: David Green

As a Schwab Fellow of the World Economic Forum, David Green has worked to sustainably, affordably, and accessibly bring medical technology and healthcare services to the poor, who make up two-thirds of humanity. His *humanized capitalism* or *compassionate capitalism* makes use of business production capacity and surplus revenue to meet the needs of many.

For example, in 1992 Green helped establish Aurolab in India. As a nonprofit, Aurolab manufactures intraocular lenses (IOLs) which are implanted into the eye as a replacement lens during cataract surgery. Today Aurolab is one of the world's largest manufacturers of IOLs (with 10 percent of the global market share) and sells its lenses for $2 to $4, whereas in developed countries those lenses would sell for $150. Just as importantly, Aurolab, under Green's guidance, manufactures sutures and has reduced the price of ophthalmic sutures from $200 to $25 per box. With that, an enormous imbalance is beginning to be addressed — only 10 percent of suture products are sold to developing countries, which are home to 70 percent of the world's population.

If you're not factoring in population numbers into your efforts, then you're probably missing a big chunk of the social context that will almost surely affect you. In many cases, you'll be faced with the problem of ever-expanding scale; needs and wants may well outpace your ability to respond — unless you're prepared.

Issues Arising from the Major Trends

Globalizing science, urbanization, and population growth are gigantic forces shaping our collective futures. They're so powerful they can spawn "storms" of change in other areas. The good news is that social entrepreneurs are leading the way in facing up to these more focused challenges.

Consumption and waste

The big three trends discussed so far are responsible for tremendous consumption and waste-producing stresses that are rapidly and dramatically degrading our planet's environment and ecology. Consumption and waste are linked by many to what U.N. Secretary-General Ban Ki-moon calls "the greatest collective challenge we face as a human family": climate change.

Some say consumption and waste are Western phenomena, where 15 percent of the world's population hoards 85 percent of the planet's resources. Consumption and waste aren't population issues, they claim — they're cultural greed issues.

We say yes and no to that. Not too long ago, it may have been the case. But with globalization, the Asian rim, Indian subcontinent, and many parts of Africa are all racing to jump onto the Western-style consumption bandwagon. Cultural greed is no longer exclusively Western. Some estimate that humanity would need five planet earths to support the full process. No wonder we're looking longingly at our moon, Mars, and beyond. In the meantime, we need to keep our eye on the ball — this ball called Earth.

Many people are working to remind us of this truth. Here's one example: Conceived by the World Wildlife Fund (WWF) and the *Sydney Morning Herald* in 2007, Earth Hour is held every year on the last Saturday of March from 8:30 to 9:30 p.m. It asks people around the world to voluntarily turn off their nonessential lights and other electrical appliances for one hour. In 2009, the Philippines topped Earth Hour participation as 647 cities and towns and more than 15 million Filipinos were estimated to have joined in the hour-long lights-off campaign to raise awareness about human energy consumption patterns and its link to climate change. Globally, participation in Earth Hour increased ten-fold from 2008 to 2009; in 2008, 400 cities participated, while in 2009, 4,000 cities in 88 countries participated.

Some may say, "What? Turning off clocks and lights for one hour? Is this the best we can do in meeting the 'greatest collective challenge'?" No, it's not the *best* we can do, but culturally speaking it's a hugely important step in the right direction, especially when we look at the phenomenal increase in Earth Hour participation over a short period of time.

Clearly, people are getting the message. And in large part that's due to local, smaller-scale social entrepreneurs everywhere organizing families, friends, neighbors, communities, and businesses to hold candlelight or light-emitting diode (LED) parties, sell eco-friendly products for charity, or host eco-friendly office events. For more ideas on how to start something that helps, search the Web for "Earth Hour party ideas."

Another person who is pushing the idea of responsible consumption, trying to make it a cornerstone of meeting environmental challenges, is Helio Mattar, of the Akatu Institute for Conscious Consumption (www.akatu.org.br). Mattar is moving social and environmental change forward using a two-pronged approach. On the one hand, the Akatu Institute promotes conscious consumption by demonstrating to the public how our consumer habits challenge the limits of the natural world and threaten life on our planet. And on the other hand, Mattar partners with consumer and other social organizations, governments, and investors to press for changes in the way that companies measure success. This is done most importantly through the Akatu Scale of Business Social Responsibility, a 4-category, 60-item scorecard that companies use to demonstrate to consumers their BSR practices.

The nuclear family

One of the most important and fascinating global population developments revolves around the *nuclear family* (parents and their children). The number of nuclear families has been increasing from generation to generation as more healthy children grow up to have families of their own. Large families used to be the norm because more children meant more people to help with the work that needed to be done. In many parts of the world, these extended families persist because of cultural tradition.

Yet, as global population growth is beginning to slow, family size has been shrinking. Two of the more important population-growth countries — China and India — have instituted one- and two-child policies. Women are becoming more and more involved in mainstream economic activities, and the cost of raising children in modern economies is rising. Did you know that raising a child to the age of 18 in Western countries costs about $300,000?

What are the implications of these troubling family trends? It seems quite likely that tremendous numbers of families of small sizes, coupled with increasing family insecurity as both parents work in low-wage economies, are going to dramatically push up the value of each and every child worldwide. More and more, children will be seen as more precious.

We envision, then, a world where the "pro-family" voice will become louder and stronger with every passing year, and social entrepreneurs will be in the thick of things. Any threats to the family, whether in terms of economic, social, or environmental instability, will become more unacceptable. Remember the earthquake in China's Sichuan province in 2008? Tragically, some 90,000 people were killed or went missing in that terrible quake. But you may also remember not only the normal extreme anguish but also the great anger of the parents of more than 5,000 schoolchildren who were also killed or went missing in the quake when it was revealed that the children had died under the collapse of poorly constructed schools in a known earthquake zone. We see this pro-family trend increasing worldwide, including in the U.S.

Families will continue to push for the creation of family-supportive communities and better integration into those communities in attempts to shore up their diminishing resources. There will be lots and lots of work — and support — here for family-oriented social entrepreneurs. In the case of the Sichuan earthquake, volunteers, led by Beijing-based artist and social entrepreneur Ai Weiwei, have investigated, recorded, and accounted for the loss of children's lives. This group's social insight is apparent: "Once you have the basic facts, you know who is responsible for those kids," Ai told CNN.

The ever-rising concerns of growing numbers of families are going to be a major impetus for positive social change more than at least the next couple of generations. Consider that families themselves are the most potent and fundamental socializing force shaping the hearts, minds, and practices of future generations. Countless small nuclear families will be enormously concerned about the dehumanizing effects of misplaced, forgotten, or usurped ends. These families will also be quick to criticize negative urbanization and environmental effects.

Families will need more support and execution from governments at all levels. Despite their allegiances to other competing interests, such as those of big business, governments will likely have to attend to pro-family concerns and join with them in demanding far greater corporate social responsibility (CSR) from the private sector (which we address in the "Trends in Social Responsibility and Corporate Social Responsibility" section, a little later in this chapter). Family is, after all, the backbone of every society — and the voting base of every democratic one.

Not surprisingly, then, many social entrepreneurs are already working to protect and develop children and their families, and nurture and support communities. Here are just a couple of examples:

- ✔ Joseph Terry Williams spent his professional career helping low-income families. In 2007, when Williams retired, he set up a nonprofit program to help low-income families buy their own homes and achieve financial self-sufficiency. The Wyoming Family Home Ownership Project (www.wywf.org/WYFHOP.html) works with local churches and businesses to educate low-income families about their finances and helps them to contribute monthly, over two years, to a home-ownership account, which allows for a house down payment as well as a modest emergency fund. Williams says this about the project's efforts: "This is about the power of local people to take action and own solutions. It is also a chance to change reality for a generation of children who deserve to grow up in a safe and stable environment, and whose futures hinge upon the financial stability enabled by home ownership."

- ✔ Vera Cordeiro started Renascer Child Health Association (www.criancarenascer.org.br/ingles/Inicial-Ing.htm) in 1991. At the time, she had been working in a public hospital in Rio de Janeiro. But Vera was dismayed when children, apparently treated successfully for infectious diseases, were soon returned to the hospital where they died from the disease because they become re-infected at home. It was obvious to Vera that whole families needed to be treated, not just the sick kids. Today Renascer furnishes families with an impressive range of social services, seeing approximately 1,000 people per month. The model is so successful that it's currently being replicated in at least 24 other independent centers. A further dozen or so new centers will be added to the network by the end of 2011.

Families, of course, have deep affiliations with at least three other vocal demographic groups:

- ✔ Educated youth and young adults

- ✔ Women who no longer have child-rearing responsibilities

- ✔ Older adults (including the massive baby boomer population), who are today healthier and more keenly aware of social and environmental issues than any previous similar generation

These groups will likely join with the family in championing its causes. In the next section we briefly consider these groups.

Innovator in energy efficiency: Avery Hairston

Avery Hairston and his friends founded RelightNY when Avery realized how slow the United States has been in adopting compact fluorescent light (CFL) bulbs. CFLs, Avery discovered, reduce the cost of electric bills, generate less heat, and last far longer than ordinary incandescent light bulbs. In fact, according to the U.S. Environmental Protection Agency (EPA) Web site, "If every home in America replaced just one incandescent light bulb with an Energy Star–qualified CFL, it would save enough energy to light more than 3 million homes and prevent greenhouse-gas emissions equivalent to those of more than 800,000 cars annually."

With these kinds of justifications in mind, and sensing an opportunity to make a real difference, RelightNY was off and running — using donations to supply, among others, low-income housing project residents with CFL bulbs. To check out the kind of impact RelightNY is having, see www.relightny.com, where an interactive map of New York City shows how the light bulbs are proliferating. At the time of this writing, 57 RelightNY teams have changed more than 112,000 bulbs and eliminated more than 22,000,000 pounds of CO_2 emissions, saving New York City $5.5 million.

The discerning youth and young adults of the world

From the civil rights movement, Vietnam War protests, and social movements of the 1960s and early 1970s, to the Tiananmen Square massacre in China, to the recent pro-democracy protests in places like Myanmar and Iran, students continue to voice their displeasure with governments and big business alike. Sometimes students even shed their blood and lives for their causes.

Students and young people around the world are committing even further to positive social change. Many are counseling or talking to their peers about drug and alcohol abuse and addiction, safe sex and HIV/AIDS, alternatives to violence, poverty, staying in school, and much more.

These commitments among youth are also translating into dramatic shifts in professional and career choices. These days, for example, it's increasingly common for students to get college and university educations in disciplines such as environmental science and in community, international, and sustainable development, among other similar fields. Educated youth are on their way to bettering the world in profound ways, building bridges between the "academy" and local communities.

Kjerstin Eriksson is one of the young adults to watch — and emulate. Kjerstin, as a 20 year-old junior studying public policy at Stanford University, founded Facilitating Opportunities for Refugee Growth and Empowerment (FORGE) in 2003. Today, FORGE is an official operating partner of the United Nations Refugee Agency (UNHCR) and is working in three different South African refugee camps, serving 60,000 refugees.

Women, demanding their proper place

Just as students have for years been at the forefront of social change, so too have women. From the ones who confronted the Love Canal polluters in 1977, to the anti–cruise missile protests of the Greenham Common Women's Peace Camp in the 1980s, to the women who blocked MacMillan Bloedel from clearcutting Clayoquot Sound — the dissenting voices of women have been, and continue to be, unflinching. Women, as the deeply socialized bearers of the caring ethic, understand and respond when family and community are threatened.

Boomer power

As families have fewer children, and life expectancy increases (U.S. males are now living, on average, 75 years, only 5 years less than their female counterparts), older adults will make up a larger share of their societies. In 2006, those 65 and over numbered 500 million. By 2030, more than 1 billion of the world's population, or one in eight people, are estimated to be in that age category.

In Western societies, the graying phenomenon will be largely the result of aging baby boomers — in the United States alone, boomers comprise the 77 million people born between 1946 and 1964. Demographers have been frantically waving their arms in the air about this phenomenon for some time now.

We need to catch on: Boomers are the largest generation in human history. Imagine the good that could come from encouraging and supporting their civic engagement. The same opportunity awaits many other boomer societies around the world. What a favorable moment for social entrepreneurs to leverage their skills and philosophy!

Innovator in young women's rights: Olga Murray

Olga Murray of Sausalito, California, is an 80-something on a mission. That mission? Through her social enterprise, Nepalese Youth Opportunity Foundation, Olga is trying to end the *kamlari* system in Nepal, which sees thousands of young girls every year sold into bonded servitude by their poor parents. NYOF's method of ending *kamlari* is perhaps a little unusual, but it works: The foundation simply offers each family a piglet or a goat if the family allows a daughter to stay home and receive an education. The exchange works because the animals are easy to keep, and can ultimately be sold for more money than might be received from their daughter's labor.

NYOF's efforts are paying off on a national level as well. The foundation's Web site (www.nyof.org) recently announced a major victory in its campaign to free Nepalese girls from servitude. After much lobbying, the Nepalese government pledged $1.6 million toward eliminating the *kamlari* system and educating those young girls who've been sold into bondage.

Boomers are a bit of an enigma. They're renowned for their independence, entrepreneurial work ethic, and consuming habits. But they're far less likely than their parents (Tom Brokaw's "Greatest Generation," which battled the Great Depression, fought in World War II and the Korean War, and built up the Western industrial world) to involve themselves in volunteer activities. Some estimates claim that somewhat less than one in three baby boomers plan to give back in terms of community service after retirement.

This lack of boomer interest in community service might be due to a few factors:

✔ Boomers and other older adults may see a serious lack of resources available to support their involvement. If boomers were to start engaging in community services, many agencies would be scrambling to handle the influx. Perhaps, sensing the lack of infrastructure to facilitate their involvement, and not wanting to face endless frustration, boomers are opting out before even joining. (Charlotte Holstein would certainly agree with this idea, as we explain in the nearby sidebar "Innovator in local sustainability: Charlotte Holstein.")

✔ The global economic recession of the late 2000s has also eroded many boomers' retirement funds dramatically and forced them to continue working into their planned retirement.

✔ Many boomers see themselves as self-starters, preferring to work on their own rather than through agencies as volunteers.

Now, somebody, maybe you, can step up and take advantage of this latent, untapped talent.

Swamping governments

It goes without saying that governments, especially democratic ones, will be the target of the demands issuing from families, students, women, and older adults. There's a rising sense that people are questioning where the heck we're all going — concerns over ethics, transparency, and sustainability are a huge part of that — and that governments should either facilitate that process or get out of the way.

In the United States, the Obama Administration, with its United We Serve nationwide campaign, has decided to facilitate that process. Perhaps it will model real governmental-civic partnership to the rest of the world. The administration is calling on all Americans to participate in the nation's recovery and renewal by serving in their communities.

There is even a very explicit place for the social entrepreneur in this scheme of things. If you have a service opportunity of your own, you can register it with www.serve.gov and invite others to join.

Innovator in local sustainability: Charlotte Holstein

You might want to follow Charlotte Holstein's inspiring example. In 1998, Charlotte established Forging Our Community's United Strength (F.O.C.U.S.; www.focussyracuse.org), a nonprofit designed to engage local citizens and organizations in the major economic, social, and environmental issues facing the Syracuse, New York, region.

After much public discussion involving literally thousands of people, almost 90 goals relating to building sustainable community were developed and put into action. Among them, F.O.C.U.S.

created a no-cost ten-week Citizens' Academy that would boost community member participation and help folks recognize how government actually functions. Related to that, F.O.C.U.S. is actively involved in partnering with Syracuse University's College for Human Development and Health Professions, the New York State Office for the Aging, and various national agencies in preparing communities nationwide for the economic and social impact of baby boomer retirement and civic involvement.

Trends in Social Responsibility and Corporate Social Responsibility

If governments are getting the message and aligning themselves with the grass roots and communities in a general insistence that we all need to practice social responsibility (an admittedly hopeful but debatable statement), then it should come as no surprise that business should have similar expectations placed upon it. No one can or should be exempt. We don't anticipate that the calls for increasing CSR will quiet down anytime soon, regardless of whether that responsibility for the impact of business activity on the environment, consumers, employees, communities, stakeholders, and all other members of the public is ultimately self-regulated. In fact, a recent Institute for Corporate Culture Affairs (ICCA) CSR Globe survey of the top 100 multinational corporations indicates that 49 percent of the companies have CSR governance systems in place (www.csrglobe.com/pdf/Report.pdf).

Not everyone buys CSR as a reality. Some people believe that CSR is a farce, nothing but a public-relations campaign — all talk, no action. Others in the business community insist that the attempt to link CSR to long-term profitability is pie-in-the-sky. They claim it can't be achieved because it contradicts the bottom line, or is easily superseded by the imperative to turn a profit and keep shareholders happy.

Yet, more and more businesses, governments, and communities believe that CSR is

- ✔ An absolute social necessity, not open to debate anymore — an idea whose time has come
- ✔ Ultimately good for the bottom line, even though the positive results may not be immediately evident

It seems inevitable that the heavy hitters in the corporate world will have increasing expectations placed on them by humanity at large and its governments, to join with everyone else in achieving social responsibility. And if those corporations would serve as role models to everyone else on the supply chain and pass on those expectations as well, then we may well be on the way toward a better world.

The final sections here in this chapter discuss a few important ways in which CSR is being realized. Every one of them offers you, the social entrepreneur, many potential avenues for involvement. (For more information on CSR, see Chapter 8.)

Social impact assessments

One of CSR's most straightforward applications is the *social impact assessment* (SIA). SIAs are, as the name suggests, attempts to determine the impact on human populations before, during, and after development projects.

SIAs are tools that everyone should be picking up and using. It's incumbent on businesses to move beyond the bottom-line-only mentality and consider the impact of their ventures on communities. Just because you can make a profit doesn't mean that you *should*.

Remember the bit about how means shouldn't govern ends? The SIA provides a way to determine whether we should, for example:

- ✔ Build the Three Gorges Dam Project (the largest dam in the world) on China's populated Yangtze River
- ✔ Expand one of the world's busiest airports, Heathrow Airport, in London
- ✔ Open up South Africa to tourism
- ✔ Bring oil down from the Arctic through the Mackenzie River Valley
- ✔ Introduce predatory Nile perch stock for commercial fishing purposes in Lake Victoria, Africa

Ethical investing

Most people would love to invest in a startup company that would pay us handsome dividends as it grew! But at what cost to society and personal integrity are we willing to do so if the company operates unethically? The following types of investing attempt to address this issue:

- **Socially Responsible Investing (SRI):** SRI is about investing while following your values and ends up being a defensive posture against so-called "sin stocks" — stocks from companies that are in some way thought to be involved in unethical or immoral activities.

- **Sustainable Investing (SI):** SI is about proactively investing in triple-bottom-line stocks — ones that promote environmental, social, and profitable ends.

Both vehicles allow investors to invest in companies that are socially responsible and promote positive change even as they go about making money. (Chapter 8 discusses this topic in a bit more detail.)

Philanthrocapitalism

Wealthy people often want to pitch in, and tax incentives are usually a big reason why. People with deep pockets are finding new ways to dramatically redefine the relationship between capitalism and philanthropy, ushering in a new age of *philanthrocapitalism* (venture capital financing, high-tech business management, market economics, and an expectation of return on investment either over the long term or through secondary benefits such as corporate recognition, as these apply to social programs and philanthropic causes).

When, in 2006, Warren Buffett donated $40 billion of his holdings to the Bill and Melinda Gates Foundation, already valued at $37.6 billion, Buffett and Gates showed the world only a glimpse of philanthrocapitalism's financial might. However, there is a great debate today about the role of philanthrocapitalism in making the world a better place. Business interests and democracy have long had a tenuous relationship, and some people are understandably suspicious of philanthrocapitalism's motivations, arguing that it gives the wealthy even more power over the lives of others and the policies that govern them.

But even the philanthrocapitalists — at least the good ones — are humble in assessing the place of their practice in the grand scheme of things. The founder of eBay, prominent philanthrocapitalist Pierre Omidyar, has said, "I don't believe there is a for-profit answer to everything, but if for-profit capital can do more good than it does today, foundations can concentrate their resources where they're most needed."

How should social entrepreneurs go about forging productive relationships with this new philanthropy? You need to determine whether you need philanthrocapitalism and in precisely what way. Keep in mind that pursuing profit should be, first and foremost, for the purposes of sustaining the social enterprise. Only after that base is covered should profit flow back to the venture funders. And if it doesn't, it doesn't. At that point, as Bill Gates himself once pointed out, it may have to be enough for philanthrocapitalists to be content with seeing their return in terms of positive social recognition. Chapter 8 talks more about venture philanthropy in the context of funding social entrepreneurial activities.

Microcredit and microfinance

Western Banks have, for eons, been reluctant to lend money to the world's poor, citing concerns over the lack of collateral and entrepreneurial ethic. Luckily for the world, Muhammad Yunus challenged those patronizing assumptions — and jointly won the Nobel Prize in 2006, with the Grameen Bank he established, for doing so — by developing the notions of microcredit and microfinance, making very small loans (microloans) available to the poor and otherwise assisting them with a wider range of financial services (microfinance) so that they can engage in entrepreneurial enterprises and consequently lift themselves out of poverty. (For more on this remarkable social entrepreneurial innovation, see the nearby "Innovator in affordable business credit: Muhammad Yunus" sidebar). Kiva (www.kiva.org) has taken the microloan idea a creative step further by allowing individuals to *personally* loan money to low-income entrepreneurs.

Open access and open source

One final trend is the movement toward *open access* (equal access to information) and *open source* (equal opportunities for production). This may not be a completely new phenomenon but rather an extension of a long-standing trend in the way that societies govern themselves. That is, once upon a time, violence in the hands of elites was the key to social control and order. But these days, after generations of internal strife, the tendency is to achieve these same outcomes through equitable, widespread, nonviolent democratic dialogue (open access) and participation (open source).

It's only a very short hop from these historical developments to the *prosumer* movement. Here, consumers achieve an "open access" of sorts to businesses for a couple of reasons. Either they are sophisticated enough — professional-like in their knowledge — that their consumer demand actually shapes supply (as with prosumer digital cameras), or they're actively involved in the design and production of goods, although not as staff. Nudie Foods in Australia (www. nudie.com.au), for example, has developed a close, even interactive, continuing dialogue with its customers that blurs the boundary between the two entities. The focus is on sharing a passion for mutually accomplishing something different and meaningful with fruit — yes, fruit — including developing and playing a new online game like "Bananarama Drama," browsing interactively through the company story, suggesting new ideas or recipes for fruit smoothies, providing "Nudie addict" testimonials, and much more.

From there, it's not too far an additional hop to "open source" research, development, and production of goods and services, whereby the public actually produces the goods it consumes. The open-source philosophy seeks, as much as possible, to replace rigid corporate organizational hierarchies and exclusive ownership circles with fluid communities of owning, producing, informal networks.

Open source, then, is not limited to Linux-type software, which today makes up so much of the world's computing infrastructure. It's about how the empowerment of software communication — the ability to make words do things in the world — is viewed by global citizens as a free (economically and politically speaking) birthright for all humanity. And with that, of course, open source becomes a political manifesto for a new, collaborative, and hopeful way of doing things that just might help us meet challenges we face.

Innovator in affordable business credit: Muhammad Yunus

As a young economics professor at Bangladesh's Chittagong University, Muhammad Yunus was dismayed because his knowledge of economics meant nothing to those in Bangladesh suffering from widespread famine and poverty. Villagers were borrowing from loan sharks, and it wasn't uncommon for defaulters to become enslaved.

While visiting the village of Jobra, Junus made a list of 42 people who, all together, owed no more than $27. He gave each of them the money they owed, asking only that they concentrate on their work and repay him when they could. Later, Yunus served as guarantor for a larger loan to the villagers. It was not charity, not a handout. It was a hand *up* to those with an entrepreneurial spirit who were being systematically denied the small-business basic opportunities necessary to develop their ideas.

Grameen Bank loans, by Western standards, are usually tiny, often in the neighborhood of $50 to $100. But with the help of a local network of supporters who serve as loan "collateral" — in the sense that they cooperate to ensure that individuals repay their loans — these financial boosts are enough to get people started while making credit a basic human right. But do the people ever repay these loans? Repayment rates typically are more than 95 percent. Today, Yunus and Grameen Bank are leading defenders of the global poor, having loaned out more than $5.1 billion to 5.3 million people.

Part II
Establishing Your Organization

The 5th Wave — By Rich Tennant

"Through our organization, we hope to eliminate poverty, illiteracy, hunger, blindness, hangnails, red tide, bad hats, and comb-overs. Our motto: 'Focus and Achieve.'"

In this part . . .

So you have some idea of how social entrepreneurship works, and how others approach it. But how do you start?

Chapter 6 identifies the core types of social entrepreneurial organizations and offers advice on finding your niche. In Chapter 7, we tackle the important issue of initial planning in the enterprise. We address the question of whether to aim for profits in your enterprise in Chapter 8. The tricky but common problem of funding nonprofits is the subject of Chapter 9. Chapter 10 rounds out this part with a discussion of creating your brand and identity — the face you show the world, which can affect everything else.

Chapter 6

Finding Your Focus: Civil Society's Many Faces

. . . .

In This Chapter

▶ Discovering civil society and its organizations

▶ Finding out about health and wellness organizations

▶ Checking out groups promoting family and youth issues

▶ Looking into women's and minorities' organizations

▶ Discovering poverty, humanitarian, and development organizations

▶ Greening the planet with environmental enterprises

. . . .

*I*f you're anxious to get started but you haven't fixed on an exact direction yet, this chapter is for you. Here we offer a simplified map of a very large and rapidly expanding territory.

Social entrepreneurs and the enterprises they start are an important part of a larger social phenomenon known as *civil society* (a sector of volunteer fellowship and society building that exists outside the relatively controlling state and business sectors). Our hope is that briefly outlining the efforts of a large number of civil-society organizations will suggest avenues for you to begin exploring in your own enterprise.

This chapter is organized into six very broad, though not exhaustive, areas for social entrepreneurs to move into:

✔ **Service, community, and social organizations:** This is a general umbrella category for organizations that are peopled by volunteer members who provide gifts of friendly assistance, either through hands-on involvement or by raising money for other organizations. Examples include Boy Scouts and Girl Scouts, local community associations planning for the future of their neighborhoods, and the United Way. These affiliations are the pillars of civil society.

- ✔ **Health and wellness organizations:** These are organizations focused on improving health and alleviating health-related issues. Examples include elder-abuse hotlines, organ transplant peer-support groups, or jogging clubs that share healthy eating tips.

- ✔ **Family, children's, and youth organizations:** These organizations include the YMCA and YWCA, social activity programs for preschoolers in a community hall, and countless other religious establishments.

- ✔ **Women's and minorities' organizations:** In this category, we include groups such as the American Association of University Women, Pacific and Asian Women's Forum, and local chapters of the NAACP.

- ✔ **Poverty, humanitarian aid, and development:** Organizations in this area include those promoting advocacy for low- and moderate-income families; the National Indian Youth Leadership Project, which attempts to alleviate rural poverty; and groups such as the Pittsburgh History and Landmarks Foundation, which preserves historic buildings and neighborhoods.

- ✔ **Environmental organizations:** These organizations defend the environment from threats on all fronts. Examples include Friends of the Fox River Environmental Coalition, the Illinois Recycling Association, and America's Clean Water Foundation.

As you read this chapter and reflect on the six broad areas we cover, start creating some goals for yourself. What would success look like to you? For example, if you're environmentally inclined, which natural waterways or watersheds around you desperately need cleaning or restoration? For more help with goals as well as vision and mission statements, see Chapter 7.

Service, Community, and Social Organizations

Countless *service, community, and social organizations* (SCSOs) can be found all over the world. What do they all do? More than ever before, they work toward one big idea that can be summed up in two words: *service delivery,* by which we mean the provision of various kinds of human services.

In generations gone by, such organizations concentrated on providing local voluntarily organized benefits, self-help, or mutual aid (in the form of relief assistance). The Freemasons are a classic example of an SCSO. With obscure, secretive origins in the early 17th century, today the Freemasons still enjoy a membership estimated at around 5 million, including just under 2 million in the United States and half a million in England, Scotland, and Ireland. That old idea of service, then, is still around. (If you're curious about the Freemasons, check out *Freemasons For Dummies,* by Christopher Hodapp [Wiley].)

But these days, with governments and business professionals having a tough time living up to their own human service mandates, modern SCSOs are about much more than being "neighborly." They're recruiting themselves to collaboratively ensure that social justice reaches as many people as possible in practical ways. These organizations see their task as pulling society toward delivering services that are socially just, while providing ways to get there that value collaboration and recognize the importance of being pragmatic.

You can find SCSOs working in all the areas we look at in this chapter, too, and there are almost endless possibilities for social entrepreneurs to create similar organizations in any of these areas.

Our first examples combine issues relevant to both minorities and health and wellness (two areas covered in more detail later in this chapter).

Of those surviving a prolonged critical illness, more than 50 percent die within the next year, and 90 percent of those have never made it home to live independently.

Believing that "no one should end the journey of life alone, afraid, or in pain," the Nevada Multicultural End-of-Life Care Coalition (NMELC; www.nv multiculturalcoalition.org) provides a forum for organizations and community leaders to improve access and education on end-of-life healthcare services for diverse, multicultural communities. NMELC provides forums for resource sharing, continuing education for Nevada healthcare providers, giving members the opportunity to network and collaborate, and developing strategic plans and implementing activities that directly involve or relate to the members and their respective organizations.

The clear takeaways here for social entrepreneurs are that end-of-life issues should not be lost in discussions about healthcare spending. They should, instead, be discussed openly and commonly within society. And more privately, end-of-life discussions should always fully include the patient and their personal and family belief systems, but this is an especially neglected consideration for minorities. The role of the physician is simply to assist informed decision making by providing the best available information. Finally, whether patients should be dying in hospitals after recovering from a critical illness needs to become much more of a community and national debate.

A person cannot survive long without water — only around 72 hours — whereas he can survive without food for almost a month. Almost half the people in the world live in water-scarce countries, although on average there is enough water for everyone.

The University of Malawi's Lucy Chipeta notes that in Blantyre City, Malawi, Africa, the urban slum areas of Mbayani and Ntopwa were faced by a water crisis in 2007. Water scarcity meant that all available water was filthy, unsanitary surface water. This crisis left poor women and children at great risk of disease and death because they couldn't afford the firewood needed to boil the water (and kill the deadly organisms living in it). The Blantyre Water Board couldn't meet the cost of financing water-main extensions throughout the city, so it encouraged poor communities to raise their own funds through membership drives, nongovernmental organizations (NGOs), donors, and other funding agencies in order get water into their areas.

Because Malawi is one of the world's poorest countries, it comes as no surprise that, despite these efforts, the installed water mains were plagued by substandard materials, poor workmanship, leaks, and low water pressure. To deal with the problem of unsanitary surface water at the source, Habitat for Humanity works in partnership with local communities and governments to build simple, decent houses — including latrines. Habitat provides all the materials and skilled labor, but not as a giveaway; locals repay Habitat for the costs, and that money is then put into a revolving fund that stays in the community to build *more* houses and latrines.

Obviously, much more can be done in Blantyre and many other water-scarce and poor parts of the world. A very good start to making a difference is to make sure that your community observes and celebrates World Water Day on March 22 each year. Also, don't be fooled by claims that desalination will solve the problem of global water scarcity. The technology is currently energy intensive, increases emissions, and damages coastal and river habitats. Social entrepreneurs should direct their efforts to developing and promoting appropriate and sustainable water catchment (water conserving) and water-filtration technologies.

Another area of interest in this context would be *diaspora* (scattered) populations who emigrate out of their homelands. The three largest diaspora migrations have been the British (more than 50 million), Chinese (about 20 million), and East Indian (about 20 million). These and other immigrants typically maintain contact with their homelands, travel back and forth, and send money home (an act known as *remittance*). In other words, they're trying to keep up participation in their original social, cultural, and political lives back in their home countries. Social entrepreneurs can make that experience more positive at both ends.

In the new country, social entrepreneurs can strengthen ethnic communities against financial uncertainty (often caused by sending remittances home), racism, family difficulties, and so on.

When diaspora communities are more viable, they can better give back. And what can they give back to? You might be surprised to know that immigrant remittances are an extremely important source of development aid. Not only does money go to families back home, but it also goes to villages, communities, and larger regions. The World Bank calculates that in 2007 emigrants sent $251 billion back home. Kathleen Newland, a director at the Migration Policy Institute (www.migrationpolicy.org) in Washington, D.C., reports that many governments, including those in Mexico, the Philippines, and countries in Latin America and Africa, exploit remittances to the fullest. The Mexican government's *Tres por Uno* (Three for One) fund-matching initiative is a shining example. In 2005, local associations raised some $20 million for development, which other levels of government matched with another $60 million.

What this means is there are social entrepreneurial opportunities to close the circle in the homeland. The Norwegian government is one entity that has this figured out. It's making Norway's Pakistani diaspora part of its aid strategy. Through Pilot Project Pakistan, the Norwegian Agency for Development Cooperation is collaborating with Norwegian-Pakistani organizations and various NGOs to make sure aid flows to approved projects that make the emigrants proud. This is certainly a model that could be emulated with other diaspora populations, working local-to-local, with or without formal government involvement.

Somewhere in the middle there may also be social entrepreneurial opportunities. In late 2009, the Italian *Mando soldi a casa* ("I send money home") Web site (www.mandasoldiacasa.it/english) was unveiled at the International Conference on Remittances, held in Rome. The Web site allows Italy's immigrants to send money to their country of origin using a process that is clear and transparent. Because this is likely a first-time offering, it's clear that much more social entrepreneurial work could certainly be done in this area.

Other groups are actively looking to collaborate with grass-roots organizations in order to meet, justly and practically, human needs:

- **Healthcare professionals:** Counseling psychologists, for example, are increasingly recognizing that mental-health interventions must be bundled with social integration that also pays attention to the need for advocacy, social action, and social change. Some psychologists are in the early stages of doing just that and could probably benefit from alliances with social entrepreneurs who might be more familiar with local social terrain — especially as it applies to the complex realities of stigma. Perhaps you're one of those social entrepreneurs? For more guidance in this area, we recommend having a look at the Ashoka Foundation's 2009 Changemaker report titled "Rethinking Mental Health: A Discovery Framework," available at http://is.gd/5GhHz.

- **Corporations, colleges, and universities:** Corporate social responsibility (CSR), through such vehicles as employee volunteer programs, is fast becoming popular in business circles (as we point out in Chapters 5 and 8). Somewhat related to CSR is higher education's concept of *service learning* (a method of teaching, learning, and reflecting on how meaningful community service can combine with educational classroom instruction). Both are structured programs that promote social engagement and both are typically seen as benefitting the participants, employers, and recipient communities. As such, they may prove to be fertile collaborators for creative social entrepreneurs. A forward-thinking example of this kind of attempt to link academia and community is Belmont University's recently opened Center for Social Entrepreneurship and Service-Learning (`http://forum.belmont.edu/umac/archives/012362.html`).

- ✔ **Philanthropists:** These days, philanthropists are looking to do more than just donate money to nonprofits. They want to increase their community involvement and even invest in community initiatives. One possible outcome here is public-private partnerships (PPPs), which are designed to empower undercapitalized communities.

Social entrepreneurs such as R. K. Misra show how PPPs can work. In 2005, when he turned 40, Misra left the corporate world in order to concentrate on giving back to his home country of India. Through his social-entrepreneurial efforts, Misra advocates for and succeeds with instituting PPPs in the areas of infrastructure and job creation, working in collaboration with various levels of government and industry. To catch up with R. K. Misra's efforts, check out his blog at `http://rajendramisra.blogspot.com`.

- ✔ **Trade unions:** Trade unions — very much aware of their fading political status in Western societies — are anxious to partner with other community organizations and social movements, especially on issues of social justice and service delivery. This is extremely evident in the area of healthcare reform, where the unions are battling the "marketization" of healthcare, raising awareness on the issue, and attempting to mobilize resistance to the idea.

Health and Wellness Organizations

Broadly speaking, *health* refers to the general condition of a person in all aspects, which the World Health Organization (WHO), in 1948, defined as "a state of complete physical, mental, and social well-being and not merely the absence of disease or infirmity."

But when you consider the common modern uses of the terms *health* and *wellness,* it turns out that, often, people are really talking about *health management* (the kinds of things that doctors and nurses and other practitioners do to make us better) or wellness as associated with *wellness management* and optimizing our health the best we can. How big a deal is wellness management? According to The Centers for Disease Control and Prevention, lifestyle — which is a wellness management issue, not a health management issue — accounts for more than half of all premature deaths in adults in the United States. When social entrepreneurs (or health professionals) intervene, then, in many areas of human functioning, they can do so in one of two basic ways:

- ✔ They can avert or remove crisis conditions and restore things to some minimum acceptable standard.

> ✔ They can go well beyond that and push toward the fullness of human flourishing and positive outcomes, which are valuable in their own right, but also useful in terms of the economics of prevention. After all, an ounce of prevention is worth a pound of cure.

The concept of *flourishing* can apply to many of the ideas discussed in this chapter. Families, children and youth, men and women, minorities, the poor . . . all these groups want to be "flourishing," don't they? Social entrepreneurs can help people flourish in all these areas.

There is a further aspect to health and wellness managements these days: Both are being heavily *commoditized* (turned into commodities that turn a profit). Something's going on with health and wellness that might be laying the foundation for how we deal with other human challenges in the future. This transformation is something for social entrepreneurs to think about because it may challenge many of our most sacred assumptions about how we help one another.

Health and wellness management becoming commoditized can be seen very easily in one booming area of business: medical tourism. For a price, the folks at corporations such as WorldMedAssist (www.worldmedassist.com) can set patients up in places such as India for procedures — such as high-quality liver transplants or disk replacements — which patients otherwise would have to wait and wait and wait for at home, perhaps in vain.

Everyone is jumping onto this bandwagon. At a 2009 MedHealth & Wellness three-day international exhibition, some 65 companies from 17 countries touted their ability to make top-notch privatized medical tourist services available to consumers around the world.

Wellness is also huge business. Wellness entities are contracting out to health plans and convincing corporations that investment in employee wellness should be at the top of their agendas, along with commitments to financial and organizational health. Alere (www.matria.com), for example, is a market leader in the United States for delivering comprehensive health-enhancement (wellness) programs to top corporations and health plans. Employers are more involved in promoting worker health than ever before. Some 90 percent have some sort of health initiative for employees, ranging from a smoke-free workplace to education and training to health risk assessment.

Where do these trends leave you as the social entrepreneur? Well, you should get involved! Can you set up the next WorldMedAssist or Alere? All over the booming commercialization, privatization, and individualization trends in health, we're starting to see services, whether for-profit or not, coming to the fore. These services are offering anxious consumers the kind of critical information they need in order to make informed and intelligent decisions that are right for them.

FitSense Australia, a corporate wellness provider, suggests that there are benefits to customers receiving regular e-mails containing "specific exercise and nutrition recommendations." Given what we talk about in Chapter 11, on collaborative learning using social networking and social media, it only makes sense that such a service could easily be picked up by social entrepreneurs like you.

How about setting up something like what Outdoors Queensland (www.qorf.org.au) is up to? Its Web site is a one-stop shop for anybody interested in the outdoors in Queensland, Australia — which fits in perfectly with the idea of wellness. As a subsidiary of Queensland Outdoor Recreation Federation (QORF), any profits generated by Outdoors Queensland are returned to QORF to further its aims and objectives.

Although privatization has its benefits in terms of getting health and wellness services and products to market, history shows that "buyer beware" — especially in matters relating to well-being — is wise counsel. Someone representing consumers, or affiliations of consumers, will need to stand up for reasonable regulation, equity, and community concerns, typically the purview of health promotion. Professionally, organizations such as the National Wellness Institute (www.nationalwellness.org) play this role. Organizations that develop independent quality standards for the wellness market might also provide social entrepreneurs with a citizen-oriented template that can be applied to all of health.

Family, Children's, and Youth Organizations

No other social institution is changing as quickly or as fundamentally as the family. One of the most compelling changes in the family has been the increase in dual-wage-earner families, to the point where most American families depend on both husband and wife to be family breadwinners. Very close to 60 percent of the 121 million women over the age of 16 are working or looking for work, and women are projected to make up 47 percent of the U.S. labor force by 2016. Otherwise, with the numbers of single-parent, blended, cohabiting, and same sex-parent families continuing to rise, people's perceptions of what constitutes a family continue to change.

For these reasons and more, the state of the family is a hot topic. Some would go so far as to say that today's Western family — long considered by social scientists to be the backbone of Western society — is threatened with extinction. That may be overkill, but the prospects for children, who are the future of every society, look disconcerting.

So what's happening? Families are changing because the world out there is putting tremendous pressure on them. In an increasingly expensive and economically unstable world, single-family wage is a luxury of the distant past. For the sake of family economic stability, most families require that both partners work — and work hard. Single-parent families, especially those that are the product of divorce or death, become more prone to experiencing poverty.

Many other factors are affecting the family as well. Cultural influences promoting heightened individualism and consumerism among parents and their children, along with increasingly hectic schedules, are leading to families torn and distracted by many competing demands. Pervasive technology such as e-mail, online chat, cellphones, and so on mean that the boundaries between public life and private family life are becoming more flexible, blurred, and open. And when families look beyond themselves to formal social supports, they find less and less assistance, thanks in large part to government cuts not only to public services but also to community and faith-based services.

If you'd like to get involved in helping families, you'll find no shortage of challenges and opportunities.

Before we look at particular examples, we want to mention a basic organizing device you may find useful. As with the health and wellness distinction we mentioned — between crisis and restoration versus flourishing and prevention — assistance to families and children follows a similar pattern of intervention: crisis and restoration on the one hand, and ongoing commitments to a better future on the other. Although the bulk of SCSO work tends to focus on deficits and problems (crises and restorations) within the family and with children and youth, some important attention is now being paid to what is being called *positive* family, child, and youth development — another way of talking about flourishing. So, aside from the traditional emphases and opportunities, new ones are opening up for social entrepreneurs in the area of family, children, and youth welfare.

All that said, a good number of SCSOs do concern themselves with families who are in difficulty or crisis. There are few things more difficult for a family than homelessness, for example. Homeless Families Foundation (www. home lessfamiliesfoundation.org) is a family shelter in Columbus, Ohio. Homeless families can benefit from shelter and support services and a tutoring and enrichment program for their children. HFF provides shelter, support, stability, and nurturing for homeless families as they transition to permanent housing.

For families in severe crisis, SCSOs rally with a range of service delivery options ranging from therapeutic foster services to in-home interventions to behavioral health services, adoption services, training and education services, and more.

Specialized Alternatives for Families and Youth (www.safy.org) is a non-profit leader in the emergency services area and is expanding into communities across the nation by providing programs and services that go beyond therapeutic foster care.

Sometimes the help for families in difficulty can be quite subtle: Santa's Four Helpers (www.santafourhelpers.com) is a registered charity that puts on events for children from limited-income and single-parent families. Since 2005, the organization has been partnering with others such as the Boy's & Girl's Club, Children's Aid Society, Our Kids Count, and the Dilico Ojibway Child and Family Services.

The idea of positive family development is about more than seeing individual families flourish — it's also about seeing communities flourish.

Gang Resistance Education and Training (G.R.E.A.T.; www.great-online.org) is an important U.S. Department of Justice initiative (not a social enterprise or NGO). The program's commitment to immunizing families and communities against delinquency, youth violence, and gang membership provides the strongest possible legitimacy for any social entrepreneur wanting to do something similar within the larger community.

Houston Family Foundation (www.houstonfamilyfoundation.org), a Christ-centered organization dedicated to helping parents raise children and build families with virtue, would, in theory, fill that "larger community" bill, as would almost every religious organization.

The existence of organizations such as we've profiled previously suggests many opportunities for social entrepreneurs to get involved proactively in community, family, child, and youth development before relationship troubles spiral out of control.

On the "difficulty and crisis" side of service delivery to children and youth are many more possibilities. Aside from more direct interventions, advocates serve an important middle-man role, giving a voice to voiceless children. Here are some examples:

- Kentucky Youth Advocates (www.kyyouth.org) is a nonpartisan, non-profit children's advocacy organization. Believing that Kentucky's youth deserve the opportunities and resources necessary to ensure their productive development and health, KYA works on behalf of Kentucky's children with the state legislature, the community, and the media.

- Because being hospitalized can be a traumatic experience for children and youth, Lollipop Theater Network (http://lollipoptheater.org), a nonprofit organization, brings the enchantment of new-release movies to children in hospital beds.

✔ Foster-care placement can also be a stressful ordeal. Kids in care might be better helped with a more holistic approach than the typical state-run process. Children Youth and Family Collaborative (www.cyfcla.org) works collaboratively with youth-centered organizations to link volunteers with more than 4,000 foster and at-risk youth in Los Angeles and Compton, California. This holistic approach enriches the lives of the young participants and benefits academic and social development.

Within the concept of positive youth development, the key is to look at children and youth not as problems to solve, but rather as assets to develop.

The Laidlaw Foundation (www.laidlawfdn.org) promotes positive youth development by engaging youth in activities related to the arts, the environment, and the community. As part of that process, the foundation funds, through catalyst and project grants, youth-led initiatives for social change.

Women's and Minorities' Organizations

Why are we grouping women with ethnic minorities? Well, although women make up roughly half the world's population, their traditional subordination and historically distinct identity have earned their classification by social scientists as a minority group.

Some of the difficult issues facing women today — which occupy SCSOs — are

✔ Human and employment rights and equity (including concerns for women's safety and exploitation)

✔ Health rights and equity (including sexual and reproductive health and rights)

✔ Women's place in social, cultural, and environmental development (with a strong interest in developing women's leadership and entrepreneurial capacities)

Much of women's difficulties in the world can be traced to the violence they are routinely subjected to. In March 2006, the World Health Organization (WHO) released its "Multi-country Study on Women's Health and Domestic Violence against Women" (available at www.who.int/gender/violence/who_multicountry_study/en). The results indicate not only that many parts of the world are frightening and dangerous places for women but also that the violence perpetuated against them has rippling and damaging effects on women's physical, mental, sexual, and reproductive health. Plus, in the United States, the leading cause of injury to women aged 15 to 44 is domestic violence.

Here's what just a few SCSOs are up to in these areas of concern:

- ✔ The Women's Aid Organization (WAO; `www.wao.org.my`) is an independent, nonreligious, NGO in Malaysia. WAO is committed to challenging and ending violence against women, which it recognizes as a crime and a violation of women's human rights. Their mission is to "promote and create respect, protection, and fulfillment of equal rights for women."

- ✔ Vital Voices Global Partnership (VVGP; `http://70.32.91.35`) empowers domestic-violence victims and the women working to defend them. The VVGP also works from crisis and restoration to positive futures and prevention. In its own words: "Vital Voices Global Partnership . . . identifies, trains, and empowers emerging women leaders and social entrepreneurs around the globe. . . . We provide these women with the capacity, connections, and credibility they need to unlock their leadership potential." This organization covers many of the issues outlined in this chapter, so it should be of special interest to social entrepreneurs interested in the challenges facing women today.

- ✔ The nonprofit International Organization for Women and Development (`www.iowd.org`) is committed to bringing into being a sustainable program that surgically repairs, supplies post-operative care, and then rehabilitates (by providing literacy and vocational skills) the "fistula women" of Nigeria. (*Fistula* refers to *vesico vaginal fistula,* a rupture or hole that develops between the vagina and bladder during prolonged obstructed labor.) These women are constantly leaking urine and for that they are routinely ostracized by their communities. It's imperative to realize that this problem is widespread (not specific to Nigeria), and yet this organization is fighting the good fight almost single-handedly.

When you look at ethnic minorities, two dominant themes emerge: On the one hand are increasing diaspora populations (people spreading out from their original homelands) and the rise of a modern, demanding, multicultural reality. On the other hand are threats to cultures across the globe. If you have any doubts about the enormity of this problem, just ask Wade Davis, National Geographic Explorer in Residence. He'll tell you that the extinction of indigenous languages and cultures is a problem every bit as crucial to humanity's future as our planet's environmental degradation. All in all, social entrepreneurial second- and third-generation immigrants, especially, just need to look to their own families, communities, and homelands to find scores of opportunities for their involvement.

Partnering with government

You might notice that poverty reduction, aid, and development initiatives are either governmental or nongovernmental. Obviously, the nongovernmental side of it is where you'd fit in. We mention this because although, in theory, the boundaries between the two forms of assistance are distinct, in practice those boundaries are being continually redefined as the relationship between the two arenas is constantly renegotiated.

In fact, if there is a general trend, it is for governments to more often partner with

nongovernmental efforts. The reasons for this trend are pretty simple: When those partnerships work, governments look like geniuses for backing winners and providing valuable cash, expertise, and other resources. When things don't work out so well, governments don't have to worry about cleaning up the mess because they, as "silent partners," are far less exposed on the front lines than social entrepreneurs like *you* would be.

Here are a couple of organizations that are trying to address these concerns:

- Multiculturalism Community Service (MCS; www.mcsdc.org) was founded in 1997 by a group of concerned Washington, D.C., residents who wanted to build on the strength of the city's diversity. Since then, MCS has grown and assists in parent involvement, offering language access, youth peacemaking, and facilitation and mediation services.

- Native Planet (www.nativeplanet.org) is an NGO "dedicated to the self-empowerment of indigenous peoples and the preservation of world ethnic cultures." This organization helps these groups speak for themselves to the world. Not only is this crucial to their protection, but it may also even be key to the survival of the rest of us. Why? Because these traditional groups understand and can teach us a great deal about successful conservation, consumption, and stewardship of what remains of the Earth's wilderness and biological diversity.

Poverty, Humanitarian Aid, and Development Organizations

The patterns of social and economic inequality in our world are striking, to say the least. When 80 percent of the world's population takes in only 20 percent of the world's income, and half of *those* folks take in a mere 4 percent of that income, it's easy to see why poverty, humanitarian aid, and global development issues — and the question of social justice — should be near the very top of humanity's agenda for today and the foreseeable future.

How can you get involved? Well, to start with, hundreds, if not thousands, of organizations worldwide are working valiantly to fight and reduce local and global poverty — and having a really hard time with that — so there are many places for you to volunteer your services.

By volunteering, you begin to expose yourself to the scale and complexity of the problems and, as a result, become much better equipped to make your *own* social entrepreneurial contributions when the time comes.

Here are the poverty, humanitarian aid, and development organizations we want to bring to your attention:

- **Action by Churches Together International** (www.act-intl.org): ACT is a worldwide union of churches and their connected service agencies, all working during times of emergency to save lives and support communities. ACT members are from Protestant and orthodox churches drawn from the membership of the World Council of Churches and Lutheran World Federation.

- **ActionAid** (www.actionaid.org): ActionAid is an international anti-poverty agency formed in 1972. Since that time, ActionAid has been working in 42 countries, helping many millions of the world's poorest and most disadvantaged people.

- **Aga Khan Development Network** (www.akdn.org): AKDN is a group of development agencies with a broad set of directives. It works in the following areas: the environment, health, education, architecture, culture, microfinance, rural development, and disaster reduction. It also promotes private-sector enterprise and revitalize historic cities.

- **Asian Disaster Preparedness Center** (www.adpc.net/general/adpc.html): ADPC is a nonprofit organization that supports safer communities and sustainable development. The group accomplishes its goals through programs and projects aimed at reducing the impact of disasters on Asian and Pacific countries and communities.

- **Directory of Development Organizations** (www.devdir.org): lists more than 53,000 development organizations, with downloadable contact information. The idea behind the directory is to facilitate knowledge sharing and international cooperation regarding social and economic development and poverty reduction.

- **German Foundation for World Population** (www.weltbevoel kerung.de/en): The foundation aims to "reduce extreme poverty and help young people achieve universal access to sexual and reproductive health." The group is involved in development projects in Ethiopia, Kenya, Tanzania, and Uganda. It also produces advocacy campaigns, special events, and publications on population and reproductive health.

- **Global Development Network** (www.gdnet.org): GDN is an international organization of research and policy institutes that contributes to improved international development by advancing the production, sharing, and application of multidisciplinary development knowledge.

- **Grameen Bank** (www.grameen-info.org): GB takes a very different stance on conventional banking by not requiring collateral from the poor. The entire loan system is based on "mutual trust, accountability, participation, and creativity." The bank and its founder, Muhammad Yunus, were awarded the Nobel Peace Prize in October 2006. As of October 2009, GB has almost 8 million borrowers, 97 percent of whom are women. GB's borrowers own 90 percent of its shares; the rest are government owned.

- **IASC Humanitarian Early Warning Service** (www.hewsweb.org): HEWSweb is an interagency partnership that tries to warn of impending humanitarian and natural hazards using the most credible global-level information possible.

- **Interchurch Organization for Development Cooperation** (www.icco. nl/delivery/icco/en): ICCO works toward the global eradication of poverty and injustice and, with that, a future where people live in dignity and prosperity.

- **Institute for International Cooperation and Development** (www.iicd-volunteer.org): IICD is a nonprofit volunteer organization active in Africa, Central America, and Brazil. IICD's emphasis is on humanitarian development and community work.

- **Mercy Corps** (www.mercycorps.org): Mercy Corps supports those affected by disasters, conflicts, and poverty by providing emergency relief and development initiatives.

- **Novartis Foundation for Sustainable Development** (www.novartis foundation.org): NFSD aims, through networking and via its own think tank, to encourage stakeholder development policy dialogue intended to improve the quality of life in developing countries. The foundation also has a specific interest in healthcare and social development.

✔ **People In Aid** (www.peopleinaid.org): PIA is a network of international humanitarian assistance and development agencies. The organization helps other poverty relief organizations by improving their people management and support. PIA facilitates this process by helping these organizations see how they might improve their standards, accountability, and transparency in meeting their many challenges.

✔ **United Nations Development Programme** (www.undp.org): UNDP provides vital information on the UN's Millennium Development Goals (MDGs) through publications and special initiatives.

As you browse the preceding Web sites, you'll note that some of these folks are on the constant lookout for volunteers. Contact them for an opportunity to start really learning the ropes.

Although the organizations in the preceding list are large and well established, you should have a look at ventures that are somewhat smaller, but often just as innovative:

✔ **Boulder-Lhasa Sister City Project** (www.boulder-tibet.org): BLSCP was formed in 1986 by the City Council of Boulder, Colorado. This nonprofit public charity allows sister cities Boulder and Lhasa, Tibet, to develop and implement mutually beneficial (but nonpolitical) exchanges in the areas of "health care, education, environmental protection, science and technology, agriculture and animal husbandry, and culture and art."

✔ **Give Us Wings** (www.giveuswings.org): This organization is a small, grass-roots nonprofit organization working in Kenyan and Ugandan villages. Areas of assistance include funding community development projects, meeting the educational and medical needs of adults and children, and training folks for economic self-sufficiency. Volunteer trips may involve poverty education and assistance with sustainable development programs.

✔ **Mary Slessor Foundation** (www.maryslessor.org): This group continues the legacy of Mary Slessor's work in Nigeria, where, despite the country's wealth of resources, the masses remain poor. The foundation focuses its efforts on medical problems, employment and training, and agriculture.

✔ **The Bangladesh Relief Fund** (www.bangladeshrelief.org): The BRF is an Ohio nonprofit corporation founded by Mr. Muhit Rahman, an expatriate Bangladeshi who has emigrated to the United States. Mr. Rahman, horrified by the devastating floods in Bangladesh in 2004, organized to raise and distribute funds for poverty alleviation in his home country. To date, the BRF has expanded and funded a number of programs including a fishery, a chicken farm, and a cow-lending microcredit operation.

Issues to watch in aid and development

Beware of "phantom aid." In 2006 ActionAid estimated that almost half of global aid — $37 billion — was aid that was not "genuinely available to poor countries to fight poverty" because it was tied up in *technical assistance* (in other words, consultants, research, and training). ActionAid concluded that "technical assistance is often overpriced and ineffective, and in the worst cases destroys rather than builds the capacity of the poorest countries." ActionAid goes on to say, "... donors continue to insist on large technical assistance components in most projects and programs they fund."

Why? A couple of reasons:

✔ Technical assistance provides a "soft" lever that allows donors to direct and supervise the policies of the governments of developing countries.

✔ Technical assistance gives donors the opportunity to "own" reforms that they feel are worthwhile.

The moral of the story is to be aware that organizations that are fighting poverty with technical assistance may have ulterior motives, and that these may detract from actually getting the job done.

Another issue arises from the fact that humanitarian aid and development aid are quite different things:

✔ *Humanitarian aid* (sometimes called just *aid*) is relief that follows disasters or civil unrest or warfare. It's about saving lives in the face of calamity, pure and simple — it's crisis and restoration work.

✔ *Development aid* (or just *development*), on the other hand, works toward positive human and social flourishing: building infrastructure, putting up schools and hospitals, creating roads and dams, and so forth.

The relationship between aid and development is not always a happy one. In fact, over the past few years, a lot of development aid money has been diverted toward humanitarian aid, with the result that longer-term initiatives have often been shelved due to a lack of funds. And at least in the aftermath of conflict, it doesn't seem clear that humanitarian aid actually decreases violence — Darfur remains a chilling case in point, as increased aid to the area often invites more slaughter from marauding militia.

If you like brain-teasers, here's one to mull over: Research indicates that reducing poverty leads to improvements in participatory processes, such as civil society and politics, and in *social capital* (the usefulness of one's social relationships). However, the opposite holds, too: Work on improving civil society, participation, and social networks, and you reduce poverty. This suggests that not only do social entrepreneurs have another good reason to "sell" poverty reduction, but that you might actually reduce poverty by working on the things that poverty reduction claims to bring about.

Huh? We'll put it another way: As you reduce poverty and see benefits in civil society and social relationships, seize on and maximize those gains because they'll be the basis for further poverty reductions. Sounds like a good deal, doesn't it?

Environmental Organizations

Unquestionably, the fate of our planet is the issue beyond all others. If we don't get that right, none of the other earthly concerns we've also got to tackle will matter. And there's so much more. Just consider the scope of the environmental problems we face. We need to undo the polluting tendencies of humanity and, with that, reduce carbon emissions while moving quickly to construct environmentally responsible buildings and other lived environments — just for starters.

Since its founding in 1961, the World Wildlife Fund (WWF; www.world wildlife.org) has grown into the world's largest private international conservation organization, with almost 5 million supporters distributed on 5 continents and with offices in more than 90 countries. It's safe to say that the WWF has played a starring role in the development of the planetary preservation movement.

With people like them on the case, do you even need to worry about helping out? In fact, with the large number of organizations worldwide devoted to issues related to the environment, ecology (the relationships between organisms and their environments), habitat, threatened species, and so on, there might be a tendency to relax and leave the environment to all those mighty capable people. Fight that tendency because the stakes couldn't be higher.

Let's say that as a social entrepreneur you'd like to do something to help the environment, but you're not sure where to start. You might begin by increasing your environmental literacy through discussion with others more knowledgeable than yourself, whether they're close by or far away. Here are some resources that can help you begin:

- ✔ **Environmental Literacy Council** (www.enviroliteracy.org): The Environmental Literacy Council is an independent, nonprofit organization that helps teachers, students, policymakers, and the public find reliable cross-disciplinary information on a wide range of environmental science topics.

- ✔ **Association of University Leaders for a Sustainable Future** (http://ulsf.org): The ULSF is the Secretariat for signatories of the Talloires Declaration (signed in 1990, accessible at http://ulsf.org/pdf/TD.pdf). This declaration was agreed to by more than 400 college and university presidents and chancellors from around the world. The ULSF advances the resolution's ten-point execution plan for integrating sustainability and environmental literacy in learning, inquiry, operations, and outreach in higher education. This is accomplished through ULSF publications, research, and assessment. Its Web site is a great place to find out about what the academy is committed to (as well as a great way to hold the academics in your community accountable).

✔ **Wiser Earth** (WE; www.wiserearth.org): WE is a free online community space that works toward a just and sustainable world by connecting concerned people, nonprofits, and businesses. On the Wiser Earth Web site you can find others who may share your passions; raise your visibility; and generate support for your projects, network, or community action group.

✔ **National Environmental Education Week** (http://dev.eeweek.org): EE Week is the "single largest organized environmental education event in the United States." In 2009, almost 2,600 schools, nature centers, museums, zoos, and other educational institutions got together during NEE Week to bring environmental education to millions of students across America. The high-quality resources on this Web site — and it contains lots of them — are aimed at educators of every stripe. That *should* include you, the social entrepreneur.

✔ **Second Nature** (www.secondnature.org): Second Nature moves people toward a sustainable future by helping senior college and university leaders make healthy, just, and sustainable living the basis of higher education's learning and practice. Lots of ideas abound on this Web site, especially with regard to constructing environmentally friendly (green) buildings and enabling higher education to successfully interact with surrounding communities on the topic of sustainability.

Here are some other quality resources to explore that have a more international focus:

✔ **International Union for Conservation of Nature** (IUCN; www.iucn.org): IUCN, the world's oldest and largest global environmental network, "is made up of more than 1,000 government and NGO member organizations, and almost 11,000 volunteer scientists in more than 160 countries." Consequently, it represents an enormous bank of information and expertise in promoting conservation and finding pragmatic solutions to pressing environmental and development challenges. The union supports scientific research and manages field projects all over the world. But it does even more, bringing governments, NGOs, United Nations agencies, companies, and local communities into alignment in order to develop and implement policy, laws, and best practices.

✔ **United Nations Environment Programme** (UNEP; www.unep.org): Through its leadership and willingness to partner around the world, UNEP encourages global caring for the environment. One of its basic messages is that people and nations everywhere can improve their quality of life without risking the quality of life of future generations. UNEP is a remarkable resource for social entrepreneurs.

✔ **Living Earth** (www.livingearth.org.uk): Living Earth is an international organization that encourages practical, bottom-up, and participatory solutions to environmental issues. The important point emphasized by this organization is that every situation is different and may require a unique approach. Social entrepreneurs can learn a lot from these folks.

We leave you with three more examples of encouraging social entrepreneurial/NGO efforts:

- ✔ **Blue Ocean Institute** (BOI; www.blueocean.org): BOI urges ocean conservation through science, art, and literature, inspiring solutions and a deeper connection with nature. The reliable information on this Web site is intended to better inform personal choice, instill hope, and help rebuild living ecological richness in the oceans.

- ✔ **Bushmeat Crisis Task Force** (BCTF; www.bushmeat.org): BCTF seeks to eliminate the illegal commercial bushmeat trade (which kills rare and endangered animals for food). A growing global network allows BCTF to inform nations, organizations, scientists, and the general public about the catastrophic effects of the illegal bushmeat commerce. Though habitat loss is a huge threat to wildlife, for-profit hunting wild animals for their meat is now the most important present threat to the future of wildlife in Africa and perhaps worldwide. The pursuit of bushmeat has already led to local extinctions in Asia and West Africa.

- ✔ **Forest Stewardship Council** (www.fsc.org): FSC is an independent, nongovernmental, nonprofit organization that promotes the responsible management of the world's forests. Founded as a concerned response to global deforestation in 1993, FSC is considered one of the planet's best organizations for promoting responsible forest management.

Chapter 7

The Ground Floor: Doing the Initial Planning

. . . .

In This Chapter

▶ Creating an organizational strategy

▶ Considering whether to aim for profit

▶ Identifying who (or what) will benefit from your efforts

▶ Defining your organization through mission and vision statements

▶ Establishing your goals

. . . .

*Y*ou've probably heard the saying, "Failing to plan is planning to fail." We couldn't agree more.

This chapter centers on planning for your social enterprise during its early stages. Planning can be boiled down to three steps:

1. **Identify future goals.**

2. **Evaluate various means for reaching those goals.**

3. **Choose the best course of action.**

After you complete these three steps, you've arrived at your basic plan for establishing your social enterprise.

Of course, planning isn't something you do just once in the life of your organization. After you reach Step 3 of your basic plan, you'll inevitably discover the need to back up and redo steps 1 and 2. Many organizations undertake formal planning annually, but the reality is that you'll be planning (and replanning) your endeavor on a daily basis.

In this chapter, we start by looking at ways you can think strategically about forming a social enterprise. We help you consider if profit will be one of your goals or if you plan to live without it. We show you how to identify the people (or animals or parks or whatever) who will benefit from your efforts, and we walk you through the process of developing mission and vision statements.

Finally, we get you thinking about how to set realistic goals that are just lofty enough to keep you inspired for the long haul.

Planning Strategically

Whether your ultimate goal is to develop a for-profit or nonprofit organization, you need to think strategically. (Strategy isn't something you can ignore if you're planning to start a nonprofit.) A *strategy* encompasses a long-range set of some or all of the following:

- ✔ **Goals:** Desired ends or results

- ✔ **Policies:** Courses of action adopted because they're advantageous or expedient

- ✔ **Programs:** Planned sets of activities and actions

- ✔ **Actions:** Doing what is necessary to realize goals (including setting timelines for taking these actions)

- ✔ **Decisions:** Settling or resolving a question in dispute

- ✔ **Allocation of resources:** Allotting the means to solve a problem

You need to think *broadly* enough that you cover all these items. For example, you shouldn't consider goals without also considering the resources and programs you need to reach those goals.

A social enterprise's strategy describes *what it is, what it does, and why it does it*. More specifically, *strategy* refers to setting long-term, overall planning goals and implementing the means of achieving them.

Strategic planning in social enterprises is an ongoing process. After you come up with your initial plan (by thinking about your goals, policies, programs, and so on), you continue to plan strategically. This continued strategic planning commonly includes the following:

- ✔ **Setting broad policy and direction for the enterprise:** Decide on advantageous courses of action that will lead to realization of the enterprise's goals.

- ✔ **Allowing for internal and external assessment:** Successful enterprises arrange for routine evaluations of their programs, first from internal sources (such as a supervisor, division head, or respected senior member) and then from expert individuals or groups outside themselves.

- ✔ **Paying attention to key stakeholders:** Stakeholders are those people and groups who have an interest in the success of your social enterprise. Be sure to learn about what they think of it and what they want from it.

- **Identifying critical issues:** Determine the most important problems that your enterprise must deal with. These problems typically include finding funding, reliable and effective volunteers, avenues of influence with government, and ways to sensitize the public to the enterprise's mission and goals.

- **Developing strategies to deal with critical issues:** Create strategies that will solve as effectively as possible the important problems facing your enterprise.

- **Making decisions:** Organize and direct members of your enterprise so that they can find a way to settle or resolve the issues facing it.

- **Taking action:** Having made a decision on how to solve an issue, take the necessary steps to reach the solution.

- **Monitoring the results of those actions:** Successful problem solving requires giving continuous feedback to the people involved about how they're progressing toward resolution of the issue.

Part of a social enterprise's strategy is to develop a clear set of goals (a topic we cover in the next section), but equally important is to evaluate periodically the means by which you're reaching these goals. With a critical eye, examine the means you'll be using to meet your goals and ask yourself some questions both at startup and at least once per quarter after that:

- Are the means for reaching our goals appropriate?

- Are more effective means available?

- Are certain means generally effective but in need of some tweaking to make them better?

This kind of evaluation is often left to the board of directors, if there is one. (We discuss boards of directors in Chapter 14.) If your organization doesn't have a board of directors, evaluation falls to you and/or other senior leaders of the organization.

Such an evaluation will also be helpful in determining how well your enterprise is moving along toward reaching its goals. After you're up and running, you'll want to ask yourself the following questions:

- How far have we come toward reaching our goals?

- How long has it taken us to reach this point, and is that faster or slower than we had planned?

- How much more time will we need to achieve your goals?

- Are there any ways of speeding up the achievement of our goals?

Funding bodies (which provide money to nonprofit enterprises — see Chapter 9) often request assessments with information of this sort, which is just another reason to be sure that you periodically assess your progress.

Strategic planning at startup and from then on tends to be most effective in larger social enterprises of around 30 or more members. Why? In smaller organizations, especially nonprofits, good planning can often take place without having to be strategic — planning can occur without setting broad policy and direction for the enterprise, without allowing for internal and external assessment, and without paying attention to key stakeholders (three important subprocesses of strategic planning).

Setting Goals: The Foundation of Planning

We note earlier in this chapter that goals are desired ends or results. In this section, we focus on the nature of the official ends, results that your enterprise is striving to realize, and the nature of the unofficial ends and results that some of your organization's members are also hoping to achieve.

When you're in the midst of planning, you'll likely hear people using two words to refer to your organizational aims: *goals* and *objectives*. As far as we're concerned, the two terms are synonymous. Some people try to differentiate their definitions, but we suggest treating the terms as if they mean the same thing.

Official goals: What you tell the world about where you're headed

In social entrepreneurship, the goal is to change society in such a way that this change will benefit a *target* (the beneficiaries of your work). (We explain what a target is in the "Anticipating Who Will Benefit from Your Work" section, later in this chapter.) State clearly and *in writing* the official goals — those presented in formal statements — of your enterprise. Set out your goals in a separate formal statement that is distinct from your mission and vision statements (see "Developing Mission and Vision Statements," later in this chapter).

The very act of writing about your goals helps clarify them for yourself and others.

The best way to start setting goals for your enterprise is to list, as clearly and simply as possible, the concrete changes you want your enterprise to achieve for your target. Try to list these changes in order of importance (but don't worry if some goals seem equally important). Keep it brief — two or three concrete, manageable goals are better than five or six goals that you can't effectively pursue at the same time.

Make sure that your list consists *only* of the goals you can actually achieve — set aside your pie-in-the-sky thinking for now. How do you know if a goal is possible or impossible to achieve? Consider the following:

✔ **The actions that you must take to reach the goal:** For each goal you've listed, also list the actions you (or someone in your organization) will need to take to reach that goal. Ask yourself how the target group will be realistically affected by those specific actions.

✔ **The financial costs of reaching the goal:** Identify how much money you need and where the money is going to come from.

✔ **The people you need to put your goals into action:** Ask yourself:

- Who in the enterprise is going to do what to bring a given goal to reality?

- What kind of person or persons will we have to recruit to help reach a given goal?

- What will the target of our benefits have to do to bring to fruition the pursuit of a particular goal? (For example, if education in a third-world village is a goal, students must study; if political change in your government is a goal, politicians must vote in new legislation.)

Write down the answers to these questions next to each goal.

If you discover that you don't have the resources to achieve a particular goal, you know that it's unrealistic — at least for now. But don't throw away the list — down the road, the resources you need may become available.

You'll have time for your pipe dreams later. At the start, you need to develop clear and obvious objectives — objectives that you can easily measure the progress of.

Clear evidence that your enterprise is advancing toward a goal is an inspiration for everyone in the enterprise. Taking time to carefully set up a detailed, achievable plan can be a great source of motivation for the people in your enterprise.

Unofficial goals: Stuff you secretly hope to also achieve

Note that your *official goals* may not be the only goals driving your enterprise, even at the beginning. Unofficial goals may exist at that time as well. *Unofficial goals* are unstated, secret, or hidden objectives that are nevertheless important for some of the people personally involved with your enterprise. They may include your pie-in-the-sky goals.

For example, you may have the official goal of developing a number of microbusinesses in a poor South American community. But also, some of the women in the enterprise intend to work hard to involve local females in these undertakings. Having that secondary, or unofficial, goal is perfectly okay and natural. You'll pursue unofficial goals through your operating procedures, whether intentionally or not.

Identifying unofficial goals in an enterprise often requires special effort, perhaps even including some research using interviews with its members or drawing inferences from expenditures of resources such as time and money.

Getting off-track: Avoiding goal displacement

Nonprofit social enterprises, as well as in other kinds of nonprofits, tend to stray over time from pursuing official goals into seeking such unofficial goals as maintaining the group's current personnel arrangements, organizational procedures, or organizational structure. This tendency is known as *goal displacement.*

We can explain this tendency, in part, by the fact that nonprofit groups find it extremely difficult if not impossible to actually achieve some of their official goals — so they just add in goals that they *can* achieve. For example, maybe the official goal of raising money is displaced by a more realistic goal, such as living off of government grants.

Nonprofit groups are capable of seeking and even achieving many goals, but ones that are especially hard to reach involve money. For example, David Horton Smith, a well-known researcher on nonprofit organizations, notes that, however prominent the objective of raising money, most nonprofits have difficulty raising much of it (and none can collect taxes).

Avoiding goal displacement in your enterprise requires constant vigilance. Your best defense is in knowing that this tendency exists in organizations of all kinds, and that you have to keep official goals front and center in the minds of all your staff and volunteers (more about this in Chapter 18). Be on alert for actions on the part of your personnel that suggest they have unofficial goals that could undermine the organization's pursuit of its official goals.

Unofficial goals can become a problem when they come into conflict with the organization's official goals. If you suspect that some of the members of your organization have hidden agendas that may be hindering the enterprise's pursuit of its official goals, a common and often effective solution to the problem is to meet with them face to face to discuss those agendas and their effects on official goals. An example of a conflicting unofficial goal would be where a member wants your enterprise to use his or her professional service, when that same service is available elsewhere at significantly reduced cost.

Only you can judge the compatibility between your official and unofficial goals.

Planning on Profit — Or Not

Chapter 8 is devoted to the question of whether you should develop your social enterprise as a nonprofit or a for-profit business (one from which you'll be able to gain all or part of your livelihood). We briefly introduce the question here so that you recognize that you need to deal with this question in your initial strategic planning work.

What we have said to this point about basic planning applies to both nonprofit and for-profit social enterprises. Still, some entrepreneurs at this stage of developing their enterprises have already begun to think about making them profitable. More and more, their early strategic planning centers on profitability within the altruistic framework of social entrepreneurship.

What exactly is profit? We define *profit* as the money left over after expenses have been covered — money that is not plowed back into financing the enterprise. Profit is money that, if your enterprise's legal status permits, may go into your pocket. Of course, the legal status of a nonprofit prevents this kind of transfer of proceeds. (We discuss the different types of legal status in Chapter 14.)

Even if you envision for-profit status at the get-go, you may still want to begin as a nonprofit, with the long-range goal of converting to a business when financial conditions warrant. (This possibility is an advantage that social entrepreneurs have over traditional businesses.) Starting as a nonprofit enables you to receive funding from nonprofit funding sources while testing the waters to see how difficult it is to make a profit from your goods or services. If you realize that your enterprise can profit — that is, make more money than you need to run it — you'll have proof of that fact. At that point you can approach a bank for further profit-oriented funding, if you need it. Alternatively, you might create a for-profit arm of the enterprise so that the nonprofit status of the main organization is maintained.

Our advice is this: If at startup you know that your enterprise is going to need funding, strive as soon as possible to make money if you can. If, down the road, you find you're routinely bringing in more cash than needed to meet expenses, you can decide at that point whether to become a for-profit enterprise — in other words, a business.

Here are two blunt facts:

- ✔ The vast majority of nonprofits need money to operate.
- ✔ The vast majority of nonprofits are chronically short of money.

Many nonprofits try to survive on grants from public or private sources, or both. The problem is that grants are too often undependable. In the meantime, income from the sales of goods or services can help reduce dependence on these sources. (See Chapter 9 for more on grants and funding nonprofits.)

Anticipating Who Will Benefit from Your Work

Part of generating a solid strategic plan is identifying who or what will benefit from the work you plan to do. If you want to impress your friends and family with jargon, refer to the beneficiaries as your *target of benefits* (or *target group,* or simply *target*).

Your target may be a specific population, a group of people, or a set of organizations — for example, all elementary-age children in your city or all of its agencies that serve abused women. But some targets aren't people at all. We explain the array of possibilities in this section.

Defining a human target

Say the social problem you're trying to address is homelessness in your city. You set up End Homelessness, which aims to assist men, women, and children who hang out and sleep in public places. Your target population is very clear, and you even know how to locate them: You can often find homeless people on park benches, in doorways, in alleys, in spaces under bridges, and near heating grates (in the winter).

On the other hand, you may find that your target is easier to define than to locate. For example, say you want to initiate a social enterprise designed to educate female high school dropouts. You know from data published by the local school board that a certain percentage of females in local high schools never earn a high school diploma. But how do you find these people so you can encourage them to take advantage of your services? That's a challenge you must address in your strategic plan.

Think through the possible avenues of contact with your target population before you set up shop. Otherwise, you're throwing a party without an invitation list.

Focusing on nonhuman targets

The beneficiaries of your work don't have to be humans. Many environmental enterprises have targeted trees, rivers, birds, animals, and even the air we breathe. You can make the argument that these organizations do, ultimately, target humans, because we all benefit from improvements to the natural world. But in terms of strategic planning, you want to focus your energies on the first-tier beneficiaries, whether they're human or not.

Just to make things really interesting, keep in mind that *ideas* may be your target of benefits, too. For example, many social enterprises have been formed to fight for the teaching of either evolutionary science or creationism in schools. And enterprises whose mission is to convert people to a particular religion may be regarded as targeting ideas because they try to change how others think about supernatural powers. (See the nearby sidebar, "A creationist social enterprise," for an example.)

A creationist social enterprise

You may think social enterprises are always liberal and progressive undertakings, but that's not necessarily the case. Consider the example of a conservative idea-based social enterprise established by Paul Abramson called Biblical Creation Apologetics Program at Master's Divinity School. The object of this program is to instruct students on creationism, or what Abramson calls *creation theory*. The social problem he sees and is trying to solve is the dominance in Western societies of the evolutionary theory of human origin and development. He believes that theory is wrong and that

people in the West should be informed about the alternative creation theory and why, in his opinion, it's a better explanation.

Abramson's plan for reaching his entrepreneurial goals has been to establish the Master's Divinity School. That plan also includes a Web site he established for disseminating the creationist view (www.creationism.org), which provides links to other creationist sites and even a few evolutionist sites. Abramson has written numerous books and articles on the creation theory.

Moving on to new frontiers: Understanding goal succession

Sometimes a social enterprise changes one or more of its basic goals. When this happens, it's known as *goal succession*. Goal succession can occur when an enterprise has achieved one of its original goals, or it can occur because a goal has been made irrelevant by changes in the surrounding social or physical environment of the enterprise.

Goal succession becomes more likely as the group ages. Changes in the social or physical environment can take place any time, raising the possibility that certain goals may become obsolete.

Here's an example of goal succession in a social enterprise: The Marching Mothers of Ontario conducted their Canadian campaign in the 1950s and 1960s. It was part of the larger North American March of Dimes, whose fundraising mission was to collect money to be used to find a cure for polio — a highly contagious, disabling, and sometimes fatal disease. The money raised went toward research on polio. The Marching Mothers and their counterparts elsewhere in Canada and the United States went door to door in their neighborhoods, collecting donations (often much larger than a dime) for the March of Dimes. These funds supported the research of Dr. Jonas Salk, who eventually developed a polio vaccine, which brought a halt to the polio epidemics that had been plaguing North America. Suddenly, the volunteer work of the Marching Mothers was no longer needed; their goals had been reached. If their enterprise were to continue, it would need to find a new goal — or arrange for goal succession, which is what they did. Still marching, the Mothers now collect donations that support a wide range of vital services for adults and children with physical disabilities.

Look to the future to anticipate which, if any, of your present goals are soon likely to be reached. As you engage in initial planning for your social enterprise, you can't anticipate all the possible developments that may happen down the road. Besides, your time and energy are better spent dealing with the immediate and diverse challenges of reaching goals, conducting evaluations, and carrying out many of the other aspects of strategic planning. Still, it's good to be mindful that the world can change, sometimes suddenly, and successful goal succession requires a lot of advance planning if the transition is to be smooth and effective.

On the other hand, many nonprofit social entrepreneurs, when they've reached their goals, are quite content to call it a day. They set out to solve a finite problem — for example, to clean up a river, build a shelter for the homeless, or establish a set of summer recreational programs for children with physical handicaps. After your goal is reached, you may decide to move on to another social problem requiring a new enterprise for its solution. After all, you've already proven you can do it!

Developing Mission and Vision Statements

The *mission* of your social enterprise is, quite simply, its central purpose as defined now. The *vision* is how you foresee your organization operating in the future — the needs it fulfills, the target it serves, and so on.

As you develop a strategic plan for your enterprise, your challenge is to craft a mission statement and a vision statement that capture your ideas effectively enough to convey them to the rest of the world. In this section, we show you how.

Mission and vision statements aren't carved in stone. Although you want to strive toward consistency, especially in your mission, you can modify these statements if your enterprise's mission or vision changes.

Short and sweet: Crafting a mission statement

Mission orientation is the basic distinguishing characteristic of nonprofit groups — it's what sets them apart from the for-profit organizations, which, not surprisingly, have as their central purpose the pursuit of profit. (That's not to say that corporations and companies don't also see themselves as having missions — usually serving customers and so on — but their *real* bottom-line mission is to make a profit.)

Some businesses start out purely as businesses with a mission to make money. Some of these, especially in today's moralistic climate, have later added social missions (see Chapter 8). But they aren't social enterprises. Other organizations — both nonprofit and for-profit — start out as organizations designed to solve a particular social problem.

Coming up with the mission of your social enterprise may be easy: It's simply a statement of what you want to change in this world and why. For example, say your organization's goal is to fight homelessness. The mission statement of such an enterprise may read: "The mission of End Homelessness is to establish suitable shelter for all street people in Seattle."

Not all social issues are as easy to communicate to the public, though, and not all mission statements are so simple to craft. So if your mission statement hasn't popped into your head already, read on.

Recognizing the characteristics of a great mission statement

Your challenge is to present your mission in such a way that it's easily and quickly understood by the people who will benefit from your work, your funders, potential volunteers, and anyone else who can influence your success. The best statements are

- Short
- Simply worded
- Unambiguous
- Interesting to read

Although shorter is better, you may need a longer mission statement if your work is more difficult to explain. Some mission statements, for example, must contain definitions of key concepts that are not widely known. Otherwise, they risk being misunderstood or clashing with definitions that are too simplistic or inconsistent with the organization's mission.

Drafting a mission statement of your own

See what you can do in, say, 25 or 30 words to create a succinct and catchy mission statement, using the criteria in the preceding section. Practice writing mission statements for other organizations — not just your own. Writing effective mission statements is a skill that you can polish with a little practice.

After you have something written down — a mission statement that applies to your organization — circulate it to others in your enterprise for their evaluation. And don't forget to show drafts of the statement to folks outside the enterprise because the statement will ultimately be read by all sorts of outside people who must also understand it. Getting feedback from some outsiders early in the game can help you avoid having to redraft the statement later.

Here are three model mission statements for three different kinds of social enterprises. Each statement has been written to be short, simply worded, unambiguous, and interesting to read.

- **Human target:** Self-Directed Learners League (SDLL). The SDLL was formed to promote self-directed learning at all ages.

  Mission statement: Self-directed learning — learning that is intentional, planned, and controlled by the learner — is a main highway to deep personal development. The Self-Directed Learners League encourages self-directed learning at all ages in all areas of life, fosters opportunities to learn in this way, and develops and promotes resources by which this can be achieved.

✔ **Idea as target:** The Jazz Appreciation Society (JAS). The JAS was established to promote understanding of and love for jazz music in all its forms

Mission statement: Jazz is one of the world's most original and vibrant forms of music. The Jazz Appreciation Society encourages people to listen to this exciting art — both live and recorded — as well as to learn about its nature, history, styles, and key performers.

✔ **Non-human target:** Save the Black-Footed Ferret. This organization was born to find ways to save from extinction one of North America's most endangered mammals.

Mission statement: The black-footed ferret — once a lively, omnipresent resident of the Great Plains from Mexico to Canada — is now on the verge of disappearing. Save the Black-Footed Ferret sensitizes politicians, environmentalists, and the general population to this imminent tragedy. We also foster research into habitat preservation for and optimal breeding practices of this mammal.

A glimpse of your future: Writing a vision statement

Unlike a mission statement, a vision statement is future oriented. Your vision statement presents your enterprise's ideal picture of itself in the future, as an entity that's already successfully carrying out its mission. It provides an ideal toward which you're striving.

The same criteria that guide your construction of a mission statement (see the preceding section) also apply here: You want a vision statement that's short, simply worded, unambiguous, and interesting. However, your vision statement will undoubtedly be longer than your mission statement.

Your mission statement and vision statement will most often be presented in tandem on your marketing materials, your Web site, your grant applications, and so on. For this reason, you don't want the two to overlap significantly.

As with your mission statement, we suggest that you draft a vision statement or two as an exercise in forming such a document.

Vision statements center on already realized goals. Therefore, your draft should portray this outcome, while also saying something (quite general) about the actions you took to reach them. Here, too, practice makes perfect.

The three model social enterprises, whose mission statements we review in the preceding section, also have vision statements. As with a mission statement, a vision statement should be short, simply worded, unambiguous, and interesting to read, as exemplified here:

- **Self-Directed Learners League:** People of all ages everywhere in the community routinely shaping their own education by reading, listening, and viewing material that interests them and leads to their growth as unique individuals.

- **The Jazz appreciation Society:** People throughout the community listen to live and recorded jazz and learn about it by reading, listening, and watching informative books, articles, CDs, DVDs, videos, and television programs.

- **Save the Black-Footed Ferret:** A healthy, reproducing population of black-footed ferrets is distributed throughout its original native habitat such that it fits well within the larger ecosystem.

Marketing reusable shopping bags for profit

Judy Lazar, a mother of three, was looking for a new business opportunity. She had abandoned a career in Montreal's fashion industry to be a full-time mother. One day while she was grocery shopping, she realized that the supermarkets shared considerable responsibility for the proliferation of plastic bags, which pollute urban environments everywhere.

Judy knew that reusable plastic bags were catching on in Quebec in supermarkets and other businesses. Still, the produce section of the supermarkets and the various farmers' markets presented a special problem. Dispensers holding rolls of plastic bags were all over the produce aisles, and even shoppers with reusable grocery bags used the plastic ones to wrap their produce.

So Judy decided to create produce bags that would change grocery shopping, making it more environmentally friendly. She developed a bag consisting in part of cotton. At the time of this writing, Judy has sold more than 30,000 of her produce bags.

Chapter 8

For-Profit and Nonprofit: Considering Your Options

*E*veryone needs money, and everyone likes to be paid for doing what they like. So, the question naturally arises: Should you try to personally profit from your proposed social enterprise? For some entrepreneurs, the answer is "Of course!" For others, the answer is an equally strong "Of course not!" If you're not sure, this chapter's for you.

Here, we explain the key differences between running a nonprofit business and running a for-profit business. We help you consider how your decision will affect the people or things you're trying to benefit. We also lay out some pros and cons of each option for you to consider. Then we turn to considering the moral dimension of running a social enterprise, including choosing which and how many bottom lines to consider when making decisions about how to run your organization.

Introducing the Different Types of Socially Conscious Organizations: Nonprofit and For-Profit

When you're getting ready to launch a socially conscious organization, one of your first decisions needs to be whether to profit. Nonprofit and for-profit social enterprises both have pros and cons, but before we launch into our discussion of these pros and cons, you need some background information.

At startup, you can choose from one of three types of organizations. (Later, you may want to change to a different type, but we're getting ahead of ourselves.) We cover these organizations in the following sections. For more-detailed information on these types of organizations, turn to Chapter 14.

Unincorporated nonprofit groups

An unincorporated nonprofit group is a group that has no legal status and whose mission is to solve a social problem.

When we refer to a *group* here, we're talking about two or more individuals who share one or more goals and have a sense of common identity (distinct from other groups and the population at large). The group is organized around a set of rules and roles.

Nonprofit corporations

No, *nonprofit corporation* is not an oxymoron — it's actually a legally established group (that is, a nonprofit organization that has a charter and may also have a governmental tax-exempt status). The people responsible for directing the organization (often called the *board of directors* or *trustees*) can't be paid — they're volunteers. They may, however, hire staff for pay, including an executive director, who implements board decisions and policy. The executive director doesn't direct the organization, though — that function is filled by the volunteer board of directors.

For-profit corporations

A for-profit corporation is a legally established group. The key difference between a nonprofit corporation and a for-profit corporation is that, in a nonprofit corporation, members of the board of directors, owners, and shareholders (if there are any and if they also help direct the group) are legally prohibited from being paid from the profits gained by the corporation. In a for-profit corporation, everyone may be, and usually is, paid for his work, including the board of directors, owners, and shareholders. A for-profit corporation, therefore, cannot qualify as a charity and doesn't have governmental tax-exempt status.

Profit is the money left over after all the expenses of the enterprise have been met, including the wages and benefits of paid staff.

Weighing the Pros and Cons of Nonprofit and For-Profit Organizations

Being a social entrepreneur doesn't necessarily mean you're going to spend the rest of your life in jeans, T-shirts, and a beater car. But here's what you need to know: If you incorporate as a nonprofit organization, you and other members of your group who own it or on your board of directors cannot legally receive personal income or other financial benefits funded by your organization. Instead, any profits from sales of goods and services must be returned to the enterprise for use in ways that advance the enterprise. If you incorporate as a for-profit enterprise, you and the members of your group can be paid and can receive a share of the profits.

By *profit* we mean the money left over after all the expenses of the enterprise have been met, including the wages and benefits of paid staff.

Nonprofits: Everything goes back to the organization

The idea of the nonprofit group has been around since the dawn of the for-profit corporation (which we discuss in Chapter 14), when it became necessary to distinguish the two kinds of organizations. The nonprofit has since acquired a rather saintly aura of fostering good in the community rather than blindly pursuing profit. But here we take a more realistic and detailed view of nonprofits, looking at their advantages and disadvantages.

The advantages

Here are some of the key benefits you gain by opting for nonprofit status:

- ✓ **A clear conscience:** You avoid the potential uncomfortable feeling of making money off the social problem you're trying to solve.

- ✓ **A keen focus on your target population:** Any money the organization makes is funneled back into solving the social problem and helping your target population.

- ✓ **Lifestyle balance:** Commitment to running a nonprofit social enterprise is very likely to take a good deal of time away from making a living. Under such conditions, some social entrepreneurs experience a shift in values as the "hobby" gains in importance compared to the "job." You may decide that you and your family can live comfortably on a smaller income. The lifestyle of a nonprofit social entrepreneur is rarely opulent, but you don't have to take a vow of poverty.

✔ **The ability to nurture the enterprise:** You can invest some of the earnings from your enterprise in a bank account, mutual fund, or money market fund to increase the value of your *idle money* (money not immediately needed for operations or that is ineligible for the support of your operations, such as restricted endowments — see Chapter 9). To retain nonprofit status, all interest on such investments must be returned to the enterprise and not to individual members.

✔ **Decreased financial risk:** As a nonprofit social entrepreneur, you avoid the risk and hassle of going into business and taking on the responsibility of running an enterprise for profit. You probably aren't investing your own cash in the organization, so you aren't risking losing your own money if it doesn't succeed.

✔ **Less bureaucracy:** When profit is removed from the picture, you may have an easier time keeping your enterprise small and the bureaucracy minimal.

✔ **Credibility**: As mentioned in the introduction to this section, the nonprofits have acquired a rather saintly aura compared with profit-seeking businesses.

The disadvantages

Running a nonprofit isn't a cakewalk. Here are some of the disadvantages to setting up and running a nonprofit organization:

✔ **You're limited when it comes to how much money you can make.**

✔ **Free time may be a thing of the past.** Because you can't make a ton of money when you're running a nonprofit, you may need to hold down a day job while you're running the organization. Every spare minute you have when you're not at your day job will have to be poured into your nonprofit, which doesn't leave you much time for a life outside the nonprofit.

✔ **The growth of your organization is limited.** Because you don't have much to risk (see the preceding section), you can grow only so big, which means the number of people you can help may be limited as well.

✔ **You must rely on volunteers.** Although some entrepreneurs may consider volunteers purely as an advantage, others give them a mixed review. As we discuss in Chapter 17, volunteers do pose some special managerial problems.

Helping society while turning a profit

You may be more familiar with for-profit corporations than you are with nonprofit groups. We all know about businesses, which seem to be everywhere in life, but many people have little if any contact with nonprofits. Most of your friends and relatives probably work for a for-profit organization of some kind. But specifically what are the advantages and disadvantages of the for-profits?

The advantages

Here are some advantages of running a for-profit business:

✔ **The money:** You can use the profits from your social enterprise to achieve a more comfortable life for yourself and your family. In fact, your social enterprise may enable you to devote yourself full time to your entrepreneurial work — something that may or may not be possible in a nonprofit.

In for-profit organizations, financial returns from invested idle money (see "Nonprofits: Everything goes back to the organization," earlier in this chapter) may be distributed among owners, paid staff, or both.

✔ **Access to credit:** Banks and other financial institutions will lend money and issue credit cards only to legally established groups who show a level of profit sufficient to repay a loan.

✔ **Greater benefits for your target population:** Running a for-profit enterprise lets you expand faster and have a bigger impact on your target population, partially because you can afford to pay salaries and haul in more investment capital.

✔ **Stability:** For-profit organizations have greater stability, with less employee turnover, than their nonprofit counterparts because the for-profits are supplying a livelihood. Except when jobs are plentiful, employees are reluctant to leave positions that, for example, pay well and offer adequate benefits.

If you're entertaining the possibility of making your enterprise a for-profit business, you probably don't feel particularly hamstrung by the moral issues of making a profit from the social problem at hand or channeling profits away from your target population. Rest assured that we don't take a stand one way or the other in this book: Both nonprofits and for-profits contribute to society in positive ways.

If you're considering becoming a for-profit corporation, head over to Chapter 14 to find out the ins and outs of legally incorporating.

Aiding the poor in a profitable way: The Kuroiler chicken

In March 2009, *The Economist* ran a story about the Indian social entrepreneur Vinod Kapur. To help feed India's rural poor, Kapur invested $1 million to breed a super-chicken called the Kuroiler. Kuroilers are disease-resistant and cheap to feed. They also produce twice as much meat and lay five times as many eggs as regular Indian chickens do.

Kapur established a firm called Keggfarms (*Kegg* is a combination of *Kapur* and *egg*), which produces the Kuroiler. The chickens have been welcomed by 700,000 rural households in various states in northern India. The system Kapur set up works like this: Kegg Farms supplies chickens to 1,500 mother units located throughout northern India. Local entrepreneurs own these units, buying between 400 and 2,000 birds in a single purchase. The entrepreneurs then sell them in the nearby villages, via vendors on bicycles. The typical entrepreneur of a mother unit makes a profit of 3 Indian rupees (about 6¢) per bird, and so does the vendor on the bike.

The disadvantages

So, what are the negative effects of seeking profit in the field of social enterprise? Here are a few to consider:

- **Complexity:** One major consequence of seeking profit is the accompanying complexity of operating procedures. Profit-seeking enterprises have to pay taxes, which certainly adds a layer of bureaucracy. For-profits also have more access to credit than nonprofits, which means debt can become more of an issue. And because banks are often involved in funding for-profit businesses, you may have to do more formal (and more frequent) financial reporting.

- **Tighter markets:** The market is much more competitive and restrictive for for-profit businesses than it is for nonprofits — if for no other reason than that ordinary businesses are much more dependent on sales than nonprofits.

- **The risk of tyranny:** Businesses are not democracies. Nonprofits, by dint of their constitutions (see Chapter 14), are democracies. In nonprofits, groups of members govern. Nonprofits experience more leadership turnover than for-profits as a result, but that's not necessarily a bad thing. In for-profits, the risk is that one person (or a small group of people) rules, and that person simply may not be the best leader for the group.

✔ **Resentment among your target population:** If the people you're trying to help know that you're making a profit, they may feel exploited. They may lament or even vocally protest that outsiders are making money from their misery.

✔ **A snowballing preoccupation with profit:** All the time and effort that you put into thinking about how to get more or bigger subsidies or maximize return from investments, products, or services may come at the expense of more effectively serving your target population.

The wise and thoughtful entrepreneur (that's you, right?) steers a course between two distinct goals: making money and serving the target population. If you keep your enterprise's mission squarely in sight, you should be able to steer your organization successfully.

A delicate balance: Nonprofits that charge user fees

User fees are fees that a nonprofit organization charges for the use of its services. Examples include park and museum admissions, hospital bills, daycare fees, and even college tuition fees. When you're trying to decide whether to charge user fees, you have to weigh the cost of administering them. The organization either has to pay someone to collect the fees or find volunteers to do it.

An even bigger problem with user fees is that they sometimes run counter to a nonprofit group's mission. You want people to use your services — that's why your social enterprise exists in the first place, right? Token fees may not be much of a hindrance, but substantial user fees can discourage would-be patrons, patients, students — whoever your users are.

The decision you have to make is whether the additional revenue from user fees is worth the loss of some users. This dilemma is unique to nonprofit enterprises because most for-profit ones have no choice but to rely on such fees as a main part of their revenue.

One way around the dilemma is to try to determine what level of fee users will tolerate — in other words, at what price level will they refuse to patronize your nonprofit enterprise? There's no magic formula here — each case is different. All you can do is ask a sample of patrons what they think of a fee set at a certain amount. Or start charging the fee and watch what happens to your patronage.

You may want to consider charging based on the ability of different categories to pay. For example, you may charge less for children than for teenagers or adults. Or you may want to charge based on a *sliding scale* (higher fees for families with higher incomes).

Looking at the Moral Dimension in For-Profit Enterprises

Running a social enterprise has a moral dimension to it. This moral dimension stems from the fact that social enterprises — whether they're nonprofit or for-profit — are created because someone wants to solve a social problem (feed the hungry, house the homeless, care for those in need).

The moral side of for-profit social entrepreneurship is expressed in, among other ways, the kinds of bottom lines that the entrepreneur seeks. We discuss three bottom lines in the following sections. The moral issues supporting the mission of your enterprise help determine which type of entrepreneurial organization you'll want to create. These moral issues also help determine which bottom lines you choose to favor.

Plus, the moral dimension in for-profits extends well beyond the concern about bottom lines. So, later in this section we also discuss practicing corporate social responsibility and marketing with a conscience.

Double and triple bottom lines: Adding social and environmental good to your goal of turning a profit

Traditional corporations have one bottom line:

> How much money are we making after paying everyone we have to pay?

The for-profit social business has that same bottom line, but it adds a *second* bottom line to it:

> How much *good* is the enterprise doing? In other words, how much is the target being helped?

Adding that second bottom line is very impressive — it's like riding a unicycle and juggling at the same time.

Can a for-profit social enterprise not only earn money (the bottom line) and serve a social good (the second bottom line), but *also* serve an environmental good (the third bottom line)? Isn't that like juggling while riding a unicycle along a tightrope? The environmental benefit we're talking about is, for example, an improvement in the condition of some part of nature such as water, air, soil, or animals. You accomplish this improvement in a way that is sustainable, that will endure over time, and that does not, in the process, undermine another part of nature.

Is a triple bottom line possible? Yes! Two nearby sidebars — "Terra Nova: A Brazilian success story" and "Symbio Impex: The triple bottom line in agriculture" — give examples.

Terra Nova: A Brazilian success story

André L. Cavalcanti de Albuquerque established an organization in São Paulo, Brazil called Terra Nova Regularizações Fundiárias. He wanted to establish a procedure to legalize, in a sustainable way, urban land that is illegally occupied, most notably in *favelas* (urban slum communities).

Terra Nova mediates between the people who legally own a piece of property and those who have come to live on it illegally. The goal is to find a solution to this problem that both parties can accept. Terra Nova is the first nongovernmental organization in Brazil to become involved in land regularization. Before, the service was almost exclusively offered by government, but given inefficiency, shortage of funds, and overloaded staff, government was often unable to deliver as needed. Those deficiencies were part of the social problem that inspired de Albuquerque to found Terra Nova.

Terra Nova has been a success story. Every community regularized by de Albuquerque has seen a rise in the quality of low-income family life. As soon as the town council sees a title deed provided by the local land office, it begins offering such necessities as water, electricity,

basic sanitation, public transport, and even a postal code.

What is environmental and sustainable about the Terra Nova project? What is its triple bottom line? Local soil and water have been improved by providing sanitation services and purified water from an external source. Other benefits relate to the second bottom line: improvements in public transport, mail service, and lighting.

For-profit enterprises have a bad reputation in Brazil, so it took courage for de Albuquerque to establish a social business. He says that Terra Nova is not out to build up and hang on to capital. He believes the problem should be viewed independently of the power and attractiveness of money. With a for-profit approach to solving this kind of social problem, he can make enough money to stretch the service to many more people than would be possible were the enterprise founded on a nonprofit basis. De Albuquerque says that, if his profits allow, he would like to expand Terra Nova's operations to the rest of Latin America and to Africa.

Symbio Impex: The triple bottom line in agriculture

Tokya E. Dammond is the president of Symbio Impex Corporation, which he, Symbio Polska, and Artur Tyminski founded in 1998 in the United States. Using a Polish/American venture-capital fund, the three created a company that contracted small family-owned farms and landscape parks to produce and process Polish-grown organic fruits and vegetables.

Symbio started with 20 farms, but today the company works with more than 300 farms, selling produce to the European Union and North American industrial and retail markets. The company gained $4.5 million in revenues in 2006 — taking care of the first bottom line.

The company also helps solve a social problem by paying a fair price to small family farms for their organic produce, which addresses the second bottom line. Small family farms are in danger of disappearing in the face of competition from giant factory farms.

And, when it comes to the third bottom line, Symbio achieves environmental sustainability through organic farming. Healthy soil is created to produce healthy plants, which have high immunity against plant diseases and pests. Organic farming recycles natural materials back into the soil, thereby sustaining fertility and creating a natural approach to controlling pests and disease. This cyclical process, say the Symbio executives, eliminates the need for artificial fertilizer, chemical pesticides, growth hormones, and similar unnatural additives.

Practicing corporate social responsibility

The phrase *corporate social responsibility* (CSR) means different things to different people. We define it as the way businesses (including for-profit social businesses) coordinate their organizational values and actions with the needs and expectations of the *stakeholders* (customers, shareholders, other investors, employees, regulators, the community at large, and special interest groups).

If you plan to set up a for-profit social enterprise, you may want to develop a statement describing and proclaiming your CSR. Doing so demonstrates to your stakeholders a commitment to monitoring the effects of your operations on your local community and society at large. Your statement should declare how you'll maximize societal benefits while minimizing the costs to the community. For example, your statement may emphasize the large number of people you employ who make a reasonably priced product using pollution controls that keep local air and water acceptably clean.

Enlightened employment policies can also be a part of your enterprise's CSR. Your statement on CSR may contain information on, for example, how your company fairly handles employee grievances, assures equity in pay and promotion, and exceeds industry-wide health and safety standards.

Some CSR statements contain passages concerning a company's relations with the community — for example, in support of the arts, youth activities, or municipal parks. The statement may include information about how your company helps workers' families and provides them with company-sponsored events such as Christmas parties, summer picnics, and special outings.

 Post your CSR statement conspicuously on your Web site, summarize it in your corporate brochures, and speak about it at public gatherings involving your enterprise. ***Remember:*** You'll always have to live down the popular image that businesses are greedy entities strictly concerned with their own interests, and your CSR statement can help you do exactly that.

Because CSR statements, at least in the larger corporations, tend to be lengthy, we suggest you go online to view examples. For example, McDonald's has one at `www.aboutmcdonalds.com/mcd/csr.html`. Ford Motor Company pitches its CSR in terms of corporate sustainability at `www.ford.com/about ford/company-information/corporate-sustainability`. And Walmart Canada offers a 24-page report titled "Corporate Social Responsibility" at `www. walmart.ca`.

 Showing CSR is not pure altruism. Certain advantages accrue to companies that parade their CSR. Some of these advantages include the following:

- **CSR can improve access to capital.** People like to invest their money in companies that show CSR.

- **CSR can reduce bad publicity.** Showing social responsibility can lower the risk of opposition from parties outside the company who are upset with a company's disagreeable policies and practices.

- **CSR can increase good publicity.** The public relations impact of high CSR can be worth its weight in gold. That is, the company's product basks favorably in the light of exemplary behavior in the community.

- **CSR can expand markets and save money.** Exemplary CSR may even generate new markets for a company's product. CSR may also generate previously unknown opportunities for saving money in production, manufacturing, or distribution. (For example, switching from oil-based to soy-based manufacturing can save a company money.)

- **CSR can help recruitment and hiring.** Many people want to work for an enterprise known for its fine CSR. Conversely, they don't want to work for companies whose CSR leaves much to be desired, such as those who have a bad reputation for environmental pollution or exploitation of employees.

 The form of CSR that may be of most interest to you as a social entrepreneur could be a partnership between your for-profit social enterprise and a private company with no social mission. Such a partnership can create profit and social value. Can you team with a corporation to advance your entrepreneurial mission so that the corporation can both profit and demonstrate its responsibility to community or society? It may be worth a try.

Some companies, inspired by the principles of CSR, prefer to support a social enterprise related to their interests instead of giving unspecified donations to foundations and other nonprofits. Philip Kotler and Nancy Lee present a variety of examples of successful partnerships in their book *Corporate Social Responsibility: Doing the Most Good for Your Company and Your Cause* (Wiley).

Marketing with a conscience

The most obvious and common way for your social enterprise to become involved with the market and make some money is to try to sell one or more of your products or services. (We illustrate this approach in the sidebar "Aiding the poor in a profitable way: The Kuroiler chicken," earlier in this chapter.) But you have to sell with a conscience. In addition, there are several other approaches that social enterprises may take to exploit the market.

Beyond just starting to sell your goods and services in the marketplace, you can market your products or services with a conscience. The main idea is that you want both to promote your enterprise and make some money in a manner that is morally acceptable to you, your colleagues in the enterprise, other stakeholders, and the wider community:

- **Rent out your brand.** A social enterprise can make available to a for-profit (non-social) enterprise its reputation as a trustworthy and socially beneficial organization. The business then pays the social enterprise for use of this asset. Affinity credit cards are a well-known example, as are some minibuses that serve disabled people.

- **Endorse someone else's brand.** A social enterprise can endorse a particular business brand and receive payment from the company selling the branded good or service. The American Cancer Society entered into such an agreement with several manufacturers of nicotine patches. What would prevent a hospital from naming a visitors' lounge in recognition of the local corporate sponsor who pays for its construction and operation? (You could imagine the "Caravel Room," after a local dairy, or the "Lakers Lounge," after the professional basketball team.)

- **Form an exclusive brand partnership.** A social enterprise may sell or license its services to a corporate sponsor, for which the corporation pays the nonprofit. A common example these days is corporate support of educational programs and institutions, such as Coca-Cola gaining the exclusive rights to the sale of soft drinks on a university campus or a caterer gaining exclusive access to all catered food in a large museum.

- **Sell or license intellectual property rights.** A social enterprise may earn money from certain intellectual property rights. This contested practice is evident, for example, when a company offers a research grant contract to a university if the university gives privileged access to the results of the research. There may even be some advantages for the company in terms of eventually gaining patents through such an exchange.

What do non-social businesses get out of such liaisons? If all goes as planned, they can add to their profits in new ways. They may also want to bask in the *greenwashing effect,* or enhanced public image that can sometimes develop from being positively linked with a respected community good or service.

These ideas are best suited for established social organizations. If you're a small startup, you won't be able to do these things until you grow large enough.

Sometimes, making liaisons like this can be like selling your soul to the devil. Such partnerships can change the culture of the nonprofit. People who raise money through these external funding sources can easily lose sight of the enterprise's goals. Plus, if they succeed in getting the funding, they're likely to get all kinds of kudos within the enterprise — possibly at the expense of other volunteers and employees whose contributions are directly related to the enterprise's mission, which can send mixed messages about what the group really values.

Considering Capitalistic Concerns in Nonprofit Enterprises

Capitalism, it turns out, can be quite useful to the development and running of social enterprises. The traditional goal in investing is simply to make money, but making money isn't always possible in social entrepreneurial missions, which may make a little money, break even, or lose money. Here's the good news: Some capitalists with a conscience and funds to donate want to help organizations reach their socially oriented missions. Their chief interest is to make the world a better place, and they're willing to put their money where their mouths are.

Philanthrocapitalism: Capitalism with a twist

Philanthrocapitalism is different from mainstream for-profit capitalism. Philanthrocapitalism is the realm of individual philanthropists who have money to burn and a burning desire to help solve key social or environmental problems, but who are — for one reason or another — unable to tackle these problems on their own. They can work with nonprofits to reach their charitable goals.

Philanthrocapitalism is about applying business principles to using large amounts of money in solving social problems and, in the course of doing so, fostering social change.

Still, the philanthrocapitalist's relationship to nonprofit social entrepreneurship is complicated. A philanthrocapitalist is not opposed to making money through a social enterprise, even though his first goal is to help solve a social problem. Philanthrocapitalists, when not working through government, work through the nonprofit sector — but if a good or service produced there also becomes profitable, they're typically quite pleased to make money on their investments.

Among the most celebrated philanthrocapitalists today are Warren Buffett, Bill Gates, and Bill Clinton. Buffett gave a large proportion of his enormous fortune to the foundation established by Gates: the Bill and Melinda Gates Foundation. Internationally, that charity has donated large sums of money to social enterprises whose missions are to enhance healthcare and reduce extreme poverty.

Founded on the financial acumen of Bill Clinton, the William J. Clinton Foundation operates in four areas: health security; economic empowerment; leadership development and citizen service; and racial, ethnic, and religious reconciliation. The William J. Clinton Foundation works mainly in partnerships with like-minded individuals, organizations, corporations, and governments.

These are among the most dramatic and publicly visible manifestations of philanthrocapitalism. But smaller fortunes may be deployed the same way, usually directed to problems more local in scope. Mathew Bishop and Michael Green's book, *Philanthrocapitalism: How the Rich Can Save the World* (Bloomsbury Press), profiles a number of philanthrocapitalists, all of whom have vast fortunes to give to social entrepreneurial causes.

The point in all this for you is that you can't overlook philanthrocapitalism — large scale or small — as a source of funding for your mission. But how do you find a philanthrocapitalist? A good way is to write to them. You can reach Matthew Bishop and Michael Green, for example, at www. philanthrocapitalism.net/contact. Or write the New York office of the Clinton Foundation at William J. Clinton Foundation, 55 West 125th Street, New York, NY 10027. Whomever you write, tell them who you are and what your enterprise does, and ask whether they would be interested in receiving a more detailed proposal for funding. It can't hurt, and you'd be surprised at the response a modest personal request can generate.

Venture philanthropy: The work of fairy godcapitalists

In venture philanthropy, a capitalist applies venture capital approaches among nonprofit groups to help them obtain not just grants but also technical assistance, networking opportunities, and other support services. Venture philanthropy is a way to improve the effectiveness of philanthropic foundations. Such philanthropy becomes a kind of *social investing* because it uses the discipline of the investment world in a field that has traditionally relied on trust and good faith.

Venture capital, by the way, is risk capital, or money put up for speculative investment.

So what's the difference between a venture philanthropist and a charitable foundation? The equity holders in venture capital enterprises serve as partners, coaches, and guides of the new business supported by their capital. In other words, they don't just give money the way foundations do — they follow the money and make sure it's being spent wisely. In addition, this kind of hands-on approach leads to long-term sharing of risk and investment in organizational structure and growth.

If you want to establish your enterprise as a business, and you can find venture philanthropy to support your mission, consider yourself very lucky. Go for it! In the United States, check out the National Venture Capital Association (www.nvca.org) and search for those capitalists possibly interested in investing in social enterprise. The Canada Venture Capital and Private Equity Association provides a long list of members (venture capitalists) on its Web site (www.cvca.ca/membership/directory).

Foundations often fail to gives grants as effectively as venture capitalists do. Foundations often invest haphazardly in new ideas. Plus, they rarely give organizational support or demand accountability.

Granting agencies never move out of the role of *funder* to that of *partner*. Whereas a partner — a venture philanthropist — shares the risks of the enterprise. Of course, that partner also shares in any successes and hopefully, as a result, makes a profit. This kind of partner takes an active role investor role there. For example, Cordova Ventures says its partnership includes ownership with "a minority stake" in the funded enterprise. Moreover, venture capitalists usually provide expertise on how to achieve entrepreneurial success and make valuable connections to people, agencies, and organizations that can also help you reach this goal.

Socially responsible investing

Socially responsible investing (SRI) is an investment process that considers the social and environmental consequences of investments, both positive and negative. Consideration of the consequences takes place within the framework of rigorous financial analysis. SRI involves both nonprofit and for-profit organizations through different arrangements.

SRI is often referred to as a *holistic* approach to investing because it takes account of financial, social, environmental, and ethical criteria when choosing investments.

What does SRI have to do with social entrepreneurship? As a social entrepreneur, you stand to benefit from SRI in two ways:

- ✓ **Some investors seeking responsible investments donate their money to venture philanthropic organizations.** Individual philanthropic venture capitalists are, by definition, engaging in SRI. For example, the Investor Education Fund lists "community investment" as a method of social investment. In this case, a person invests money in community development or micro-enterprise initiatives that contribute to the growth and well being of specific communities. Your enterprise could become the object of such investment.

- ✓ **Your enterprise may want to invest money that's not immediately needed for operations or not eligible for support of operations.** Investing using SRI is a perfectly legitimate process for nonprofit organizations of all kinds.

When a nonprofit enterprise hires a new financial advisor or new manager of its investment portfolio, the board of directors has to make sure that the person is qualified and that she's serving your enterprise well. When considering any financial expert:

- ✓ Make sure you understand all the risks associated with any investment made by you and your enterprise.

- ✓ Never turn over money to a manager whom you believe lacks experience, appears incompetent, or is known to be unethical.

- ✓ Always assess on your own each investment made by your enterprise and the manager of your enterprise's portfolio. This rule is especially important when she's still new on the job.

Your enterprise, when and if you eventually turn it into a business, won't ever be a typical for-profit corporation. It has an important public mission, and this mission may well be expected by the public to influence its investment decisions. Therefore, always consider socially responsible investing as it relates to that mission.

Chapter 9

It Doesn't Grow on Trees: Funding Nonprofits

*T*he vast majority of social enterprises need external funding of some sort. By *external funding,* we mean financial support that comes from sources other than (a) the pockets of the social entrepreneur and his partners, or (b) the revenues from sales that are plowed back into the operating costs of running the organization. Most social enterprises need to supplement such *internal funding* with money from outside sources.

Exceptions include the diverse small enterprises that are formed to make limited changes in the local community. These social enterprises are sometimes established to transform an aspect of municipal government, local industry, school policy, or community habit (such as littering, panhandling, speeding, or loitering). Don't get us wrong — such undertakings may well require considerable time and effort, but they're often all-volunteer affairs and can succeed with little or no money.

If your social enterprise is a nonprofit, you'll likely need outside funding — and this chapter is for you. (If your enterprise is a social business or is a small, limited concern such as the ones just described, and you don't think you need to raise money to succeed, you can safely skip this chapter.)

Achieving Charitable Status

A social enterprise can obtain charitable status only after becoming a legal entity — that is, after it has been officially incorporated. *Charitable status* refers to legal recognition of a social enterprise as a special kind of nonprofit group known as a *charity.* (We cover the details of different types of legal status in Chapter 14.)

Legal and charitable statuses are closely intertwined with funding. To obtain external funding, your enterprise must usually

- ✔ **Be incorporated:** Becoming legally incorporated establishes your legal status.
- ✔ **Be established as a charity:** Many, though not all, funders require charitable status for funding.

Most of the best funding out there depends on having charitable status.

A *charity* usually has the following characteristics:

- ✔ It's formally organized as an incorporated nonprofit.
- ✔ It provides one or more public benefits (as opposed to member benefits).
- ✔ It receives a significant amount of its revenue from donations.

In the United States, many charities (technically called *public charities*) are registered with the Internal Revenue Service (IRS) as 501(c)(3) groups and qualify as such under IRS Section 509(a). Charities registered like this are eligible to receive tax-deductible charitable gifts of money or in kind. (*In-kind gifts* are something other than money, such as goods or services. Donating rare books to a public library or land for a nonprofit homeless shelter are examples of gifts in kind.)

If a charitable gift is *tax-deductible,* it means the donor gets to deduct the amount of the donation from her taxable income, thus lowering her own tax bill. Tax deduction is a substantial incentive for potential donors. Of course, people or organizations may donate to nonprofit enterprises that lack charitable status, and some individuals and groups do precisely that — but they don't get a tax deduction for it. The possibility of a tax deduction, especially for large donations, is a powerful incentive to give. So, if you can achieve 501(c)(3) status, you should — it'll increase your chances of getting charitable donations.

Be aware, however, that 501(c) identifies 26 types of nonprofit organizations exempt from some federal income taxes. The types vary as to their impact on the mission of your enterprise. For example, a 501(c)3 cannot lobby a legislative body (or endorse a specific candidate for president), but others can.

Several of the grants available are open only to 501(c)3s that have been in existence for more than a year. If your organization is newly formed, you may want to "borrow" the charitable status of another organization. This is perfectly legal, and there are organizations, such as Acterra (www.acterra.org) that openly advertise for this type of fiscal sponsorship. Going this route is a way to get around those grants requiring a minimum period in business.

You Gotta Pay Your Dues

Many social enterprises require their members to pay dues — normally an annual fee — for rights of membership in the group. Dues are usually the main source of revenue for national enterprises. For smaller, grassroots enterprises, dues are often the only source of revenue. A major question, then, especially at the beginning of a dues-based social enterprise, revolves around how much a member pays in dues.

By way of example, to join Amnesty International, members must make a donation. Benefits include a subscription to *Amnesty* magazine, members-only specials at the Amnesty online store, and exclusive access to the Members Area at www.amnestyusa.org. The Sierra Club — dedicated to protecting America's natural resources — gives the following benefits to its dues-paying members: a one-year subscription to *Sierra* magazine; access to members-only outdoor adventures; automatic membership in the local chapter; and discounts on Sierra Club calendars, books, and other merchandise. People who pay the fee to join the Association of Children's Museums, which represents and advocates for children's museums, receive various benefits. These include: access to the members-only Web site, discounts on publications and programs, subscription to *Hand to Hand* (a professional and scholarly journal), and subscription to *E-Forum* (a newsletter of museum news and marketing opportunities).

Deciding how much to charge in dues

Where dues are the only source of revenue, they must cover your *overhead* (the costs of operating your enterprise).

One way of keeping dues to a minimum — which helps attract and keep members — is to minimize your costs. Of course, you have to be careful that your cost cutting doesn't lead to inefficient or ineffective delivery of benefits to the target, because that could undermine your mission and upset your members. You have to strike a balance.

Your members have joined the enterprise to help it achieve its mission. So the ball is often in your court as leader of the enterprise to try to persuade members to accept annual dues that are high enough to enable its work, but not *so* high that they turn off potential members.

The more members you have, the more dues the enterprise takes in. So, another approach to keeping dues as low as possible is to recruit more members. This strategy spreads the expense of running the enterprise across more pocketbooks. Plus, increasing membership is a good strategy, as long as you can find enough new members — and as long as you can still manage the organization when it grows in size.

Maximizing the efficiency of your dues

You have a few ways to tinker with your dues in order to find that perfect balance of enough members paying reasonable dues.

Membership drives

One way of raising the number of members is to conduct a *membership drive* (a formal campaign designed to bring in new dues-paying members). In a typical membership drive, each dues-paying member may be asked to recruit one or two new members. Alternatively, a member who brings in more — say, five new members — would get a free membership for that year or win a prize.

For smaller grassroots enterprises, membership drives are often disappointing. The fact is, raising money for any cause is difficult. The average citizen is bombarded almost daily with such requests. Plus, he doesn't have nearly enough money to give to his favorite causes, let alone to the others that are (sometimes disagreeably) brought to his attention. Professional fundraisers are trained to avoid the many hurdles that spring up while trying to raise money in the community, but their services aren't cheap.

Dues structure

Another option for raising enough money through dues is to develop a *dues structure* (a sliding scale of payment that changes according to the annual income of members). The size and range of categories of income depend on how well off your members are.

If your enterprise consists of lower-income people trying to establish microfinancing for local small businesses, then maybe your members will pay nothing, or very little. (An exception might be asking higher dues from those with viable businesses that the enterprise helped develop.) On the other hand, if your enterprise attracts compassionate people from the middle and upper-middle classes, then you may be able to ask for an increasingly higher membership fee based on their annual income.

A sliding scale like the following is common, with each successive level paying higher dues:

- Under $40,000
- $40,000 to $59,999
- $60,000 to $79,999
- $80,000 to $99,999
- More than $100,000

That's just a typical setup. Feel free to invent your own scale to suit your members' economic situations. A sliding scale is also typically used for companies that join as members, and is based on each company's revenue.

The income category a member claims is self-reported. Don't try to try to verify the figures using some external measure because that can lead to awkward revelations and even confrontations. A dues structure is an honor system among people eager to do their best for the social enterprise and its cause.

Keeping dues low with additional funding

You may be able to keep dues affordable if you can find other money to supplement them. Eliminating dues is not usually a viable alternative, and keeping some dues can actually help you find additional funding: Funding agencies normally like to see some tangible commitment from members, and dues are clear evidence of that.

The average number of volunteer hours per member may also serve the same purpose. In that case, funding agencies may ask that, using a standard formula, you estimate the monetary value of the hours your volunteers have given to your enterprise during a specified period of time, often the past fiscal year.

Special corporate fee

Still another option is to establish a *special fee* for corporate members — this fee is typically higher than the fee paid by ordinary members. A special fee works well in situations where having corporate members is feasible. Here, too, the amount of the fee depends on what the traffic will bear, as well as what the corporate members get from participating in your enterprise and whether they're willing to pay the special fee.

Dues can often be offset by "member benefits" — when you donate to PBS, for example, you get a free DVD or tote bag. Other social organizations secure a discount at sympathetic business (for example, a 10 percent discount at a local bookstore for members), which is another way to maximize dues efficiency. Additional examples of such benefits were presented earlier in this section on paying dues.

Putting the Fun in Fundraising

Simply put, *fundraising* is successfully persuading an external individual or organization to provide financial support for your enterprise. There are four basic types of fundraising:

- ✓ Ongoing funding
- ✓ Episodic funding
- ✓ Capital campaign
- ✓ Planned giving

Ongoing funding

There are four types of ongoing funding:

- ✓ **Annual fund:** You make an annual appeal to known or likely contributors.

- ✓ **Ongoing sales of products or services:** Girl Scout cookies are a well-known example of ongoing sales of products. More ordinary examples may include holding a weeklong car wash every May, selling chocolate bars in September, and conducting a recycling drive at six-month intervals.

- ✓ **Program and project grants:** This type of funding is earmarked for a certain program or project and is commonly designed to last for the duration of the project or, in the case of programs, a specified number of years.

- ✓ **Raffles, lotteries, and auctions:** In each of these events, your enterprise, as sponsor, keeps a portion of the money that people pay to participate.

In the typical raffle, each participant buys a ticket that has a chance of being randomly selected. The holder of the winning ticket wins something (for example, two passes to a cinema or dinner for two at a local restaurant). The money collected also pays for the prize. With a lottery, a sum of money is usually the prize. In a charitable auction, people donate objects of value such as art, books, or recordings that are auctioned off to the highest bidder.

We classify raffles, lotteries, and auctions as ongoing funding. Some enterprises may hold them as one-shot or sporadic events, which would be episodic funding (see the next section).

Episodic funding

Episodic funding may occur as a one-shot grant given by a foundation or corporation. A program or a project of yours may benefit from episodic funding, but you also may look for such funding for special events (such as conferences, festivals, or training sessions). The sometimes lavish awards given nowadays by a variety of corporate donors for excellence in social entrepreneurial work are also a kind of episodic funding.

Google **social entrepreneur awards** to find lists of donors and their programs.

Capital campaign

A *capital campaign* is solicitation of money for something specific that is important to your mission, such as a building, parcel of land, or expensive piece of equipment. Fundraising of this type also includes money to augment an endowment fund or to support a major research project.

Capital campaigns can be very successful, even if the amount of money you're seeking is substantial. Often what makes contributing to them enticing for donors is the prospect of receiving permanent recognition for their generosity. For example, you name a building, room, endowment fund (see the next section), or space (such as a park, forest, or garden) after the principal benefactor.

You can use a sliding scale for these campaigns — smaller donations are given relatively minor recognition (such as the donor's name etched on a brick or a chair or bench, whereas larger donations are recognized by, for example, naming a room or building after the benefactor.

Another way to make capital campaigns more effective and more appealing to donors is to locate matching funding from, say, government or the private sector. For example, if your enterprise can raise $10,000 for a piece of equipment, there may be a program in your state government that will match that sum, giving you the $20,000 you need to buy it. The fact that matching funding exists is a selling point for would-be individual donors because they see that they may double the value of their donation.

Make sure to frame the capital campaign in terms of your mission and the needs of your target of benefits. In considering the possibility of donating money for research or a new building, for example, donors may lose sight of the larger purpose of your enterprise. So you should be sure that they understand how that research or building will aid in the pursuit of your mission.

Planned giving

In *planned giving* a donor arranges to legally give money or other assets to a social enterprise at a specified time in the future, such as upon the death of the donor.

A bequest like this one can also be said to be a kind of episodic funding — because you die only once.

Planned giving may wind up in an endowment. In an *endowment*, one or more donors give money to a nonprofit group. They typically intend for the fund's principal to be held in an interest-bearing account for a long period of time, if not permanently. They also intend for earnings from investments of the principal to be used to cover operating expenses, which may include those incurred in getting grants. Endowments, whose principals are not to be used, are usually invested in some way, the interest from which is often restricted to helping further the mission of the enterprise.

Social enterprises may also use the interest from their endowments to run certain aspects of the organization, as long as they conform to the conditions of the endowment. Colleges and universities are examples — they sometimes use interest from their endowments to finance professorships ("chairs") as well as scholarships and fellowships for students.

Hiring out your fundraising

You may try your own fundraising or rely on the efforts of an intermediary. A *fundraising intermediary*, itself a nonprofit group, is an organization that specializes in raising funds from the public. It uses the money gathered to make philanthropic grants to other nonprofits. The most celebrated example of a fundraising intermediary in North America is the United Way. Catholic Charities USA and the Combined Federal Campaign are also intermediaries.

If you're interested in seeking funding from a fundraising intermediary, contact it directly about this interest. For the United Way, visit `www.unitedway.org/worldwide`, where you can contact your local branch. The Combined Federal Campaign invites national and international independent organizations to apply to participate in its annual campaign.

Fundraising intermediaries generate money by way of payroll deductions. In the typical case, workers authorize deduction of a portion of their paychecks. The money accumulated in this manner is sent to the intermediary. The charity then distributes the money to various charities in the local community.

A *fundraising alternative* is a nonprofit organization that attempts to serve as a viable alternative to the larger, well-established federated fundraising intermediaries like the United Way. *Alternative federated funds* are usually distinctive in their focus on a coherent set or "package" of charities and nonprofit groups as the ultimate recipients of the money raised. Health charities, international aid/development charities, nonprofits focusing on women's issues, African American nonprofits, and environmental nonprofits are all examples of fundraising alternatives. Many alternative federated funds are social-change-oriented and, thus, are naturally receptive to social entrepreneurial initiatives.

Finding a fundraising alternative suitable to your needs may take a bit of research. As is often the case, the Web is as good as a resource as you'll find. Using *charities* as your base word, search for the package that best describes your enterprise. If it's in the field of religion, for example, search for "religious charities" or "Jewish charities." In the area of sports, search for "sports charities" or more specifically, "baseball charities."

The United Way strongly resists such alternative federated funds competing for charitable donations gained through corporate and governmental payroll deductions. As a result, alternative funds, which are smaller and more focused, have found it difficult to gather money in this way. One reason is that they lack the broad, traditional acceptance in industry and government that the United Way and the other well-established federated intermediaries enjoy.

There are professional fundraisers for hire who raise funds for profit. They typically act like agents and take a percentage of what they bring in. In order to work with your organization, they'll want to make sure your mission, goals, and messaging are all in order before they're willing to work with you.

Finding Donors and Preventing Their Fatigue

A *donor* is a person or group who makes, not surprisingly, a donation. In the eyes of the person or group receiving the donor's donation — in other words, you! — the donor is a benefactor. In social entrepreneurship, *donations* (also called *philanthropy*) tend to be gifts of money, goods, or property to a non-profit group without expectation of direct, immediate economic benefit for the donor. Donations are a central source of revenue for charities.

Strictly speaking, a donation is a non-labor contribution — meaning, it doesn't involve volunteer time. Many donations qualify as charitable contributions and are tax deductible, though that's only the case — and you know this by now, right? — if the enterprise has acquired charitable status.

Donors are great, but often they're people who have a lot of money, which means you aren't the only enterprise vying for their attention. Sometimes donors get tired of being donors and feel they're being asked to do too much for too many organizations. *Donor fatigue* is the reluctance of a donor to give any more money to a particular charity. Such a condition commonly results when a charity has made excessive financial demands on the donor — and the definition of *excessive* is really dependent on the donor (some donors tolerate more requests for money than other donors do). When donor fatigue hits, the result is temporary loss of interest in making donations. Donors suffering from such fatigue have made one or more previous donations but have decided that they've now reached their monetary limit. (Donor fatigue differs from compassion burnout — see Chapter 18.)

Fundraisers often focus on *donor renewal,* targeting return donors, in their attempt to attract them again to a particular cause. Donor renewal requires significantly less effort than trying to entice new donors does. The logic behind this strategy is that fatigued donors are usually still sympathetic to your cause — they've just run out of money. With the passage of time, they'll probably be in a position to give again. Give the wallets of fatigued donors a rest, and given their favorable attitudes toward your charity, they may contribute anew.

What about trying to find new donors? The only problem here is that you don't know how potential new donors feel about your cause. Some people will be inclined to give, and others won't. So, spending time and money trying to generate new donations often has an even lower rate of success than trying it with fatigued donors does.

So how do you combat donor fatigue?

You might want to try persuading government entities to create temporary tax breaks for contributions made to specified causes — a strategy that works well with natural disasters and other emergency hardship situations. Visit www.irs.gov and search for the file entitled "Disaster Relief — Resources for Charities and Contributors" (or go to www.irs.gov/charities/charitable/article/0,,id=149938,00.html). You may also want to allow donors to direct their money toward certain aspects of the target of benefits. Maybe if they know that their money is going directly to buy school supplies for kids this fall, they'll be more likely to donate.

Another good way to keep a fatigued donor involved is to ask her to donate her time and connections instead of money for a specific fundraising event. For example, opening up the donor's home for a fundraising dinner party allows the organization to acknowledge the past generosity of the fatigued donor, while being introduced to several potentially new donors.

In the final analysis, relieving donor fatigue is most effectively accomplished by getting to know your donors and learning what motivates them to give to your enterprise. We aren't suggesting that you mount a research project to gather such information — although that might well produce some useful results. But you can accomplish a great deal by chatting informally with a reasonably representative, but small, sample of potential donors about how they view your enterprise and its mission. Such information can help you frame a donor appeal to these people, in harmony with their views on life and your target of benefits, such that they'll be more inclined than otherwise to respond with a donation.

Finding External Financial Support

If dues, fundraising, and donors don't cut the mustard, you may want to seek external support for your social enterprise. You may do this by contacting one of more of the following sources:

- Foundations
- Government entities
- Private sector sources
- Individuals or corporations who will give in-kind donations

Foundations

The word *foundation* has a variety of meanings, but in terms of social entrepreneurship, we mean a nonprofit group, usually one with a substantial endowment and (in the United States) a special tax status as a private foundation. Basically, a foundation is an organization that manages a pool of money and gives it away through philanthropic grants to individuals, non-profits, or both. Such foundations have a long history in the United States and many other countries.

Many foundations are national in scope. *Community foundations* are local nonprofit organizations established to grant money to other, usually local or regional, service-producing nonprofit groups. These foundations differ mainly in their lack of a sizeable endowment that is the hallmark of large private foundations. Community foundations raise money through (mostly local) donations and grants. They also receive money from donors who don't care to bother establishing an independent foundation themselves, whatever its geographic scope.

Another kind of foundation not to be overlooked is the family foundation. Its funds come from members of a certain family, typically with at least one family member being on the foundation's board of directors/trustees and playing a significant role in governing the foundation. It is the most common type of foundation in the United States. Among the many family founda-tions in the United States are the Henry J. Kaiser Family Foundation and the Rockefeller Foundation. These charities often are devoted to a funding a spe-cific category.

A good place to start looking for foundations in your community or country is the Internet. Entering the name of your community or state plus the word *foundations* into your favorite search engine is likely to turn up a number of foundations. You can also check published directories of national and local foundations — many libraries stock these directories — but the Internet gives more complete and updated results and is certainly easier to access.

Foundations have specific annual deadlines for their grant application pro-cess. In doing your research, note the deadlines ahead of time and create a grant-writing calendar, so you're prepared and don't miss any deadlines.

Examples of published directories include *The Foundation Directory,* 29th Edition, edited by David G. Jacobs (Foundation Center) and *The Europa International Foundation Directory,* 17th Edition, by Cathy Hartley (Europa Publications). Local, state, and regional foundations also publish directories, as do foundations devoted to supporting certain groups such as Jewish inter-ests, educational research, and the disabled. See also the Foundation Center (www.foundationcenter.org), with offices around the country offering free or cheap classes for organizations looking for funding.

If you're fortunate enough to run a large, long-established social enterprise, you can establish your own private foundation. Many such social entrepre-neurial foundations have earned fine reputations in their fields of operation. Some people with money are more willing to donate to a foundation that has been specifically established to aid the enterprise in question. Naturally, to do this you have to do some considerable searching and persuading — first to find and then to move potential donors to the point of giving to your foundation and its cause. Charitable status for both your enterprise and its foundation is absolutely essential.

Governmental entities

Governments, unlike some corporations, don't normally have one big specialized unit whose mission is to give money or services to social causes. Instead, at least in democratic countries, governments operate programs through various related departments or other, often far-flung units that are aimed at helping target groups in the population.

Government help may be advisory or monetary or both. The groups targeted are often the poor, handicapped, elderly, undereducated, underemployed, people in need of recreational instruction and facilities, and so on. Government or, more precisely, politicians may want public acknowledgment of any help they give you. Funding operating expenses usually generates little obvious benefit for politicians, whose chances at the polls may be favorably influenced by more evident, splashy generosity. Still, most governments do have a few programs designed to fund such costs.

If your social enterprise bears on such a target and you want governmental advisory or monetary aid, your first step is to track down the relevant governmental unit. Unfortunately, doing so isn't always easy. The Web pages of the government in question are a good place to begin. Here are a handful of places to start:

- ✔ **Grants.gov (www.grants.gov):** This Web site offers the closest thing to one-stop shopping for U.S. government aid for various activities. Use the search function to enter appropriate keywords relating to your field of interest.

- ✔ **USA.gov (www.usa.gov):** This is the overall Web site for the U.S. government, with many, many links to its various branches, bureaus, departments, programs, and agencies.

- ✔ **Catalog of Federal Domestic Assistance (www.cfda.gov):** This site provides online access to more than 1,800 programs administered by federal agencies and links to many offerings for nonprofit groups seeking grant money.

- ✔ **Your state or city government:** The URLs will vary, but Googling the name of your state usually brings up the official state Web site, which should link to funding agencies. It may require some digging to find them.

Google can also come to the rescue if you search for your specific criteria and include the word **grant.** The unit in question may also publish a brochure or, more rarely, maintain a phone line for inquiries. We discuss different kinds of grants later in this chapter.

Set up a free Google Alert to search for the words *grant* and your area of involvement (go to `www.google.com/alerts` and enter your information). Google then e-mails you any time those words pop up in their news crawlers. This is a great way to keep abreast of new grant opportunities.

The private sector

The *private sector* is the business, or corporate, part of society. As a social entrepreneur, you may want to approach a corporation to get monetary help for your enterprise — say, for an event, project, service, or piece of equipment. You can get funding out of the private sector but only certain kinds, and it's tricky.

Private enterprise is seldom interested in funding your operating expenses, which tend to be publicly invisible and, therefore, unlikely to call attention to the corporation's generosity. They will *always* want some credit.

In order to get a private corporation to donate to your operating costs, you should offer the company some *placement* — such as adding their logo to your Web site and to every piece of printed material you distribute. Be prepared to answer questions as to how the corporation will be recognized. You may want to prepare a sponsorship package in advance, illustrating how the corporate logo will be featured on your Web site and brochures. If the corporation doesn't want its logo listed alongside its competitors (called an *exclusive sponsorship*), ask for a larger donation to guarantee that.

To get corporate monetary help, you have to contact the unit in the corporation responsible for charitable donations. That's often easier said than done. Most corporations *are* involved in some kind of community work — the most notable examples of which they often promote prominently on their Web sites. But it usually takes some digging to find the name of the person you should contact. Note that many large corporations have established an independent foundation to handle their numerous requests for charity. Most external inquiries are sent to that foundation. Home Depot set up its Home Depot Foundation to fund affordable housing projects, for example.

Though you should research and pursue grants through its foundational arm, a large company may also be willing to provide money to sponsor specific things for a social enterprise. These requests are handled through that company's marketing department. For example, the marketing department might be willing to sponsor a cocktail reception fundraiser for your organization if their logo is prominently displayed on the invitation. Find the name of the VP of marketing for that company because he or she will be the appropriate contact for such requests. Ask friends, board members, and volunteers if they have connections to a specific company you're targeting. A personal introduction into a company will be handled much more swiftly than a cold call from a stranger.

Don't simply e-mail your request. Follow up with a phone call, asking for a time to present your proposal to the company. Again, they'll direct you to their grant-giving foundation arm, but make it clear this request is for a specific event or purpose.

Start on the particular Web page of the corporation's site that discusses its history and general structure (as opposed to the pages devoted primarily to selling its goods or services). If there is a site map, explore it for pages with titles such as *Community Involvement, Benefits to the Community,* and *Corporate Social Responsibility.* Some corporate sites also have a Frequently Asked Questions (FAQ) section, which may contain an answer to the question of how to contact the corporation for charitable support. You may e-mail, make a phone call, or write a letter, but the key is to keep at it until you find your way in.

When you find information on the company's charitable work, you might be able to tell where the corporation's interests lie. That can be a valuable way of seeing which areas the corporation has been attracted to in the past. If your new proposal falls outside the corporation's past involvement, don't worry — they may still be interested. You never know — a contribution might follow.

Gifts

Gifts may be monetary or *in kind* — such as equipment or building space — and may be donated by individuals or corporations. Legal charities are normally in a position to issue a tax receipt for such donations, which enhances the likelihood of receiving them.

The better known and the more celebrated your social enterprise, the better your chances of receiving individual or corporate gifts, especially monetary ones. Donors typically want their largesse to be publicly visible and honored. Big contributions to well-known causes tend to have this effect. If you're just starting up, the chances of receiving a large monetary or in-kind gift are rather slim. But small gifts such as a hand-me-down computer or a check for, say, $100 are certainly possible.

In-kind contributions

In-kind contributions are made to nonprofit groups and typically take the form of physical commodities or physical space or facilities. More rarely, a special service might be donated, with pro bono legal and accounting services being two common examples. Legal charities may issue tax receipts for in-kind contributions as well; that way, the monetary value of the gift can be estimated.

Both the United States and Canada have major organizations devoted to making in-kind gifts to other charities. Gifts In Kind International (GIK) is the seventh-largest charity in the United States, according to the *Chronicle of Philanthropy.* In 2006, GIK generated and placed close to $900 million in in-kind donations. In Kind Canada (IKC) is a nationwide Canadian charity whose mission is to provide smaller charities and nonprofits with access to practical resources typically only available to larger organizations. Both operate with donations received from numerous large and small companies. At the time of this writing, GIK distributes donations to more than 150,000 community charities across the United States and, because it is an international organization, to charities in many other parts of the world.

To learn more about how organizations like GIK and IKC function and whether you might want to contact them to help fund your enterprise, check out their Web sites: Gifts in Kind International is at www.giftsinkind.org; In Kind Canada is online at www.inkindcanada.ca.

Keep in mind that there are some minor legal restrictions on in-kind donations. For example, the organization can't resell donated materials for profit.

Writing Successful Grant Proposals

So, how do you get your hands on the grant money we've been making you drool over? Well, you have to tackle the fine art of grant proposal writing. Writing grant proposals is a tremendously involved and exacting undertaking — so much so that numerous books have been published on the subject, and entire Web sites are devoted to it. For a far deeper look into this process than we have space for here, we recommend Beverly A. Browning's *Grant Writing For Dummies,* 2nd Edition (Wiley).

Grants follow the 80/20 rule. Grants will consume 80 percent of your time, and provide only about 20 percent of your funding. But that effort is worth it because grants are reliable and can be a consistent source of funding for an organization.

In the meantime, to get you started on the right track, here are ten essential tips for writing successful proposals:

- ✔ **Read a decent sample of previous grant proposals in your area, especially ones you know have succeeded.** Proposals are rarely available online to the public. Instead, seek out the nonprofits you know (they may be local or national) that have been awarded grants and ask permission to read their proposals.

- ✔ **Be sure to write your proposal so that it harmonizes well with the granting agency's mission and goals.** You'll need to look up the mission and goals of the granting agency. You should be able to find both on the Web site of the agency you intend to approach. But, if not published there, e-mail them.

- ✔ **Write your proposal so that it will stand out as much as possible against the many competing proposals.** This means, in part, stressing the uniqueness of your enterprise and its mission.

- ✔ **Show your compassion/sympathy for the target of benefits (but don't overdo it), and convey clearly the urgency of your mission.** Try to make your would-be benefactor feel obligated to help.

- ✔ **Show your commitment and your determination to realize your goals.** Show how much time (days, months, years) has so far been devoted to realizing your mission, how many people have been involved, how much money has been spent in the process, and so forth. You may also mention some of the more difficult problems you've faced and how you managed to solve them.

- ✔ **Write simply and as non-technically as possible.** The reviewers of your proposal may be unfamiliar with all the terminology and issues of your particular field and enterprise. And everyone appreciates an easy-to-understand style of writing.

- ✔ **Closely follow all technical requirements set out by the granting agency.** These guidelines may be as detailed as using the right type size and page margins. If sections of the proposal have word limits, never exceed them.

- ✔ **Keep the proposal as short as possible.** In fact, there is often a prescribed page or word limit, which you should religiously respect.

- ✔ **Have other people read your proposal before sending it.** Someone from outside your enterprise should be among the critical readers.

- ✔ **Hire a professional grant writer if you have the resources and don't trust yourself or your partners in the enterprise to do the job needed to succeed.** You can Google grant-writing services to pull up an extensive list. Ask for references and find out how successful the grants have been in getting money for the applicants.

   If you can find a local grant-writing service, all the better. You can meet face-to-face, which may help personalize your relationship with the writer and possibly enable that person to gain a more profound sense of your enterprise and its uniqueness. For these reasons, we suggest you first try a local service and, if not satisfied, then go online. Whichever approach to grant writing you end up selecting, ask around among friends, relatives, and acquaintances about their experiences with writers and agencies, whether local or online.

Grants take time to apply for and more time to wait for the results. Expect it to take a year for the fruits of your labor to result in funds being granted to your organization. Due to this timing, start your grant writing early on in the development of your enterprise and from then on do it continually and regularly.

As laborious as it seems, every single grant proposal should be tailored to the specific grant application. Don't think you're going to be able to make one master proposal and submit it as is to each granting organization. Do your research and customize it to the unique requirements of each grant. It's worth it.

Check out Non-profit Guides at `http://npguides.org/guide/index.html` for a free site offering guidelines and samples of preliminary proposals, full proposals, letters of inquiry, and cover letters.

Getting grants in hard times

We can't ignore the fact that, at the time this book is published, a major recession is raging worldwide. Moreover, there is plenty of evidence that the nonprofit sector is taking a beating. The investment base of many foundations has withered, and many governments are putting money into job creation rather than into social enterprises relying on volunteers. Furthermore, a recent issue of *The Economist* raises the specter that the rich, who have also taken a sizeable hit on their wealth, may be growing much less charitable.

However, the cloud has a silver lining, and the situation can also be worked in your favor. True, such dire conditions put a premium on superior grantsmanship, because there is now much less money to share among ever more applicants. And ever more applicants are turning up because social needs are greater today than they are in economically stable times. More people than before are greatly stressed by their lack of work, loss of a home, decline in

investments, reduced income, and other woes. And many are falling into categories needing help that may very well fit your target. For such reasons, the ingenuity of social entrepreneurs like you to institute change remains in high demand. But you may have to rely more than usual on volunteers and minimal funding (low dues, ongoing sales of product and services, money from your own pocket and those of your partners), especially at startup.

Angel-investor groups and networks may be interested in the social entrepreneurial work that you do or want to do. (An *angel investor* is a wealthy person who provides capital from his or her own resources to start a business. Some of these people organize themselves into groups or networks.) Among them are Investors' Circle (`www.investorscircle.net`) and Good Capital (`www.goodcap.net`). True, they receive hundreds of applications annually and accept only a handful. But they *definitely* won't accept yours if you don't submit it.

Chapter 10

Creating Your Brand

. . . .

. . . .

*A*s a social entrepreneur, you have the fire and determination to convince many people you meet about the urgency of the problem you're trying to solve. The problem is, you can't be everyplace at once. In order for your organization to thrive, you need your message to be heard even when you aren't around.

Getting your message across effectively requires creating a strong organizational identity, or *brand,* from the start. That brand needs to make your mission clear to the people you're trying to serve, the funders you're trying to persuade, the volunteers you're trying to recruit, the community you're trying to get support from — from absolutely everyone who potentially influences your work.

Starting with the name of your enterprise, you have only one chance to make a first impression. People will make judgments about you and your mission based on surprisingly little information. That's just the way it goes, and it means *marketing* (the way you define and control how customers perceive your goods and services) is critical to your success. You control your image as a social entrepreneur largely through marketing.

In this chapter, we show you how to craft your brand expertly, from choosing a name to using the Internet to creating brochures, posters, and business cards that represent you well. This is all part of marketing and promoting your group's external image, and it's a process in which you simply have to invest time and money.

What's in a Name?

We can answer Shakespeare's question in two broad ways:

- ✔ **If your enterprise is a nonprofit, *description* is a primary consideration in naming it.** Your name must convey to all interested parties what your enterprise does and for whom or what, such as animals, birds, the homeless, the environment, and so on.

- ✔ **If your enterprise is a for-profit entity, sales are the primary consideration.** You want to choose a name that promotes the good or service you're selling. An element of description is involved here, too, but *appeal* is the main thing you're after. In short, a for-profit's name should help attract buyers.

Consider an example: What does the name *Secular Humanists of the Lowcountry* tell you about this social enterprise's mission and goals? The Secular Humanists of the Lowcountry, based in Charleston, South Carolina, was established in 1994. Its members consider themselves free thinkers on a wide range of subjects. Some identify themselves as agnostics; others as atheists; and still others as skeptics, secular humanists, rationalists, or scientific naturalists.

The mission of the enterprise — which is classified as nonprofit and educational — is "to promote the non-theistic, human-centered viewpoint as a valid contribution to public discourse and to strive to maintain the First Amendment guarantee of separation of state and church." The organization is committed to the use of science, reason, and experience as the best way to understand this world and the universe, as well as to conquer social problems. It scorns any attempt to deprecate the human intellect, as in claims that "God knows best."

When seeing only the name of this enterprise, you might mistake it for a club formed strictly for the benefit of its members instead of an external target (a set of ideas). In fact, we think that this group might be able to find a better name — for example, Society for Secular Humanism or Society for the Advancement of Secular Humanism. Compared with its present name, either of the other names makes clearer the educational, political, and philosophical aims of the organization.

Here are some points to keep in mind when considering what to call your enterprise:

- ✔ **Short is good.** Your name is best kept short. This rule applies to both for-profits and nonprofits.

- ✔ **Simple is good, too.** Your name should not be ponderous, drawn out, too ornate, or filled with jargon or big words. Small words in everyday language communicate best.

- **The name should mean something.** Especially if you're a nonprofit, your name must be meaningful to the people you hope to help, as well as to any involved and potentially involved third parties, such as foundations, corporations, or investors. Any enterprises named after a person or town or identified by a number run the risk that the name won't be meaningful to the people who need to support it.

- **Catchy is good . . . usually.** Your name should be attractive, if not downright catchy. But be careful: Catchiness can obscure the nature of the enterprise. Believe it or not, Throx of San Francisco sells colorful sox in packs of three as a cure for a missing sock, and Yelo of New York City offers harried urbanites reflexology, massage, and 20- to 40-minute naps in sleep pods.

  Creating a catchy name can be inappropriate when your enterprise's mission is a sobering one, such as eliminating starvation or stopping genital mutilation or child slavery. In those cases, direct and simple are best.

- **Exciting is good.** Your name should communicate the urgency and compassion of the enterprise's mission.

- **Grandiose isn't always good.** Your name must acknowledge the scope of your enterprise. The name Save the Children suggests that the scope of the enterprise is universal. But if you plan to work toward saving children only in Germany, the name of your enterprise should reflect that.

If you manage to honor all these points in naming your own enterprise, you'll be off to a great start! Reflect on each of these points as you cast about for the best name.

Trademark and copyright considerations are also important. A quick search of the U.S. Patent and Trademark office Web site (www.uspto.gov) is a great place to make sure no one else is using your desired name in a conflicting manner.

Finally, don't forget to decide on the domain name that you'll use for your Web site — and make sure that someone else doesn't already own that name. You want your domain name to bear a decent resemblance to, if not be the same as, your organizational name. You have to pay to register the domain name you want (multiple domain name registrars offer this service, including, for example, Register.com). If the name you want is available, buy it as soon as possible to prevent it being claimed by someone else.

We cover the legal process of registering your enterprise's name in Chapter 14. Note that the name you choose *can* be changed if necessary, but if your enterprise is incorporated, the new name will have to be filed with the governmental agency responsible for registering corporations. Ideally, you'll get it right the first time because changing an enterprise's name can create confusion in the target group and interested third parties.

Some unforeseen change could force you to modify your group's name — total success being one of them. As we discuss in Chapter 7, some social enterprises eventually manage to eradicate the problem they set out to conquer. Not wanting to cease operations, they then find a new problem to master, which may force them to tinker with their name.

Creating an Online Presence

These days it seems like every person and organization on the planet is somehow involved with the Internet. Your social enterprise has to be online, too. And by online, we mean in the following ways:

- ✔ **E-mail:** At an absolute minimum, your enterprise should have an e-mail address. And even when you first start out, don't make it your personal e-mail address. Not only does using a personal e-mail address look unprofessional, but it leads to intrusion into your personal or familial account. Get a free Gmail or Yahoo! Mail account and use it only for your enterprise. The address should include the name of your enterprise, a recognizable abbreviation, or maybe a short, memorable, pertinent phrase.

- ✔ **Web site:** Be honest: When you're looking for information about an organization or company, if you can't find its Web site, do you even take it seriously? The public expects you to have a Web site, and you almost certainly should have one. We discuss details of social entrepreneurial sites in the "Creating content" section, later in this chapter.

- ✔ **Blogs and social networks:** Efficiently and effectively taking part in "Web 2.0" features has become much easier in recent years. Your Web site likely should feature a blog or discussion board, for example, that discusses subjects that relate to the goals of your enterprise. As Chapter 11 points out, you can and should also think about joining social networking services such as Facebook (www.facebook.com), LinkedIn (www.linkedin.com), and Twitter (www.twitter.com).

Check out *Web Marketing For Dummies,* 2nd Edition, by Jan Zimmerman (Wiley), to find out a whole lot more about using the Internet in your marketing efforts.

Reaching the right folks

Ask yourself this question: Who do I want to attract to my enterprise's Web site? The pool of visitors should include the following:

- ✔ **The target of benefits:** Of course, some targets may have little or no access to the Web. If you're in the for-profit sector, your target is your market — the buyers of your good or service.

✔ **Interested third parties:** These include the media, as well as potential funders and investors. For some entrepreneurs, politicians also constitute an interested third party.

✔ **Potential new members:** These are the people who can contribute to realizing your mission by participating in your social enterprise.

✔ **Potential employees:** This audience may be especially important for enterprises relying on paid staff.

Reaching these four categories of people is the entire purpose of your online presence.

Creating content

What should you put on your Web site? at a minimum, the following should be there, pretty much in the order in which the following sections appear.

Home page

On your home page, you present a short, crisp introduction to the site that encourages visitors to click at least a few of the other pages. You should also include an overview of what the site covers. And, of course, the home page is where most of your links to the rest of your site are, in one handy place.

Your home page is much like a cinema marquee or the cover of a book. It should invite potential viewers or readers to venture inside. To see examples of social entrepreneurial Web sites that exhibit all or nearly all the features in this section, visit the following Web sites and poke around to see how they did it:

✔ Keggfarms (www.keggfarms.com) raises and sells chickens in India.

✔ IONA Senior Services (www.iona.org) aids seniors.

✔ LetITHelp (www.letithelp.org) outsources the talents of Filipino IT graduates.

✔ Elevyn (www.elevyn.com) is a gallery of online trade stores in developing countries.

Mission and vision statements

You should put your mission and vision statements on their own separate page of your Web site. You may also put your organizational goals, or a sample of them, on this page.

You may be tempted to put your mission and vision statements on your home page, but if you do, you may end up cluttering it excessively. They're better off on their own separate page.

For more on writing a mission statement and vision statement, turn to Chapter 7.

Your products or services

For-profit enterprises should at least promote the goods and services they're selling, including prices and information on how and where to purchase them. You should also seriously consider selling directly on your site.

If you're interested in really getting into selling on the Web, check out *Web Stores Do-It-Yourself For Dummies,* by Joel Elad, and *Starting an Online Business For Dummies,* 5th Edition, by Greg Holden (both published by Wiley).

History

Your Web visitors may be curious about how your enterprise came to be and how it reached its present stage of development. But avoid excessive detail and length in this portrayal — the typical visitor isn't *that* fascinated with your history.

Founder

If your enterprise has existed for many years, and its initial entrepreneur and founder (is that you?) has become well known, a separate biographical page on this person is usually of interest.

News and events

This page shows the level and scope of your enterprise's activity. It may contain a list of pertinent conferences, major successes related to mission, recent funding arrangements, noteworthy changes in leadership, new publications by the enterprise or its members, and so on.

You may decide to make your news and events page a blog instead, which will allow readers to subscribe to an RSS feed in a feed reader. If you want to find out more about blogs, check out *Blogging For Dummies,* 2nd Edition (Wiley).

Links

On this page, you link to other Web sites that are related to your mission. And to help spread the word about your enterprise, encourage those other sites to reciprocate with a link to your own. There's no guarantee they will, but it doesn't hurt to ask.

Contacts

This is where you list all the fax, e-mail, snail-mail, and telephone contacts for your enterprise. From the standpoint of the people in your enterprise, e-mail contact is the most vital, flexible, and least obtrusive of these four. But if your enterprise has an office and someone regularly on hand to deal with faxes, snail mail, and telephone calls, then also listing the other three enhances efficiency of communication with third parties.

Donations

One common and surprising mistake many organizations make is forgetting to include a page that asks for donations. So, include a Donate page! You can set up a PayPal account to receive the donations and include an address for donors to send checks. If you're ambitious, you can even set up an e-commerce section and accept credit and debit card donations.

Developing an appropriate appearance

Your home page should lure visitors, but the allure should be appropriate. Web sites of nonprofit social enterprises don't need the commercial flash that at least some for-profits may find necessary.

For-profits may require entertaining mechanisms on their sites (such as catchy music, short videos, and professional, cutting-edge graphic design) that could be regarded as poor taste for many nonprofits. Imagine such flashiness on the home page of a social enterprise whose mission is to ban cruelty to animals or end political corruption. For those enterprises, education — not entertainment — is a top priority.

You may be creative, but when it comes to marketing your enterprise online you probably shouldn't do it all yourself. Matters of online taste, aesthetics, and design should not be left to amateurs. Plenty of professional services are available on the Internet and in the Yellow Pages that can help you set up your enterprise's Web site, often quite reasonably.

If you're a bit of a Web geek, though, go for it. You can buy Web page templates at sites such as www.buytemplates.net and www.metamorphozis.com.

Focusing on functionality

Your Web site won't be successful if it isn't functional — in other words, if visitors can't get the information they need there. Functionality is complex and beyond the scope of this book — we'll leave it to your professional Web site designer, should you hire one, to ensure it.

Because Web sites of for-profit enterprises tend to be more elaborate than the Web sites of nonprofits, for-profit enterprises have a greater interest in establishing decent functionality. But very broadly you want two kinds of functionality, whether you're a nonprofit or a for-profit enterprise: content management and reporting.

Content management

Through *content management,* you can manage the content of your Web site without having to acquire the special skills and knowledge of design and programming. The key here is to develop a simple *interface* (the product of a well-developed content-management system), which allows you to maintain and update the structure, navigation, and content of all the pages comprising your Web site.

Reporting

Reporting is an extremely important part of your enterprise's Web site. Reporting provides vital information about the many features of your site and how well they're working. In other words, your well-functioning Web site should automatically and routinely provide you with information about every aspect of its performance, including all sorts of useful data about who is visiting your site and what they're doing on it. Reporting tells you what is working and what could be working better.

Seeking commercial support and advertising

On a Web site, commercial support is usually accomplished through selling advertising on the site. You can then use the proceeds from those advertisements as a source of revenue for your enterprise.

You have three options for pursuing external commercial support:

- ✔ Advertising directly on your site
- ✔ Acknowledgment on your site
- ✔ Advertising on other Web sites

The first two options bring in revenue directly to your enterprise through fees paid by others (usually for-profits and regular businesses) whose goods or services you advertise or who supply goods or services to your group. The third option should produce revenue indirectly after you spend the money on advertising. You hope for an increase in visits to your site and a corresponding increase in sales of your own goods or services.

We cover each of these options in greater detail in the following sections.

Advertising directly on your site

This includes placing ads in sidebars, *interstitials* (separate Web pages that display just before an expected content page appears), and pop-ups.

The main bone of contention here — of concern primarily for nonprofit social entrepreneurs — is whether trying to make money by such commercial means is a good idea. Would including direct advertising on your site deflect attention from the messages you're trying to convey? Would such advertising reduce the sense of urgency and seriousness of your enterprise's mission? Is that mission too important, too dignified, to be keep company with anything commercial? Or should you accept the consequences of advertising, justifying it as a necessary evil that comes with bringing in badly needed money to run the enterprise and succeed at your mission? We can't answer this question for you, but you should certainly think about it.

There is also the touchy matter of your appearing to endorse the goods and services advertised. That could be risky, depending on the good or service being advertised. For example, if your social enterprise is devoted to promoting improved nutrition for children, and you inadvertently accept advertising from a company that produces an energy drink that causes dangerous elevations in heart rate, you're sending a mixed message to your visitors. An enterprise that animal lovers have established to save the grizzly bears of the Rocky Mountains should definitely avoid advertisements aimed at promoting the sale of hunting guns and ammunition — even if bear hunters are also interested in such a project (because its success should give them more grizzlies to hunt).

Acknowledgment on your site

This is public acknowledgment on your site of commercial sources of services and equipment purchased by your enterprise.

Acknowledgment, if reasonably subtle, probably avoids most of the consequences associated with direct advertising. But then, because of low visibility, the commercial enterprise you're acknowledging probably receives a lower return on its money compared with direct advertising, such as a pop-up or interstitial. Because of this possibility, that commercial enterprise will probably offer a smaller fee to your social enterprise for acknowledging it than it would if you accepted its advertising.

Put simply, you probably won't make as much money on an acknowledgment as you would on an ad.

Advertising on other Web sites

Here you purchase ads on other sites in order to promote your enterprise.

Buying advertising space on another Web site is a calculated chance at succeeding in drawing more hits on your own site. This is spending money to make money, and you can think of it as a sort of investment.

Getting Your Identity on Paper

Your paper identity is created mainly in the form of brochures, flyers, posters, banners, and business cards. For all the popularity and utility of the Internet, paper doesn't appear to be going away. Your paper marketing efforts offer certain advantages: They're portable, they don't require electricity, and they can be larger and more attractive than a computer screen. Perhaps paper's greatest advantage is that it's easy to distribute on the spot — such as at a rally, meeting, conference, spontaneous gathering, or even along a pedestrian thoroughfare.

Use the same designer for all your paper marketing, if possible. It provides an overall consistent look, and it makes it easy to make changes to all your marketing at one time. You may also get a discount on design and printing services if you become a loyal customer at one place.

Brochures

Brochures may be slick pamphlets with multiple pages or a single (usually folded) page printed on both sides. Compared with flyers, brochures commonly take more time and effort to produce, pack more information, and have a more polished look about them. But for those reasons, they're also not as flexible for addressing immediate events and developments. Brochures are more permanent. Brochures are usually more expensive to produce than flyers, although modern computer technology has narrowed this gap.

Flyers

You can think of flyers as cheap brochures. You can use them wherever brochures are appropriate, but if you have a choice, the brochure better represents your enterprise. Still, there are occasions when the flyer is the more effective tool. One is *mass distribution* — for example, as a handout to people exiting a concert or sporting event; giving out brochures in this number may be too expensive. Another is when you want to take immediate advantage of recent events. Maybe your enterprise against environmental pollution wants to show how it relates to an oil spill that has just occurred. Your strategy would be to distribute flyers showing this relationship.

Posters and banners

As with brochures, making attractive, informative, inspiring posters and banners takes time, effort, and often a good bit of money. For posters and banners, use the services of a professional designer and printer.

Even more than most brochures, posters and banners are destined to have a long life. Some are even so attractive and artistic that they become collectors' items. But they're the least versatile of the various forms of paper identity (or "fabric identity," in the case of some banners). By and large, they're limited to being hung on walls and then, if ideally displayed, only where there is proper space and lighting and the social environment is compatible with the message you're trying to disseminate. Plus, both posters and banners are susceptible to being damaged and soiled, which tends to undermine the positive publicity you're looking for. Finally, they're often subject to theft, which increases your cost.

Business cards

Your enterprise's business card is the most portable of the five kinds of paper identity and conveys the least amount of information. Most commonly it serves to associate a member of the enterprise with the enterprise itself, doing so with a personal name linked to the enterprise's name, street address, e-mail address, and Web address.

 With the space on the front of the card largely consumed by that information (especially if you also place a logo there), consider printing a short version of your mission statement on the back.

Business cards sometimes end up where the other four identity media fail to, such as on the dressers and kitchen tables of the people you give them to. In general, a business card is especially useful in interpersonal relations, including parties, meetings, informal gatherings at conventions, and spontaneous conversational encounters with people who show an interest in your mission. Good times to give out your card are on airplanes, in restaurants, and while waiting in lines.

Letterhead stationery

Letterhead stationery should have, at minimum, your enterprise's name, street address, telephone number, e-mail address, and Web address. Letters may go to people and organizations that would otherwise have little opportunity to contact your enterprise on the Internet or by means of your other paper identifiers. Examples may include city officials, members of the clergy, school administrators, local businesses and organizations, and government offices. The more attractive your letterhead, the better it will serve your enterprise as one of its paper ambassadors. For this reason, you may want to hire a professional designer to create this kind of paper identity.

It doesn't hurt to ask the printer to consider making an in-kind donation of services in exchange for acknowledgment on your organization's Web site. The printer may not be able to provide the printing for free, but it should be able to provide it at cost or at a discount.

Marketing the Old-Fashioned Way

Traditional marketing methods are the tried-and-true, old-school tools that can still be an important part of promoting your enterprise. Typical ones used by social entrepreneurs include logos, networking, slogans, and apparel.

Logos

An attractive, versatile logo is a wonderful marketing tool. By *versatile* we mean a logo that can be easily placed on the various forms of paper identity, as well as online.

You have to be able to reduce or enlarge the logo without losing its visual impact. It should be colorful, though tastefully so. A garish logo can easily overwhelm the rest of the content on your business card, poster, letterhead, and so on. Here, too, we recommend that you seek expert advice, especially because the most effective logos visually communicate both mission and goals. The best logos summarize visually, though abstractly, what a social enterprise is all about. Good logos can power your marketing.

Services that design logos are available on the Internet and in your city's Yellow Pages. Logoworks.com offers a commercial online service for designing logos, business cards, stationery, brochures, and a variety of promotional products (including apparel, discussed later in this section). The site also features online galleries containing numerous specimens of these different kinds of paper identity. To register your logo, look in the Yellow Pages for "Trademark Agents — Registered."

Don't copy someone else's logo. Many logos (among some other kinds of paper identity and marketing devices) are trademarked, which means some person or group owns them. To use such a logo without its owner's written permission could have unpleasant legal repercussions. (Later in this section, we discuss finding professional help for copyrighting and trademarking paper and marketing identities.)

In a pinch, and if you have no money, the Web site www.vistaprint.com offers free logo design. You won't find a unique or great one here, but you will possibly find one that is attractive.

Networking

We devote an entire chapter to networking (Chapter 11), but we want to mention it here, because it relates to marketing your social enterprise. As you and members of your enterprise circulate in your daily rounds, you do so, in part, as links in various social networks of friends, business associates, and acquaintances. Sometimes you'll make contacts within a network and you'll have the chance to talk, perhaps only briefly, about your enterprise and its work. If you're given that chance, do so, always. You may, in these encounters, even hand a flyer or brochure to other people present, but usually you spread information on your enterprise simply by talking about it.

Here you want to be concise. So consider the elevator pitch. Create a 30-second statement that crisply explains your organization's mission and goals. Know how to effectively explain your enterprise to someone in an elevator in under 30 seconds.

Slogans

Slogans, mottos, taglines, punch lines, catchphrases — these are all snappy verbal utterances that ring well in the ear and can simultaneously communicate something of the essence of your enterprise. A good slogan is worth its weight in gold.

Earlier in the chapter, we list four impressive social entrepreneur Web sites. Two of them have pretty good slogans. IONA Senior Services goes by the slogan of "Experts on Aging." That makes it sound reliable and informed — the slogan provokes confidence when you hear it. LetITHelp has a somewhat longer slogan: "Providing financial and spiritual transformation to Mindanao's youth." Not too grandiose — it acknowledges the local focus. The Keggfarms slogan — "Engineering rural prosperity" — is more vague, but it has the merit of being accurate, short, and catchy.

Your slogan should be short, clear, and contain wording that everyone can understand.

You and your collaborators in the enterprise will probably enjoy many lively sessions trying to think up an acceptable slogan. If you hit a wall, you may want turn to a professional for assistance — such as the online service www. kristofcreative.com (click Services and then Branding). This company also offers service in the design of logos, stationery, posters, T-shirts, and other marketing and identity tools.

Slogans, like logos, are very likely to be protected, in this instance copyrighted, as you'll probably want yours to be. To obtain copyright protection for a slogan, look in the Yellow Pages for services that design and copyright logos as well as on the Internet.

Apparel

As with the other forms of marketing and paper identity, custom-designed apparel — T-shirts, caps, sweatshirts, and so on — wind up being viewed in places where other promotional items fail to reach. Wear your T-shirt with your enterprise's name and logo on it to the supermarket, the dry cleaners, the bookstore, to lunch, and while playing golf or doing other activities with friends. Your friends may know about your enterprise, but how many other people who saw your shirt that day knew about it? Obviously, this is another fruitful way to market your social enterprise. You may even be able to sell your apparel and multiply this effect. You can find services for custom-designing apparel in the Yellow Pages under such headings as "Apparel," "Caps," and "T-Shirts." Or go online to CafePress (www.cafepress.com) for such products.

Public Relations: Imaging Your Enterprise

In the business world, you hear a lot of talk about *corporate image,* which refers to how third parties perceive a particular for-profit enterprise. Concern about image is a matter of marketing, promotion, and public relations. A favorable image is believed to increase sales of goods and services. After all, people are more inclined to buy a product from a company they like, right? Promoting a product or service is easier when the company selling it is respected — or at least not particularly disrespected. A good corporate image also helps ease public relations problems with third parties, such as politicians, consumer groups, regulatory agencies, and environmental activists.

You may think that corporate image applies mostly to for-profit social enterprises because their nonprofit counterparts often have nothing to sell and profit from. But the picture is more complicated than this. Some nonprofits *do* have goods or services for sale, even if the money made this way is returned to the operating budget of the enterprise. And whether they sell something or not, nonprofit enterprises must still tend to their *organizational image* for the same reasons.

Nonprofit social enterprises may not be marketing products, but they *are* marketing their missions and their capacity to make a difference and solve a social problem. Having a favorable image helps a great deal in your marketing effort. Imagine what might happen to your image — and therefore to marketing efforts — if your enterprise were publicly exposed for internal embezzlement, or if a bitter power struggle among its leaders spilled out into the media? That most definitely wouldn't help you sell or promote your mission.

Unfavorable events and problems with a social enterprise demand skillful handling. They demand extraordinary efforts in public relations. Consider these two examples:

- ✔ In May 1995, *The New York Times* reported a case of embezzlement by an erstwhile treasurer of the Episcopal Church to the tune of $2.2 million. The money, taken over a period of five years, belonged to the church. The treasurer spent it on trips, clothing, jewelry, real estate, and limousine services. The fact that no one discovered the embezzlement for so long was traced by the bishop of the church to the "absolute control" the embezzler had over auditing at church headquarters. This condition prevented other people from scrutinizing the books.

- ✔ In August 2007, *The Chronicle of Philanthropy* reported on fraudulent activities in the United Way of East Lansing, Michigan. The report observed that, had this charity divvied up the responsibilities of its department of finance, the culprit, a former vice president, might have been apprehended earlier. As it was, she alone controlled this unit of this chapter of United Way. She ran its internal accounting system, through which pledges were recorded, as well as a computer program that registers the donations given to the group. She also routinely balanced the checking account, though she lacked the authority to write any checks.

In both instances, the two charities involved seem to have pulled through their moral ordeals without long-term negative consequences. But those ordeals did discourage some donations in the short run.

Even if all is going well, public relations is still an essential process for effectively imaging nonprofit enterprises. Your marketing is, in effect, a part of your public relations portfolio. The same may be said for demonstrating corporate social responsibility. Public relations usually involve working through third parties, normally the media. The media sector of the third-party group is so important that we devote a chapter to it (Chapter 12).

Beyond the media, keep in mind that public relations may need special attention with reference to labor unions. (For coverage of enterprises that are unionized or contemplating unionization, see Chapter 18.) Another group meriting delicate handling is governmental agencies and the elected politicians who ultimately are responsible for them. And don't forget your relations with other kindred social enterprises and nonprofit groups. They can be important allies in helping you realize your mission but will act that way only if they respect your group.

Should you seek professional help for imaging your enterprise? You can probably wait until trouble strikes, or if your image in third-party circles is somehow tarnished. Professional services of this sort are costly, and many nonprofit social enterprises have far too little money for their missions, let alone for propping up their images professionally. Just keep in mind the ideas in this section and market, promote, and foster public relations where you can in the course of routinely pursuing your mission. That should suffice in normal circumstances.

If the need does arise for professional help, waste no time in seeking it. The Yellow Pages typically contain a fairly long list of public relations services and agencies — as does the good old Internet (search on "public relations services").

Part III
Growing Your Organization

The 5th Wave   By Rich Tennant

"We're working with several organizations to get our message out there. Gossips Anonymous has been particularly helpful."

In this part . . .

When you have your basic plan going, if you're like most entrepreneurs, your job becomes improvement, expansion, and growth — as long as those things don't come at the expense of the folks you're trying to help.

Chapter 11, on networking, acknowledges that nobody works in a vacuum — and that goes double for social entrepreneurs. Chapter 12 is chock-full of advice on working with the media to achieve your goals. In Chapter 13, we look at that monster called bureaucracy and see that it can be beneficial if kept in check. And if you want to really go for it and formally organize as a corporation, Chapter 14 is your ticket to finding out your options.

Chapter 11

Mixing It Up: Using Social Networking and Social Media

*I*t's not what you know but who you know that makes the difference. That old cliché is just as true in the field of social entrepreneurship as it is in the rest of the world.

As we mention in Chapter 2, humans as a species are intelligent, sure, but the real wealth in our intelligence comes from its social and cultural aspects. The fact that we can *share* our intelligence, collaborate, and see that wealth multiply many times has got to be one of the greatest joys and enchantments of the human experience. That's the reason why "who you know" makes the difference. And that's also where social networking comes into play.

What is social networking? A *social network* is a group of people held together by something they have in common. Social networks are all around — most of us are embedded in a whole web of them. Family life, work, church, school, volunteer work — even chatting with neighbors, shopping, group e-mailing, you name it. Wherever you're having a conversation with someone in one of your social networks, you're doing a basic kind of social networking.

Social networks are powerful tools in social entrepreneurship, and now is the perfect time to harness the power of the latest form of social networking — online sites such as Facebook and Twitter, which are called *social media*. You need to mine all your social networks to your advantage. In some ways, your success as a social entrepreneur will hinge on your ability to tap into conversations and social networks of one kind or another. In this chapter, we look at how you can develop your social networks through online social media as well as face-to-face interactions.

Social Networking and Social Media

Unless you've been held captive by aliens for the past half decade, you've probably at least heard about, if not experienced, *Web 2.0,* the type of online networking and collaboration also known as *social media.* The first wave of applications of the World Wide Web (called Web 1.0) was mostly about just putting information "out there" — getting corporate, educational, government, entertainment, and seemingly every other kind of information online and distributed as widely and as quickly as possible.

Web 2.0 is about making it possible for people to *do stuff* with what they encounter online, which includes, at a basic level, the ability in engage in group conversations. More and more such interaction takes place in real time, boasting an immediacy that's very close to what you find in a face-to-face conversation. Web 2.0 represents a phenomenal advance in communication technology, and just about everyone is embracing it.

Signing up with the most popular social media sites

Social media today includes the following online tools (although this list does not by any means exhaust the possibilities of the fast-growing world of social media):

- **Blogs:** Online journals, kept by individuals or groups, which give readers the means with which to respond, often resulting in lively conversations

- **Discussion boards:** Sites designed to foster conversations about specific topics, often connected to products or services

- **Social bookmarking services:** Places to share and discuss favorite links and other online resources, often focused on specific topics

- **Facebook** (www.facebook.com): A vastly popular social networking site revolving around each participant's social network (called *friends*) and enabling everyone to share their thoughts and observations, along with photos, videos, links, and other content

- ✔ **Flickr** (www.flickr.com): A public space to share photos and keep in touch with those who are interested in them

- ✔ **LinkedIn** (www.linkedin.com): A mostly business-oriented networking site, in which you expand your social network to include your contacts, plus their contacts, and *their* contacts. . . .

- ✔ **Meetup** (www.meetup.com): A network of more than 5 million members in 11,500 cities, who meet in the real world because of their shared interest or circumstance (for example, new moms, environmental activists, or book lovers)

- ✔ **MySpace** (www.myspace.com): Similar to Facebook, though somewhat more geared to groups (bands use it to share their music) and featuring a younger user profile

- ✔ **Skype** (www.skype.com): A free communication platform that hosts telephone-like abilities, chat, and live video feeds

- ✔ **Twitter** (www.twitter.com): A "microblogging" service, in which users write short (140-character) messages, can "follow" anyone on Twitter, and search for topics being discussed

- ✔ **Wikis:** User-generated, collaborative knowledge centers where people share and discuss what they know about a topic (www.wikipedia.org being the biggest and most famous)

- ✔ **YouTube** (www.youtube.com): A huge online video-sharing site, where users post videos and viewers respond with comments — and sometimes videos of their own

We recommend you get started by visiting each of the sites listed in the preceding section and signing up. Facebook, MySpace, LinkedIn, Twitter, Skype, and YouTube all feature easy-to-use interfaces that are self-explanatory and that have detailed help links if you have trouble. You'll likely have hours of fun setting up your accounts and watching as your social networks in each medium begin to grow. That's the easy part, actually.

We also recommend signing up for Google Alerts. All you need is a Google account (if you don't have one go to www.google.com/accounts/NewAccount). After you've got your Google account, go to the alerts sign-up page (www.google.com/alerts) and enter some keywords you're interested in monitoring. From then on, every time your keywords make a new appearance on the Web, you'll be notified by receiving a link through e-mail, along with enough information to see whether that's something you'd like to have a further look at. We recommend choosing the once-a-day notification option — that way, all your results are compiled together, and you just get one message a day (as opposed to being peppered with e-mails throughout the day).

Many other news services (BBC, CNN, *The New York Times*), Web sites, and blogs will alert you about new material as well if you sign up with them. Some do this through what are called Really Simple Syndication (RSS) feeds, indicated by an orange RSS icon usually located at the top of the organization's home page. You can certainly sign up with as many of these as you want, though we recommend signing up with Google Alerts at the very least.

The four functions of social media for the social entrepreneur

As a social entrepreneur, using and engaging with social media boils down to a four-function approach:

- ✔ **Research:** Investigating issues and developments via *social bookmarking,* a method for Internet users to share, organize, search, and manage bookmarks of Web resources
- ✔ **Integration:** Becoming directly involved in various social networking outlets
- ✔ **Production:** Creating and distributing original content on blogs and wikis
- ✔ **Notification:** Staying up-to-date on developments via e-mail alerts, RSS feeds, and microblogs such as Twitter

The research function is important in gathering the information your social enterprise and like-minded people in your social network. Social bookmarking sites are a key part of this function, and we return to that subject later in this chapter. We cover the integration function in the next section.

The production function involves creating and disseminating various interactive knowledge pieces. Over time, production can include the development of a collection of learning that you and your collaborators have pulled together. You can post this information and supporting opinion or commentary to blogs and/or wikis (which may be the perfect social media expressions of the production function). Producing collaborative content is the natural expression of the process begun by the research function and sustained by the integration function. It is also the legacy of that whole process, what is left behind for others, which may be relevant enough to fuel more bookmarking research by your community or someone else at some point.

The process of collaborative learning through social media is made convenient through the notification function. Here, you and your collaborators can update each other — and the public or other groups if you want — about your activities in adding to the mutual learning process in nice, short, easy-to-receive-and-digest bursts of communication. E-mail is still the old standby for being notified (and really struts its stuff with e-mail lists). RSS feeds and micro-blogging (with Twitter as the archetypal example) are also becoming incredibly valuable in keeping everyone updated.

If social media began as a way of creating new and ever more fanciful ways of conversing online, many services are now edging more toward providing a technological platform that can support real collaborative work on many levels.

 The startup Power Text Solutions (`http://iresearch-reporter.com`) provides a cluster of Web-based individual research tools, such as information categorization and summarization. Its goal is to roll out an unprecedented platform supporting collaborative Web research.

 Google Wave (`http://wave.google.com`) — as of this writing, the "next big thing" in social media — is intended to allow people from all over the globe to interact, collaborate, and exchange almost any type of information in real time.

Perhaps no one has signaled the advent of the trend toward flexing the muscles of social media better than President Barack Obama. His 2008 presidential campaign was a pioneering model in "government 2.0," where citizens collaboratively learned and contributed to the campaign decision-making process.

Following Followers on Twitter

You may well ask: "Being all modern and fancy with social media is well and good, but how do I move past keeping in touch to making things happen for my social enterprise?"

The most basic first step is to find others who share your concerns. People you should be collaboratively learning with are out there. How do you find those folks?

 Probably the easiest, fastest, and most productive way to get started in collaborative learning via social media is through Twitter (`www.twitter.com`). If you're new to social media, Twitter will get you up and running, meeting and talking with like-minded folks, in very short order. Even if you're a veteran to social media but haven't really given Twitter a sustained shot, we urge you to do so for reasons that will soon become clear.

Twitter hashtags

A *hashtag* is a small alphanumeric string preceded by the number sign (#). A hashtag serves as a topic identifier for finding and tracking tweets on Twitter. People looking for tweets on the 2009 Copenhagen United Nations Climate Change Conference, for example, would search for #Copenhagen and find all sorts of tweets on the summit. Note that a long hashtag like #Copenhagen eats up some of the precious 140-character limit on Twitter. A better hashtag might be something like #cop15. And, in fact, that *was* the hashtag for that conference (the conference being the 15th one on climate change). The problem, though, is that unless you were in the know and realized that "cop15" was the official moniker of the Copenhagen conference, you might not see the significance of the hashtag. You can remedy that problem by clicking the hyperlink and checking the context in which the hashtag is being used.

The generation and use of hashtags is not officially supported by Twitter — no one is really keeping track of their use. Instead, hashtags are a user convention. It may require a bit of detective work to figure out what a particular hashtag means to the folks using it.

When you're on Twitter (the signup is simple from the home page) you can begin finding people who should be in your social network. To start finding others who share your interests, we recommend doing a keyword search at http://search.twitter.com in the box at the top of the page. Use combinations of words that are of interest to your organization (for example, search for **sustainable development**, **community hospitals**, or **soup kitchen Detroit**).

You should get at least a page full of relevant *tweets* (what the mini-blog posts on Twitter are called). Take a good look at the results, focusing on those that boldface the terms you searched for in ways that are meaningful for you. Of the good hits, look to see if there is a hashtag embedded in those tweets. (If you're not up on Twitter hashtags, have a look at the nearby "Twitter hashtags" sidebar.)

When you've found hashtags you can relate to, make a note of them for later use because you can easily forget what they mean. For example, you naturally might want to try a Twitter search for **social entrepreneur**. Pretty quickly you'll notice that the hashtag #socent often appears. Clicking the #socent hyperlink confirms that this particular hashtag is one that is used, appropriately, to refer to topics of interest to social entrepreneurs.

Why all the emphasis on Twitter and Google Alerts and RSS? We're trying to get you acquainted with online communities of your choice so that you can begin to collaborate on learning with others who share the concerns of your social enterprise. You'll very likely find individuals and communities through Twitter hashtags and Google Alert links.

Becoming a valued tweeter

After your inbox is filling up with Google Alerts, if you see something of urgent interest to you and others who are like-minded, why not open up your Twitter account and tweet about the alert? Say a few (a *very* few) words to grab reader attention and then invite them to click your link to read more.

That 140-character tweet limit can be a killer. Check out `http://140it.com` if you need help shortening your prose. And what about that long Web address you copied from your Google Alert e-mail — the one that's 800 characters long? Copy that humungous monster, take it to `http://tinyurl.com`, `http://bit.ly`, or `http://is.gd` and paste it into the little boxes provided. Then click the conversion button, and presto! You've got a teeny-tiny Web address that you can now paste into your tweet.

Don't forget to include those hashtags you made a note of before. Squeeze as many as you can into your tweet; with each one, your tweet will be picked up by more members of the communities that understand and are looking for the hashtag topics of interest.

If you tweet in the way we've just described, regularly and fervently, something really important will start to happen: You'll be *followed*. Unlike being stalked, being followed is potentially a very good thing. It means someone has chosen to receive all your tweets automatically. Sometimes a single tweet can generate a handful to a dozen or more followers. Before you know it, you'll have dozens, or even hundreds, of followers.

Turning followers into collaborators

Followers are the key to using Twitter for social networking. You'll be sent an e-mail notification every time someone chooses to follow you, which includes a hyperlink to that person's profile. Click that link — this is the moment you've been waiting for! Browse your follower's tweets, and if you like what you see, follow them in return. The two of you are now part of the same social network. *Voilà!*

Your collaborative learning can even now take a more personal turn because when people follow each other they can send *direct messages* to each other (small private messages). After getting to know each other a little, the time will come for one of you to direct message (or DM) the other to say hello and express admiration and appreciation for the other's tweets. See how receptive they are to your friendly introduction. If there seems to be an open door to further communication, then you may be ready to take the next step.

What might a next step be? Think of a problem or issue about which you both are mutually interested in learning more and suggest swapping information on that topic. If you can do this with two or three or more others, you'll have the basis for a *Twitter group.* That just means that if everyone's agreeable, you can assign yourselves a unique hashtag of some sort and then designate a time to chat together. Pick a mutually acceptable time and log in to `http://tweet chat.com` or `http://tweetgrid.com`. Enter the hashtag you've assigned yourselves, and start tweeting back and forth to each other in real time. This is all very cool, of course — but also potentially very valuable to your enterprise. You never know who you'll meet or what they can offer you.

For much more information on Twitter, check out *Twitter For Dummies,* by Laura Fitton, Michael Gruen, and Leslie Poston; and *Twitter Marketing For Dummies,* by Kyle Lacy (both published by Wiley).

Networking, Online and Off

As you are increasingly followed on Twitter, and participate in and perhaps even coordinate Twitter groups (not to mention friended on Facebook, linked on LinkedIn, and so forth), you might wonder what's behind your growing popularity. Well, it's nothing but a whole lotta whuffie. No, really.

Whuffie is sort of an arcane buzzword meaning social capital or reputation (good or bad) within or specific to a particular online community. Positive whuffie refers to how helpful and therefore esteemed you're perceived to be by that community. Your whuffie is one of the measures of how much people take you seriously, and you should guard and protect it.

On the photo-sharing site Flickr, for example, your whuffie might go up with the number of photos you post, the tags you place on photos, the helpful comments you make about other people's photos, the number of useful galleries you create, and so on. With Twitter, if you follow the suggestions we make in this chapter, you should be on your way to increasing your whuffie dramatically. People who follow you, and especially people in your Twitter group, will come to see you as helpful and valuable to their own learning and progress. Other Twitterers, looking on from outside who may have searched for the topics you've hashtagged in your own tweets, will feel more comfortable following you and then joining in. The more the merrier, right?

Balancing your physical and digital lives

You do need to be careful about certain tendencies inherent in online social networking. We dropped in recently on a young psychologist and social entrepreneur we know. As we entered her office, she turned away from her computer screen and said, "I don't know why I do this to myself." She gathered up a whole mess of stickies that were adorning her monitor and stuck them all to her ten fingers, with sometimes more than one to a digit. "These are all the online favors I've committed to doing for people just this morning. What am I going to do?" Then she paused and said, "I just hope it's good for my whuffie."

Collaborative learning is something that needs to be shared. You can't do it all. As the old expression goes, "Many hands make light work."

Some people worry that all this online social media stuff is robbing us of our real-world sociability. Are we forgetting how to just sit down in F2F (that's face-to-face, of course) situations to relax, chat, and brainstorm? After all, relationships in the physical world are based on real trust and rapport — how does it work in social media, where others are not much more than a username, or at most (with Skype) a disembodied smiling face and distant voice?

Walter Schwabe, social entrepreneur and CEO of FusedLogic, the social media strategy outfit behind North America's largest fringe festival, takes the trust and rapport problem seriously. That's why after building up a followership through his online blogging and tweeting, he suggested at one point that the folks in his online community get together — gasp, yes, *in real life* — on a monthly basis to talk about social media in friendlier confines. So on a warm September evening, 14 people from his local area (Edmonton, Alberta, Canada) got together as the newly formed group Social Web Meetup. Today, that group is the second largest in the Edmonton area with nearly 160 members, and it continues to grow. A big part of the group's success is the use of the interest-group finder Meetup (www.meetup.com).

Not surprisingly, a ton of great ideas typically fly around the room at any given Social Web Meetup meeting, and the synergy level is high. Out of that come many opportunities for further collaborative learning as people from all walks of life and level of Internet savvy attend to find out more about the impact of social media. "We invite members to take one of four 15-minute presentation slots," Schwabe says. "The rules are simple: Present on anything social media– or Web 2.0 application–related." The group is exposed to new applications being developed locally, projects looking for collaborators, or just interesting developments in the space. Attending bloggers and tweeters write about what they learn and promote others within the group. Schwabe, for example, routinely blogs and comments on Twitter about the activities and people he meets through the meetings, always pushing to promote collaborative learning among members as well as their businesses or projects.

Rapport: The key to keeping it real

Always work to identify key personal traits of new contacts you make online and then follow up offline if possible. Building rapport is far easier if you "listen" to others and learn what's important to them. For example, let's say that someone on Twitter explains that they enjoy a particular type of food, hobby, or point of view. If those things align with your perspective, there is a foundation for rapport.

Don't overlook the little things that could create an atmosphere that's conducive to establishing rapport. The interesting thing about social media is that by its sheer power of numbers it has exponentially increased this capability.

If whuffie is your personal form of social currency, rapport is your interpersonal form. Both forms are steeped in the emotions that go with human relationships. People who make their livings as negotiators, for example, know well that humans are immersed in currents of emotion and that these emotions are vital to the social world.

Look to increase trust online through whuffie building. But in face-to-face meetings, generating rapport is another vital way to keep relationships and collaborative learning friendly, lively, and engaging.

But what exactly do we mean by rapport? Dictionaries may say something like "a relationship of mutual understanding or trust and agreement between people." We say it's a harmonious and freely given mutual trust and appreciation between people. The classic example is you know you have a rapport with someone when you have the feeling that you're hitting it off almost instantly with them.

Bob Rosenthal, professor of psychology at the University of California, Riverside, has found that rapport always entails three elements:

- ✔ Mutual attention
- ✔ Mutual friendliness and caring
- ✔ Mutual coordination

Mutual attention at the outset is critical — it jump-starts the process. But mutual attention isn't likely without empathy; all parties have to have the ability to relate to each other, to imaginatively put themselves in the other person's shoes. When this happens, people feel that others are "getting" them, appreciating them not only in terms of understanding them but also in terms of feeling good about them.

When the empathy and appreciation are there, it's no surprise that friendliness and caring emerge, and people align themselves with each other (which Rosenthal calls *coordination*). People with rapport don't interrupt each other, for example. Each person's body language may naturally mirror the other's.

Nonverbal signals don't clash and get in the way of engaging and communicating. Turn-taking may happen: One person allows the other to lead, and when that generosity is reciprocated, there is the potential for some real chemistry.

Building whuffie and rapport

Want some other ideas on establishing whuffie and rapport? Here are a few suggestions:

- ✔ Ask questions about the other person, listen carefully, and talk about the other person as much as you can. Be generous without being compulsive about it.

- ✔ Bringing your whuffie with you to a new community can be difficult if that group has no knowledge of who you are or what your reputation is, so draw on your friends — they can promote your authentic reputation. That helps build trust in you, which is basic to rapport. Aside from that, here's another great way to build rapport with a new group: Offer to speak to them on a topic of common interest.

- ✔ Dress well. It may sound either silly or obvious, but first impressions do count. If you and a friend are attending a networking event in which your friend has a vested interest, make every effort to add to and not diminish your friend's own prestige. When in doubt, opt for a professional look and demeanor and you'll serve your friend and yourself to your advantage.

- ✔ Keep up on the news, especially if it's related to the community you're trying to introduce yourself to. You probably shouldn't start off trying to pass yourself off as an expert, but when you know something about people's professional lives, they'll be flattered. The friend you're with can probably brief you on a few pertinent subjects beforehand.

- ✔ Have a great attitude. Be charming and exude enthusiasm, confidence, and the passionate thought of the charismatic social entrepreneur. When people see this in you, and your focus remains solidly on them, you should have little trouble building rapport.

- ✔ Let others know you care. Find some way, however small, to help whoever you're meeting. Is there some favor that you can do for them? Build that whuffie — just don't overdo it. If you've been listening closely and asking the right types of questions, something should suggest itself.

- ✔ Keep at it. The rapport you establish should not be a one-off deal. You shouldn't hesitate to let the people you meet know that you've appreciated getting to know them. Exchange business cards and follow up with a professional and thoughtful "it was great to meet you" e-mail. A handwritten note would probably make an even better impression.

Collaborative Intelligence and Collaborative Learning

Many people these days give social networking a try either because they hope it will somehow raise their marketing or public relations profile — or because they've been told they should and they find that they enjoy the fun and fascination of it all. These motivations have their place, whether you're a business entrepreneur or just someone looking for casual leisure, but social entrepreneurs need to get into social networking because doing so is a great way to make good use of collaborative intelligence.

Collaborative intelligence — the cumulative problem-solving power of a group of people working together toward the same goal — can help solve very difficult, seemingly intractable social problems. Collaborative intelligence is the result of *collaborative learning,* the enhanced ability of a group to discover, absorb, and share information.

Committing to collaborative learning

Social entrepreneurs who commit to collaborative learning through their social networks find that their profile is, indeed, raised and that they can have fun and be fascinated along the way along, too.

So how do you start collaboratively learning? To create an atmosphere in your social enterprise that's conducive to collaborative learning, keep the following principles in mind as you go:

- ✔ Commit to change and enjoy the process of changing.
- ✔ Recruit diversity of opinion and thought.
- ✔ Make space for candid, respectful, and thoughtful communication.
- ✔ Always respect confidentiality.
- ✔ Value and obtain consensus and respect the role of compromise.
- ✔ Develop a shared vision and mission with your collaborators.
- ✔ Aim for clearly identified and doable outcomes, make specific action plans, and clarify roles.

Using social bookmarking sites to collaborate

When you establish and include others in your quest to achieve collaborative learning, a logical point of departure might be to involve networked friends in the research function first (see the "Four functions of social media for social entrepreneurs" section earlier in this chapter if you're not sure what we mean by _research function_).

Someone might propose a question or topic of shared interest, for example. If everyone agrees on the importance of the suggestion, collaborators can then begin to comb the Web for information, bookmarking, and sharing their findings. Eventually, those findings may become collaboratively compiled into a collection. Starting with the research function allows for your group to set clear and doable parameters for success, which, if the project is important enough in the first place, will help to sustain the effort invested along the way.

In case you're not too familiar with the idea of social bookmarking, what's involved is that you save Web page links that you want to remember and possibly share with others. If you're thinking about sharing your bookmarks, you can choose to make them public or save them privately to your account, in which case you can then choose to keep them to yourself or share them with specified people or groups.

Many browser-based social bookmarking services are available. The following are some of the better-known ones:

- Delicious: http://delicious.com
- Digg: www.digg.com
- Diigo: www.diigo.com
- Mr. Wong: www.mister-wong.com
- Simpy: www.simpy.com
- StumbleUpon: www.stumbleupon.com

You can generally view your bookmarks chronologically or arrange them by category or even _tag_ them (assign keywords to them). The advantage of tagging is that you and others can know how often certain tags are used and, in the case of public tags, access the associated bookmarks. All in all, social bookmarking proves to be a great way to get your collaborative community researching and sharing knowledge. To start, just visit one of the Web sites in the list just given and follow the directions to join the service. It's really easy, trust us.

What you need to look for in a bookmarking service is the ease of gathering bookmarks, researching features (capturing, annotating, highlighting, tagging, and so on), cataloging and retrieval capabilities, and the ease with which you can share, follow your fellow collaborators' activities, and collaborate to compile results.

With successful social bookmarking can come the recognition and celebration of a growing learning network's accomplishments. Documenting the growth and legacies of that community can take place through a social networking site such as Facebook, Twitter, MySpace, or LinkedIn, for example. Each member can have a personal profile, of course, but there should also be a hub-like group profile page to which all members of the learning community link. In this way, members can be integrated into the group's life and activities. The hub can also provide an invitational presence to those who might become aware of the group's activities and want to participate.

Whatever is happening within your learning community, be sure to always, always, *always* communicate to get your full advantage of social media. Like a pulse, the notification function (e-mail, blogging, Twitter, Facebook) is a measure of the life and rhythm of your enterprise or group. No notifications over a prolonged period of time? Be worried. On the other hand, when your learning community's lively pulse is noticed by others, it may start to spread the word about your efforts far afield. Who knows? Something your group is up to might garner so much attention that it *goes viral* (takes on a life of its own, spreading far and wide). That would be something. No marketing money can top that.

Six degrees of separation

A key idea in networking is that the world of social relationships is really a lot smaller than we think. How long a chain does it take to connect one arbitrary person to another arbitrary person anywhere in the world? Approximately six people. This is the famous *six degrees of separation* idea initially researched by psychologist Stanley Milgram. Milgram asked for a message to be passed from randomly selected people in Kansas and Nebraska to a particular target person in Boston who was completely unknown to the initial message recipient. By using a chain of acquaintances, it took only an average of 5.5 intermediaries to successfully deliver the message to the target. Weak ties can get difficult jobs done.

In his best-selling book *The Tipping Point,* Malcolm Gladwell argues that you can boost your six degrees' chances of success if one or more of the people you interface with is what he calls a *connector* — an extraordinary hub of a person enmeshed in large networks of contacts and friends. Connectors can boost your movement along the human web, whereas others may slow things down. So pay particular attention to any well-connected people in your social network — they're your connectors.

Chapter 12

Greenroom Strategies: Winning with the Media

....

In This Chapter

▶ Considering your media outreach strategy

▶ Creating media materials, including media releases, media kits, and media advisories

▶ Holding media conferences

▶ Following up on your efforts and successes

....

*W*e place a lot of emphasis in this book on the importance of culture and communication. In order to get your message out to any target audiences you may be interested in reaching, it's good for you to think in terms of introducing or entering conversations. *Conversations* are inviting, non-threatening, fluid, and often fun ways of communicating within culture. No matter who you're talking to, conversations can provide you with remarkable opportunities to promote your world-changing views and practices, often while laying the groundwork for mutual benefit.

Conversations are effective ways of socializing toward positive social change. This approach stands in contrast to, for example, paid advertising or marketing campaigns, which have the disadvantage of being perceived as naked attempts at social engineering, as sneaky "spin" or even heavy-handed propaganda.

In this chapter, we help you prepare for those times when you want to communicate with your public through various conventional, if sometimes independent, media outlets such as the press, television, and radio. For an introduction to the complex and ever-changing world of social media, see Chapter 11.

Why Media Relations Matters

Let's face it — you're not selling deodorant or soft drinks. So, you have to be subtler in your use of the media to get your message out. As a social entrepreneur, you appreciate how important it is to affect social change in a cooperative way that doesn't get people's hackles up. So it makes sense, then, to stay away from heavy handedness and steer toward more considerate, nuanced ways of communicating your message.

One of the best ways to engage in conversations with people who will be interested in your message is by channeling your messages through the media, especially independent (or alternative) media. There's a good reason for this: *Independent media* are free, or freer, of the perceived biases of corporate- or government-owned media.

On the other hand, independent media (including radio, print, TV, and the Internet) are often perceived as being more critical. So, if a report on what you're up to passes the litmus test of the integrity of independent journalism, then what you have to offer is presumably worth knowing about.

Here are a couple of starting points with which social entrepreneurs have had some success:

- ✓ **Independent Media Center:** If you have a story, a story idea, or an alert of national or international interest, the best place to begin may be with the widely respected Independent Media Center (www.indymedia.org).

- ✓ **The Indypendent:** Another option is New York City Independent Media Center (IMC), which puts out *The Indypendent* (www.indypendent.org), an award-winning bi-weekly "free paper for free people," which is, these days, the most widely circulated underground paper in North America.

- ✓ **WireTap:** If your communication has a youth twist to it, try *WireTap Magazine* (www.wiretapmag.org).

There are many independent print, TV and video, radio, online, local, ethnic, and student, kinds of media producers who would love to hear from you. Search the Web for "independent media" and the name of your city or state. You should find something of interest to you very quickly. (For example, searching for "independent media Florida" immediately turns up the Miami Independent Media Center, along with a number of other Florida IMCs.)

Social entrepreneurs are often seen as friendlier to the independent media side of things than the corporate world is. It's kind of like when a friend introduces you to someone else he knows well. Your friend is vouching for you, and that makes it easier for the stranger to accept you — at least provisionally — and that's an important foot in the door. Independent media tend to be friendlier and more receptive toward the goals of social entrepreneurs than corporate media are.

Overall, of course, in terms of your credibility, the more positive things about your cause that are communicated through any kind of media, the better.

There are other reasons why you should engage in media relations, especially through independent media:

- **Getting your message out through independent media is a really cheap way of conversing with your target audience.** It's essentially free.

- **When you provide the media with trustworthy and interesting information, they gain as well, which is great for everyone.** In Chapter 2, we talk about creating public compassion, and in this context it's nice to know that those who help you will be around to help others.

- **As journalism goes through its current economic crisis, the reputation of independent media is likely to continue growing.** This trend will probably only further the reach of anything you have to say, through them, in the future.

- **As you develop your media relations, and as you get your foot into more and more doors, you'll find that other people will be contacting you from non-media organizations to learn more, which is what you wanted in the first place, right?** Political representatives; chambers of commerce of various kinds; tourist associations; consulates or embassies; the United Way; and other nonprofit or public-sector agencies, professional associations, civic groups, and university departments will be increasingly aware of what you're up to. This provides more grist for both your work and the public compassion mill.

- **The more media coverage you have, the higher and more favorable your profile will be to current and future volunteers, supporters, and financial donors, and, of course, to those you serve.**

The next obvious question is: "How do I do that?" First, and only briefly as a basic foundation, you need to refine your pitch or story and build out some very basic assets for the media to use, such as team biographies complete with bullet point highlights and headshots. Next comes more methodical work on two major fronts:

- **Outreach:** This front deals with the very human process of making and keeping contact with the media.

- **Production:** This front deals with producing and disseminating trustworthy and interesting content into the hands of media people.

In the next sections we take a look at each of these.

Focusing on Your Media Outreach

There are two main ways to reach out to media:

- ✔ You can suggest material to them.
- ✔ You can be the go-to organization whenever the media is interested in something that has to do with your work.

Although you should definitely try to gain access to the media in both ways, the passive route (being the go-to organization) is actually much more valuable in the long run. After all, it's not going to do your cause much good to simply hand a couple of good stories to the media and then ride off into the sunset. But if you're a proven and reliable source of information for them — *and* you can also supply them with stories — then you'll be worth your weight in platinum. And that will establish valuable recognition for your cause among the media folks.

If you do manage to become a media point person for your cause, the biggest cost to you won't be financial. It'll be the cost of your time and commitment. You'll need to be on call 24/7/365, or very nearly. That is, if the media tries to reach you, you need to respond very promptly. Media have deadlines, so if you're not available, they don't wait for you — they call someone else. But if you're easy to reach, they'll learn to go to you first because it saves them time.

Be quotable and keep in mind that you're helping them write the story, so offer suggestions and other people to contact. Make the job of media people easier, and they'll come back to you again and again.

Sometimes you need to play things cautiously. If you're put on the spot, you either need to answer as best you can, refer the matter to someone more qualified to respond, or decline with a polite "no comment." Be warned, though, the media people are generally really put off by the "no comment" tactic, so use it incredibly sparingly and only when you absolutely must.

What are the best media to approach? Here are the five main options:

- ✔ **Print:** Newspapers, magazines, newsletters, internal, and trade publications.
- ✔ **Television:** News programs (regional and cable), talk shows, and public service announcements.

✔ **Radio:** News programs (regional and local), interview shows, and community calendar announcements.

✔ **Wire services:** Examples include the Associated Press (www.ap.org), United Press International (www.upi.com), Reuters (www.reuters.com), and PR Newswire (www.prnewswire.com).

✔ **Online news publications and blogs:** Examples include Yahoo! News (http://news.yahoo.com), Google News (http://news.google.com), The Huffington Post (www.huffingtonpost.com), and Daily Beast (www.thedailybeast.com). Do some research to figure out what media your target audience reads and listens to. Doing so helps you figure out which sources to target first. Many online publications such as The Huffington Post don't take pitches because they have no staff reporters per se (yet). In those cases you need to write an article and submit it for consideration (though that's hard to accomplish — they may accept material only through invitation).

Within each media type, try to identify who specializes in covering stories on topics that have something to do with your efforts. Generally, these folks are

✔ Journalists or reporters (the front-line investigators and writers)

✔ Editors or producers (who coordinate the efforts of journalists)

Both kinds of media contacts are assigned to specific areas or *desks*, such as city/region/national news, health, consumer, lifestyle, and environment areas.

Features — usually human interest stories or investigative pieces — are the responsibility of editors, and talk shows are the responsibility of producers.

Try to identify the journalists or reporters first. Get to know them better by visiting their Web sites and possibly accessing their archived writings. Nowadays, many journalists put their e-mail addresses right there in their bylines. Send an e-mail, making it short and to the point. You can also contact the appropriate editors. To figure out who's who, have a look at the media mastheads or credits.

You need to identify and keep an updated list of all the media outlets that you might be interested in approaching. You should do this well before you ever make contact with any of them. A short list of the data you may consider collecting includes the following:

✔ Media organization name

✔ Media contact name and title

- ✔ Area of expertise/interest
- ✔ Address
- ✔ Phone and fax numbers
- ✔ E-mail address
- ✔ Personal notes
- ✔ Contact log

A spreadsheet program, such as Microsoft Excel, is a good way to organize this information. You may want to assign this task to a team of volunteers, with each volunteer researching a different media sector, such as print, radio, television, online news services, and so on. Contact other partner organizations and share your lists with each other.

When you have your list, be selective when you send out material (discussed later in this chapter). Pick your spots. The media is all about audiences. They serve audiences and they buy and sell them to advertisers. Know who will be most interested in your material because it connects to their audiences.

Don't make the mistake of sending everybody everything all the time. That either annoys media folks because you're adding needlessly to their work load, or desensitizes them to anything you send. And the last thing you want them to do is stop paying attention to you.

Creating a media outreach calendar

It's also a great idea to develop a media relations outreach calendar. This calendar sets out important upcoming dates. Once they are established, you should plan on getting your press releases out two to four weeks in advance of the dates for daily and weekly publications, and eight weeks in advance for monthly publications.

And who do you send it to? Refer to your media contact spreadsheet. Typical contacts include calendar editors, assignment editors, beat reporters (always keeping in mind their interests), and radio stations that broadcast a community calendar or have a public affairs bent. For those radio stations that are music only, consider event partnerships, where the station sponsors and promotes the event.

Feeding the Media Monster: Producing Your Materials

In this section, we look at how to create trustworthy and interesting content for media. Keeping in mind that this content is designed to advance some sort of program, event, or newsworthy effort of yours, you need to think in terms of producing that content before, during, and after the effort you want to promote.

At a minimum, you want to create *press releases.* A press release is a short and snappy article sent to media outlets about something with purported news value — your latest project, for example. You should also make a media kit, or press kit, which contains updated contact info and other information about your organization. If you're planning a media event such as a media briefing or conference, you'll create and send out a media advisory, followed by a release, in anticipation of the event.

Here we briefly consider planning, execution, and follow-up.

Planning your materials

Above all, if you're going to help reporters and other media representatives help you reach your target audiences, you need to provide them with concise and complete media content.

In order to deliver that kind of content, besides identifying media sources, which we discussed in the previous section, you need to keep these things in mind:

- **Your target audience:** Whose awareness do you want to raise? Whose attitudes or actions do you want to influence? Write down a description of who you're trying to reach. What do you know about these people? What are their core values, beliefs, social expectations, and sought-after benefits? And, most important, given where they're at, how does your content meet them there and deliver?

- **Your media materials and message:** In order to figure out whether you've got something worthwhile to send to the media, ask yourself pointed questions about the following:

  - Size of impact: How many people do your news items and/or programs impact?

  - Newsworthiness: There are lots of other things going on around you. Compared to them, how important is your message?

- Locality: Is the story relevant to people living in local communities?

- Expressiveness: What is eye-catching, action oriented, or intuitively and humanly engaging about your message?

Writing press releases

The press release has been around forever because it's one of the most effective ways to get the media interested in the efforts of citizens like you. More often than many people realize, press releases serve as the basis, if not the bulk, of news stories. To be effective, the press release must contain information that's newsworthy and not just glorified advertising.

When producing a press release, strive for journalistic merit, making what you say timely, important in terms of service to others, warm, engaging, and full of human interest.

Brevity is the soul of wit, and it's also the soul of press releases. It's common for media people to reject or ignore releases simply because they're too long. These people are as busy as you are, so keep your release down to a single double-spaced page. That doesn't mean that you can't add extra background material, but the news contained in that first page should be brief and hit-'em-over-the-head transparent.

Figure 12-1 shows a generic example of a press release you can use to get started.

Be sure to write a strong lead sentence or intro. Many media folks see hundreds of releases a week, so they learn to quickly skim them and almost never read them thoroughly until they've decided to pursue the story.

Here are a couple of examples of strong leads, drawn from real media releases:

- ✔ Who says our community is indifferent? See for yourself the compassion and spirit of people in our area who are making a real difference in the lives of others near and far. Join us as we celebrate and witness the spirit of social entrepreneurship among us on October 15, 2010, at the North-South Inn, 123 Center Street, Metropolis, NY.

- ✔ The Ministry of Community Development will be committing $10 million in the coming year to support capacity building within the social enterprise sector. This comes after the Ministry reviewed and overwhelmingly accepted 20 recommendations put forward by the National Social Entrepreneurship Committee chaired by Mr. Phillip Smith and made up of members from the public and private sectors.

Don't worry about trying to write the story for the media. They won't use it exactly the way you've written it anyway — they'll likely want to do things their own way. Just make sure you get the media's attention and let them know how to get in touch with you or some other contact person.

If you have any history or familiarity with the professional you're approaching, use it to your advantage. Target the press release so that it fits that particular person's interests.

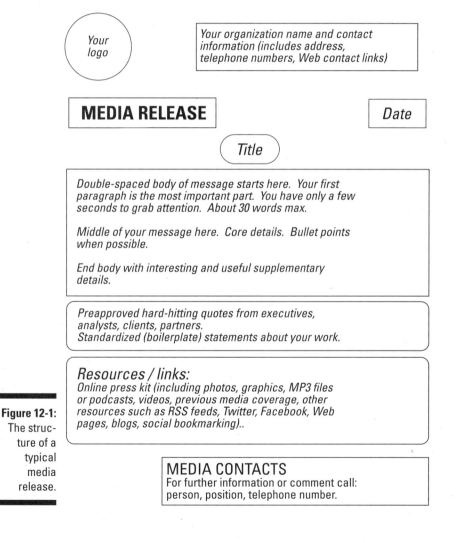

Your logo

Your organization name and contact information (includes address, telephone numbers, Web contact links)

MEDIA RELEASE   *Date*

Title

Double-spaced body of message starts here. Your first paragraph is the most important part. You have only a few seconds to grab attention. About 30 words max.

Middle of your message here. Core details. Bullet points when possible.

End body with interesting and useful supplementary details.

Preapproved hard-hitting quotes from executives, analysts, clients, partners.
Standardized (boilerplate) statements about your work.

Resources / links:
Online press kit (including photos, graphics, MP3 files or podcasts, videos, previous media coverage, other resources such as RSS feeds, Twitter, Facebook, Web pages, blogs, social bookmarking)..

MEDIA CONTACTS
For further information or comment call:
person, position, telephone number.

Figure 12-1:
The structure of a typical media release.

Assembling a media kit

Do the media know what they need to know about you or your organization? It's up to you to provide the media with accurate, up-to-date contact information and details about your enterprise. If you don't, you're leaving it to them to make something up. Make sure, then, that they have easy access to your media kit you. *Media kits,* sometimes called *press kits,* are used by media representatives in putting together their stories.

Your media kit should be a package of compact and pertinent material that includes

- ✔ Your organization's contact information, including contact person, phone number, address, e-mail address, and Web site
- ✔ Your mission statement
- ✔ Your organization's objectives
- ✔ Your organization's notable activities
- ✔ Short biographies of significant personnel
- ✔ Recent press releases, news articles, brochures, and any other materials that might help the media understand who you are and what you do

You should also put all that stuff online on your Web site and include the Web address, in case the media contact mislays some of your printed materials (see Chapter 10 for more on branding and your print and Web content).

Don't go overboard. Keep the material in the press kit thorough, but always relevant to the purpose at hand. Nobody likes to wade through reams of what, for them, is superfluous garbage, especially with deadlines looming.

Get feedback from others in your organization about ideas on what to include in your media kit. Anyone associated with you has to be on the same page with the information contained there. You don't want anyone else telling a different story — that can make your efforts look disorganized and confused. You may want to develop a set of guidelines — maybe even a formal policy. You may also want to assign key people to be the media relations contacts for your organization; if you do, everyone else should funnel media inquiries to those people (see the nearby sidebar, "Assigning a point person," for more). These assigned folks should know and keep up-to-date on the central media and reporters covering your efforts.

Assigning a point person

If you find that you're too busy to handle the duties associated with being the media "go-to" or point person, you need to assign one or more spokespeople to interact with the media in your place. Everyone else should funnel media inquiries to those people. And those spokespeople should know and keep up-to-date on the central media and reporters covering your efforts. It should also go almost without saying that spokespeople should also keep in very close contact with you, the social entrepreneur, and report to you often.

Be very picky about who should be spokespeople for your efforts. They should know their stuff about your work and the issues involved inside and out. They should also be personable, articulate, and unflappable under media fire. And try not to have more than two spokespeople. Having too many folks speaking for you risks not only diluting or convoluting your message but also confusing the people you want to reach with your message — your target audience. There should be a limited number of faces or voices officially associated with what you do.

Spokespeople serve as vital resources for the media — and target audiences — so they must be deeply involved, extremely knowledgeable, and comfortable appearing in front of cameras and microphones. Make sure, though, that your spokesperson's reputation is stellar; a good deal of your organization's reputation can be wrapped up in the spokesperson's.

Sending out your stuff

When you've convinced yourself that you've got something of interest and you're ready to send it the media, stop. Are you remembering that media people are always on deadline and are constantly being bombarded by other interests vying for their attention? Do you have something short, enthusiastic, authoritative, punchy, and clear on the ways your message stands apart from others? If so, read on.

Send your media releases and media kits by mail, fax, e-mail, telephone, Pony Express, or however your media contacts prefer — and find out their preferences beforehand.

Holding a media event

A media event is an agreed-upon occasion, either spontaneous or planned, for mass media organizations, particularly television news, newspapers, and radio, to learn more about some important and newsworthy matter. There are two forms of media events: media briefs and media conferences. There are only two good reasons why you would want to hold a media event:

✔ You've got something really, *really* important to say — and it's only with that expectation in mind that media will bother to attend. It goes without saying that you'd better not disappoint if you go this route.

✔ You need to get your message out very quickly because something fast-moving and high-profile is happening.

If neither of these circumstances is truly the case, then you don't probably need to hold a media event. Instead, you need to stick to the normal media outreach channels we've covered so far.

If you're going to hold a media event, you also send out a media advisory. A *media advisory* is simply an invitation for media to attend your briefing/conference. You should include all pertinent details about your conference and should send out your advisory three to four weeks before your event. Your advisory should be attention grabbing, but also extremely to the point. And of course, you need to describe your event in a way that clearly demonstrates its newsworthiness as well as that of your program.

Figure 12-2 shows one way to structure your media advisory.

After you send your media advisory, follow up quickly with a press release and then, just prior to the event, provide a media kit.

Media briefings

A *media briefing* is one of the best ways to have a positive impact on someone from the media. A media briefing is a short, personal, face-to-face, and dynamic meeting with a media contact. With a media briefing, you can exchange information efficiently, nip off any misunderstandings in the bud, and address further questions.

Plan ahead and set aside plenty of time: Scheduling one-on-one briefings can be tremendously time-consuming. Organizing just a handful of them can take up an entire morning or even a day if scheduling time with the media folks proves difficult.

Press conferences

A *press conference* is an event that you organize with the purpose of briefing several members of the press at once. A press conference is a lot more efficient than scheduling one or more media briefings because you get to quickly exchange information with several people across various media at once. A level of synergy and excitement can develop around a media conference that can do wonders for generating publicity and awareness for your campaign.

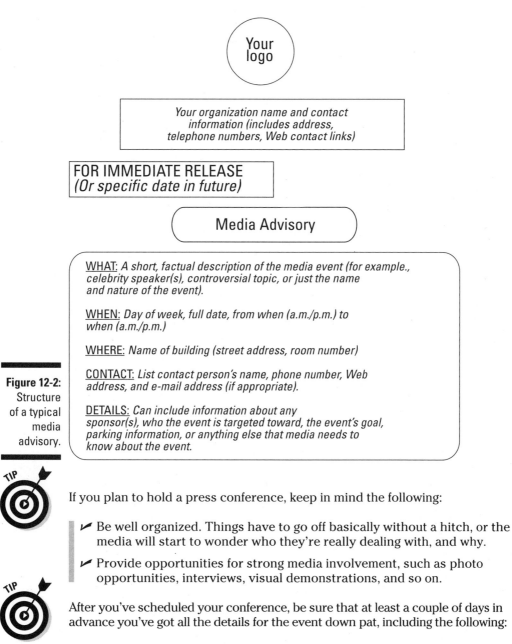

Figure 12-2:
Structure
of a typical
media
advisory.

If you plan to hold a press conference, keep in mind the following:

✔ Be well organized. Things have to go off basically without a hitch, or the media will start to wonder who they're really dealing with, and why.

✔ Provide opportunities for strong media involvement, such as photo opportunities, interviews, visual demonstrations, and so on.

After you've scheduled your conference, be sure that at least a couple of days in advance you've got all the details for the event down pat, including the following:

✔ The point person, often called a *primary program coordinator,* which could be you or someone you've assigned

✔ Contingency plans for unexpected surprises, including technology glitches

✔ Setup and rehearsal scheduled well before the media arrive — including mock run-throughs of demonstrations or speeches and reviewing critical messages and statistics

✔ The event parameters, such as who's participating, their credentials, what they'll be addressing, and what, if anything, the conference *isn't* about

✔ An agenda covering all of the important details, along with a finalized media kit to distribute to attendees

✔ Reminder e-mails that go out a few hours before the event begins

One potential downside of a press conference is that it can, especially with extremely emotional issues, manifest the phenomenon known as *pack journalism.* One vocal reporter may have a mistaken idea about something or a partisan axe to grind, and soon enough the whole agenda is taken over by that issue. If you have any sense that things might come to this, take extra time at the beginning of the conference to outline the parameters and prepare to stick to them absolutely. Any digressions from the planned agenda can be nipped in the bud and dealt with later by sending out press releases and arranging for more personal media briefings. This approach is more time-consuming, of course, but it's also far more manageable.

Following Up to Make Sure Your Message Gets Out

After you've sent out your press release or held your media event, you have to stay in touch with the media people just in case they need help focusing their story or obtaining vital but missing information. It shows care and diligence when you follow up.

Even the most compelling information requires follow-up to make sure that the material was received and was satisfactory. Be sure you're ready to field any inquiries and follow up any conversations with an e-mail or phone call. Continue to check in periodically, without making yourself a nuisance, in order to maintain interest.

Be prepared for fading enthusiasm. You don't control the media, of course, and it may be that for any number of reasons the commitment to your story that seemed so strong at first has declined. This is where you have to be ready to spring into action. Your last chance to ensure coverage for your program may rest on following up on your event or release. Don't wait too long — a few days — to do so. Be careful not to nag. Concentrate on being informative and concise.

Be prepared to be misquoted or to have points raised that you prefer to not be mentioned. Remember that anything you say to the press is likely to get used, so be mindful of your words. A casual slip in friendly conversation could become the focus of the story.

Despite your need to present yourself in the best possible light, always be honest when dealing with the media. If you're not, you lose credibility, trust, and respect — and you could be looking at a very negative story about you that could seriously compromise the success of your organization. Asking that a story that went awry be "killed" won't help you — it's viewed as an insult to journalistic integrity and freedom of speech.

If media reports do actually develop out of your efforts, congratulations. You've taken a step toward using the culture to advance your goals and the interests of your target of benefits.

Always catalog and archive your media coverage. Doing so gives you a chance to assess what kind of progress you've made with your media campaign and provides valuable reference material for future endeavors. It's a good idea to recap everything in a single document that outlines

✔ What you hoped to accomplish with your media relations campaign

✔ What you ended up accomplishing

✔ Which media contacts you garnered or successfully used again

✔ Suggested future directions for similar activities in the future

Chapter 13

Keeping Kafka at Bay: Dealing with Bureaucracy

ormer U.S. Senator Eugene McCarthy once said, "The only thing that saves us from the bureaucracy is inefficiency. An efficient bureaucracy is the greatest threat to liberty."

To us, bureaucracy shouldn't be thought of as an inevitable mass of annoying rules and procedures, but rather as an arrangement among people in a social enterprise that helps them carry out its mission and goals. This rather benign view of bureaucracy works as long as you don't allow the bureaucracy to get more complicated than necessary.

Bureaucracy can be mighty useful, as long as it doesn't eat into your freedom to pursue your mission. But you have to always watch and control it. Bureaucracy left untended has a way of swelling itself into a monster.

In this chapter, we examine different types and tendencies of bureaucracies as they relate to the social enterprise and offer tips for getting and keeping a handle on it.

Bureaucracy and the Chain of Command

Organizations, whether they intend to or not, establish bureaucracies to administrate the pursuit of their goals. So, the bureaucracy in your organization is composed of the people in your organization who carry out, or staff, this administration.

Note that these *administrators* (also known as *staff* or *bureaucrats*) don't set the organizational goals, and they don't set the policies for reaching those goals. Instead, they administer what the social entrepreneur — the owner, president, directive council, secretary general, chief executive officer, or other top leader in the organization — develops as the enterprise's mission, goals, and policy. So, bureaucracies typically consist of people lower in the organization's chain of command.

Bureaucrats do what they are told — they don't make the rules, they follow them.

Among bureaucrats you find advisors, managers, supervisors, division heads, directors of task forces, chairs of committees, and similar personnel. These workers may set rules and procedures to *implement* policy — though not the policies themselves — although rules and procedures to implement policies are sometimes set by the leaders at the top as well.

Hierarchically speaking, people in the organization serving below the bureaucracy are the ones who actually carry out policy and directly try to reach its goals. Sometimes called *line workers,* they actually produce the organization's goods or services by working within the rules and procedures set by the administrators. The administrators are responsible for seeing that the line workers perform as expected according to the rules and procedures.

Not all social enterprises are bureaucratized in any significant degree, but those that are generally look like this:

- ✔ **Leaders:** These are the mission and goal setters, as well as the policy makers. They're the social entrepreneurs — the ones who have an idea for a socially conscious business and are working to make that idea a reality.

- ✔ **Administrators:** Below the leaders are the bureaucrats — the people who make sure that the leaders' goals are met.

- ✔ **Line workers:** At the bottom of the totem pole are the line workers, or producers. They do what the administrators tell them to do, in order for the organization to reach the leaders' goals.

This chapter centers primarily on the middle section — the bureaucracy and its administrators.

Large and complex social entrepreneurial organizations often also have other kinds of personnel whose functions lie outside this chain of command. They include people providing cleaning, repair, and security services who, though not directly involved in reaching organizational goals, may nevertheless report to an administrative unit.

Many social enterprises have no bureaucracy. All the administrative services they need are supplied by the leaders. One or a few people set the mission and goals, make policy, and manage everyone. These leaders may even perform some line functions. In fact, the vast majority of social enterprises start out this way, and, typically, at this point, the founders give little or no thought to bureaucratizing.

Whereas many social enterprises never bureaucratize, some eventually do. They may develop administrative units staffed by only a handful of people — for example, a manager and a couple of committee chairs. At the other end of the scale of bureaucratic complexity are large organizations like the International Committee of the Red Cross and Amnesty International. The former presently has around 13,000 administrative and line workers, whereas the latter employs approximately 500 staff. The bureaucratic structure of the social enterprise can, under certain conditions, become enormous.

Bureaucracy tends to grow. At any point, new rules, procedures, and positions may be established, such as when a department head creates a new secretarial post or the director of finance institutes a new accounting procedure. As bureaucracy grows, the social entrepreneur and other leaders of the enterprise may lose more and more control over the administrative expansion. They may also lose more and more control over how their enterprise is managed in its routine operations. This growth of bureaucracy isn't necessarily a bad thing, as long as the administrative group remains attuned to the mission, goals, and policy of the enterprise and respects budgetary limits.

Flat Bureaucracy: Keeping Things Lean

Don't get us wrong: Even continued growth in bureaucratization is not *necessarily* a bad thing. As the enterprise succeeds, its initial flat bureaucracy may naturally begin to bulge a bit, simply because new needs emerge and new people must be found to meet them.

For example, there may come a time — after your organization has funding — when you appoint a treasurer to handle the accounting for the annual budget and explain its use to paying members and would-be funders. Incorporation as a nonprofit group (see Chapter 7) will require a formal board of directors, probably a paid executive director, and some paid staff. Similarly, the need for a recruitment officer or organizational unit could develop as the demand grows for more volunteers and paid staff.

The individuality of social enterprises makes it difficult to generalize about just how and where your flat bureaucracy will start to bulge. But you should expect that it will.

Over-bureaucratization and bureaucratic bloat come from adding more organizational functions than required and/or more people to carry them out than needed. In fact, through the ages, *over*-bureaucratization is what has provoked most of the unkind comments about bureaucracy — not its useful flat version.

Setting limits

One of the biggest problems in organizing a social enterprise is that, as the charismatic social entrepreneur inspires others to rally around and help reach the organization's goals, efforts to manage and sustain these grassroots initiatives tend to become increasingly bureaucratized. One consequence of this tendency is that the heart and soul of social change — the founding nucleus of enthusiasts — may become disenchanted. When those people start to lose their spark, the humanity and vision behind the initiatives for change can start to erode. And so can your chances for success.

Enterprises destined to grow into large organizations usually can't avoid this bloat, which is sometimes called *bureaucratic creep*. Their very size demands an increasing number of specialized units and subunits. Typical ones include the following:

- ✔ A financial department staffed by various tax, bookkeeping, and accounting specialists
- ✔ A hiring department charged with recruiting and retaining volunteers
- ✔ A human resources department to look after the needs of the swelling gang of paid workers

Unfortunately, this transformation tends to push the original, free-spirited heart and soul of the enterprise into the organization's least bureaucratized corners, if not out the door altogether. Even you, the founding charismatic entrepreneur, may find that you're increasingly shackled by these inescapable transformations.

Heavily bureaucratized enterprises may well be over-bureaucratized, but they may also still be mostly filled with volunteers and paid staff who are used to functioning under the new conditions. The founding cluster of free spirits may have adapted, found their own island of relative freedom, or left the organized side of the cause — the social enterprise itself — to work independently.

Nevertheless, whatever the stage of growth, you want to try to prune excess bureaucratic limbs. Over-bureaucratization adds needless costs while grinding down the people who have to try to get things done within it.

Staying on a bureaucratic diet

What if your enterprise is *not* necessarily destined to become a bureaucratic monster? Can the organization accomplish all that the founders and present leaders ever wanted without moving beyond the flat stage of organization? Yes.

Organizations that take this route try to preserve the inventive enthusiasm characteristic of the founding leaders, administrators, and workers, while meeting organizational needs with *minimal* addition of offices, departments, divisions, specialized personnel, and so on. Such enthusiasm flourishes best in an open environment that is receptive to new ideas as well as criticism.

Maintaining a flat bureaucracy is a delicate process. Those enterprises that manage it well constantly monitor the bureaucracy and its growth, a task that usually falls to the leaders. These kinds of leaders typically have a keen sense of oversight and an unwavering focus on the mission. And they use these two qualities to not only enable their enterprise to realize its goals, but to maintain the enthusiasm among volunteers and paid staff.

Avoiding the Tendency to Over-Bureaucratize

In this section, we discuss three main ways you can avoid creating a fat, or bloated, bureaucracy.

Having realistic expectations

One unexpected advantage of nonprofits, especially ones that struggle with funding, is that budgetary constraints themselves go a long way toward dampening leader and administrator enthusiasm for over-bureaucratization. When too little money is available for spending on underproductive arrangements or purchases of any kind — be they office rent, state-of-the-art electronic equipment, volunteers, or paid staff — then there likely will be no bloating problem in the first place.

One way to avoid the tendency to over-bureaucratize is to inquire, of every proposal that crops up: "Is it financially realistic for us to do this?" The treasurer is typically the person who asks this question (and even answers it), but any member of the enterprise may ask it. In fact, other people *must* ask it if the treasurer doesn't. An accountant familiar with the mission and everyday operations of the enterprise also often weighs in.

Asking if you can do without expansion

The group may eventually say yes to the question of whether a proposed expansion is realistic — they believe the money is there. Okay, fine. Time for another question: "Can we do without the proposed expansion?"

Even though the group may be able to *afford* it, expansion may not be *unnecessary*. The question is a reminder that, before any organizational damage is done, you need to nip the tendency for over-bureaucratization in the bud.

The "whether we can do without it" question puts up a second roadblock on the path toward fat bureaucracy. But this second question also eventually may get answered with a yes, following plenty of level-headed discussion. The group decides that the proposed new function is feasible and desirable both financially and organizationally, and no, they can't do without it (which more often means, they don't *want* to do without it). Expansion proceeds as planned. But down the road a year, two years, the bureaucratic addition turns out to be less than what had been hoped for.

A third way of avoiding the tendency is to *revisit* past expansion decisions (see the next section).

Assessing expansion

A good social entrepreneur must have the wisdom and courage to put an end to any expansion that has turned out to be anything less than promised. Governments often deal with such things through *sunset provisions.* When a law has a sunset provision, the default decision is to cancel it after a certain amount of time. After a specified number of years, new positions, departments, policies, procedures, and so on are automatically terminated, unless a case can be made for retaining them for another period of time. This method forced proponents of expansion to justify themselves.

If you want to maintain a flat bureaucracy, adopt sunset provisions in your policies. If you don't, you'll have to find the courage to reevaluate bureaucratic growth on a case-by-case basis.

Avoiding over-bureaucratization is not easy. Frequently the leader and other members of the enterprise must summon considerable courage and wisdom to respect — sometimes it's hard to even remember — the ideal of retaining their good old flat bureaucracy. Even preventing it from bulging further requires strong leadership.

Conflict can arise during reevaluation of expansions. People don't always agree that a recent addition or the one being proposed was bad for the enterprise. Some may want to grow in certain ways for reasons other than advancing the mission and may even band together to push for expansion. Catering to their special interests can strike others as favoritism (a managerial problem we take up in a bit more detail in Chapter 18). Trying to prevent these alliances from sabotaging the practical good sense of keeping the bureaucracy flat can test even the best of leaders.

Adhocracy: Alternatives to Bureaucracy

There are ways of organizing that avoid bureaucracy, but they're really effective only in the short term. In this section, we talk about temporary alternatives to bureaucracy. From the start, every participant in these types of organization knows that

- ✔ The arrangement is aimed at accomplishing a particular, practical goal.
- ✔ The arrangement will cease to exist once the goal is reached.

Task forces

A *task force* is a temporary unit within an enterprise that is assembled to complete a special informational task or work on a particular activity or problem. Senior administrators are the ones who establish task forces and set the goals the task forces are supposed to pursue. A task force may be established to gather information on the legal situation of the group's goals, to identify the most productive ways to work with politicians, or to gather information about, say, the South American tribe with which the enterprise intends to work with on a water purification project.

Task forces are now common in government, industry, and the nonprofit sector. Their duration varies depending on the nature and difficulty of the work they're assigned to accomplish. Because they're technically outside the bureaucracy, they're intended to disappear — though only when their work is completed.

Task forces are a special kind of *team* (see Chapter 17 for more on teamwork), but they're considerably more autonomous than most teams. Task force members are high enough in the bureaucracy of your enterprise to be regarded as capable of working with minimal direction or need to report to superiors. Plus, members of task forces often have to be mobile; they must be able to travel on sudden notice or even temporarily relocate somewhere to accomplish the goals of their group.

Task force members must also be flexible in their approach to realizing these goals, using their abilities and knowledge in creative ways. Because of this requirement, task forces are often staffed with people who represent a range of outlooks and backgrounds that bear on the central interest of the task force. In short, a typical task force is like a prism, where each face, or member, brings a different perspective of experience and expertise. Consequently, some task forces may be staffed with people who are not even in your enterprise.

Committees

A *committee* is a body of two or more people from a larger group or enterprise, formed to carry out a special, often temporary service. Typical committees include decorating, welcoming, nominating, planning, and organizing committees. In some enterprises, committees may be called *groups*.

In practice, some administrators — the people who usually set up committees — establish ones that are much like task forces in scope and specialization. However, committees are generally unlikely to be intentionally stocked with experts chosen for their varying points of view, whose flexibility and mobility are vital for the success of the unit. Some committees acquire a degree of permanence that's characteristic of bureaucratic departments and divisions.

Committees are handy little groups. They're comparatively easy to establish and disband, easy to add members to or take members from, and capable of giving some people in your enterprise a special identity and valued sense of participation in your mission.

Assignments

An *assignment* is a directive given to an individual member of a social enterprise to complete a special informational task or offer a temporary service. The person agrees to do something that may, in other circumstances, be assigned to a task force or a committee. When the enterprise is small, and only a handful of people are available to help with its operations, assignments become a useful alternative to expanding the bureaucracy.

Assignments are also useful when a member shows exceptional talent, aptitude, or training relative to the subject of the assignment. For example, someone in your organization may have the talent and skills necessary to set up a Web site for the enterprise. By assigning the task to her, you avoid hiring someone permanently. Of course, a Web site has to be maintained, and when the assignment is finished, the person assigned to it usually goes back to her old job. But at least it's up and running, and you may decide an intern or volunteer is sufficient to keep the site up to date.

Co-options

A *co-option* is a process whereby one or more outsiders are invited into a social enterprise to perform a specified task. Like the other examples of adhocracy, a co-option is a temporary arrangement. Many organizations co-opt an expert to give the group needed information or guidance on, for example, how to conduct a publicity campaign, approach foundations for funding, invest wisely, manage volunteers, or deal with government. A co-opted expert is like a consultant. Co-optees are sometimes said to be "absorbed" into an enterprise, albeit only temporarily.

Though co-opted experts rarely have voting rights in a social enterprise, they often do get to know in considerable depth how it works.

Co-option often carries no pay — it's a charitable, pro bono service provided by the expert — though enterprises with some cash may try to hire their advice.

Sometimes an alternative arrangement turns out to work so well that it becomes permanent. But keeping in mind the specter of fat bureaucracy, you should closely examine any transformation of that sort using the principles mentioned in the "Avoiding the Tendency to Over-Bureaucratize" section, earlier in this chapter. In other words, don't let alternatives sneak in the back door to become (unexamined) additions. If they are to become additions, let them properly earn their new organizational status.

Dealing with External Bureaucracy

Most social enterprises must deal with one or more external bureaucracies. Any entrepreneur who wants to influence a governmental entity, for example — be it local, national, or international — must work through the bureaucracy and line workers who administer and carry out his organization's mission, goals, and policy. The same goes for dealing with foundations, businesses, granting agencies, other nonprofit organizations, religious groups, and similar entities.

So, bureaucracy gets you coming and going.

To succeed, you need to learn about and live with the workings of external bureaucracies. They may be exasperating at times. You may face excessive procedures, regulations, and operational positions. You may begin to think they were intentionally created to make life difficult for social entrepreneurs. The same bureaucratic problems you're trying to avoid may have already consumed those you're dealing with.

Dealing with external bureaucracies is an area of entrepreneurial life where perseverance (see Chapter 3) is very much in demand. You can't reach your mission by railing against established institutions and their bureaucracies. These giants are very difficult to change.

In the short run, to get what you want from external bureaucracies, you have to find out how they work and learn how to cut red tape. Doing that often requires careful study and could make a worthy assignment for a willing colleague who shows talent and aptitude for it. Tap the experience of other people already familiar with the peculiarities of the bureaucracy in question. Getting to know personally some of the key bureaucrats involved is another way of expediting your interests — and face-to-face contact is the ideal way.

Governmental bureaucracy

Governmental bureaucracies have certain unique features that are relevant for social enterprises. For one thing, politicians must answer to those who elect them (in democracies, anyway) — and the bureaucratic units for which the politicians are ultimately responsible have to answer to the electorate, too.

Let's say a governmental department honors a request from a social entrepreneur to change a certain procedure, but then people affected by the change complain to their elected representatives. What happens? The change may ultimately be reversed. When you're working through governmental bureaucracies, you have to try to predict how your proposals will be received by the larger population.

Proposals unpopular in the larger community may eventually fail, even if they temporarily succeed at the administrative level. A good example would be the prohibition of alcohol in the early 20th century. At first the Temperance Movement — something akin to a social enterprise and the prime mover behind the legal change — was successful in enacting a constitutional amendment banning liquor. However, the amendment was eventually repealed because it was unworkable and caused a backlash among the public.

When working with governments, you have to think ahead , because they may change their minds.

Governments, unlike some corporations, do not commonly have a special bureaucratic unit whose mission is to provide money or services to social causes. Government aid is spread out through numerous departments and agencies. (In Chapter 9, we discuss the special challenge of seeking government help for your enterprise.)

Some social entrepreneurial causes, when faced with stubborn governmental authorities, have resorted to civil disobedience tactics, such as marches and sit-ins. *Civil disobedience* is active but nonviolent refusal to abide by particular laws, requirements, or orders set out by a government, whether the legitimate government of the country or that of an occupying power. It is one of the central tactics used in nonviolent resistance. Mohandas Gandhi used civil disobedience to help change the attitude of the British governmental bureaucracy toward his campaign to win the independence of India.

Corporate bureaucracy

You may face a corporate bureaucracy if you're trying to get the corporation to change how it operates. For example, maybe you're trying to persuade an industry to reduce air or water pollution. In this case, your best bet is usually to avoid the corporate bureaucracy entirely and schedule a personal visit with the leaders of the corporation. You may also need to organize a public pressure campaign, possibly using media sources (see Chapter 12), influential politicians or other public figures, leaflets and flyers, and the like.

Civil disobedience may be the last recourse against a stubborn corporation. For example, protesters against logging companies that clear-cut large sections of forest have sometimes taken up temporary residence in selected trees as a way of preventing them from being cut down. Earth First, a radical social enterprise, has used, among other tactics, this form of civil disobedience. Operation Rescue, a pro-life Christian activist organization, occasionally engages in civil disobedience to discourage and even block access to clinics where abortions are performed. And Greenpeace has used nonviolent tactics in its attempts to bring an end to seal hunting and whaling.

Chapter 14

Going Corporate: Formally Organizing and Incorporating

*I*n Chapter 13, we touch on the subjects of formally organizing a social enterprise and going corporate. This chapter is where we present the ins and outs and pros and cons of these potential transformations of your enterprise. Formal organization and incorporation are quite involved undertakings with far-reaching consequences. But a formal organization and a corporation are two very different things. And your social enterprise might not even be a formal organization yet. In this chapter, we sort all this out and help you decide which path is right for you.

Forming a Group: Formal or Informal

Forming a social enterprise is really about forming a *group,* which is just two or more people who share at least one goal, have a sense of common identity, and are organized around a set of rules and roles. A two- or three-person social enterprise, if it meets these criteria, would qualify as a group.

Groups can be formal or informal. According to David Horton Smith, an expert on nonprofit organizations and the nonprofit sector, a *formal group* is one that has

- ✔ **A proper and unique name:** The carefully chosen name publicly identifies the group.

- ✔ **Clear membership boundaries:** These boundaries outline who the members are or how large the group can be. The members are those people who regularly provide services that help meet the group's goals.

- ✔ **A clear leadership structure:** This structure is how the group makes binding group decisions.

Eduardo Fritis's family exemplifies an *informal* social enterprise. As reported in the *Calgary Herald,* Fritis, his wife, and his 19-year-old son plan to sail throughout the Pacific handing out shoes, clothes, and eyeglasses to children living in poverty. He calls his enterprise Shoes for the World. The idea came to him after he saw a photograph of a happy boy showing off the first pair of shoes he ever owned. Fritis has sold nearly all his possessions to finance this humanitarian voyage. At the time of this writing, he plans to set sail over the next two years to Mexico, South America, French Polynesia, and elsewhere in the South Pacific. His enterprise *does* have a unique name and clear membership boundaries, but it lacks a clear leadership structure, so the group is informal.

Many social enterprises are no more formally organized than Fritis's. Indeed, he and his family might not even think of themselves in social entrepreneurial terms. They just want to mobilize themselves and distribute certain humanitarian necessities to children in need.

Consider another example, this time a *formal* group, but unincorporated. It, too, fits our definition of a social enterprise.

The Emeritus Association of the University of Calgary was founded in 1992 to serve its members, the university, and the public. Its objective is to be a vehicle that brings together emeriti for the betterment of the membership and their families, and to foster ways for its members to contribute to the life of the university and the larger community. This group has both a constitution and a set of bylaws, annually elects a slate of officers, holds an annual general meeting, collects dues each year, and has many other attributes of a formal group. But it isn't incorporated, even though it has successfully operated for 17 years as a lively outlet for the interests and concerns of former university faculty and administration.

These two examples show that you can solve problems and achieve social change, even if your enterprise remains unincorporated.

So, should you turn your social enterprise into a corporation? To answer this question, first you have to know what a corporation is.

Introducing Corporations: Nonprofit versus For-Profit

A *corporation* is a formal organization with a charter (a written document that creates an organizational entity such as a nonprofit group or a for-profit company). A *nonprofit* corporation may also have a governmental *tax-exempt status* — which means that the corporation doesn't have to pay federal and state or provincial taxes on money left after all expenses have been met.

All types of corporations are legally established entities within political jurisdictions such as a state, province, or national government. The key difference separating a nonprofit corporation from a for-profit corporation is that distribution of profits gained by nonprofit corporations to members of those corporations is prohibited. Instead of being paid out, profits must be retained by nonprofit corporations and used strictly for financing further production of the services that the group was founded to provide.

The nonprofit may use its profits to hire paid staff (see Chapter 13). These people are not members of the organization — they're employees. (*Members* of a nonprofit are the people responsible for directing the organization — the board of directors or trustees — and other volunteers, who may not be paid by it; see Chapter 8.) Otherwise, nonprofit corporations are similar to for-profit corporations.

There are four main types of corporations:

- ✔ **Nonprofit corporations:** These corporations are unable to distribute profits to members — that is, to its directors (see "Identifying and recruiting directors and trustees," later in this chapter). They can earn money; they just have to reinvest it back into the organization. But employees of the nonprofit are paid, just as are employees of businesses, but then they are not members of the corporation.

- ✔ **General corporations:** This is the most common corporate structure. The general corporation is a separate legal entity owned by stockholders, who are protected from the creditors of the business. A stockholder's personal liability is usually limited to the amount the person has invested in the corporation. General corporations are large-scale organizations.

- ✔ **Close corporation:** The close corporation tends to be limited to, say, 30 to 50 stockholders. The close corporation is well suited for one or more owners of a small corporation, usually a small business, only some of whom will actively manage it.

- ✔ **Limited liability company:** In this type of corporation, the owners' personal assets are protected from the corporation's liability for business debts. The owners may also benefit from the tax advantages of corporate partnerships.

What people mean when they talk about legal and charitable status

The *legal status* of a nonprofit social enterprise refers to whether it is formally incorporated within a state, province, nation, or other governmental jurisdiction. In the case of nonprofits, legal status may also refer to whether the enterprise is formally tax-exempt. Paid-staff nonprofits are nearly always incorporated and tax-exempt, whereas many grass-roots associations are not incorporated and, therefore, not officially tax-exempt. Small grassroots organizations are usually "informally tax-exempt," however — they generate little money and don't always report to the tax authorities any money they do generate.

If your social enterprise is incorporated, it may apply to government for formal exemption from taxation and thereby be recognized as a charitable group, or charity. A *charity* is formally organized, provides one or more public benefits (as opposed to member benefits), and receives a significant amount of its revenue from donations. Charities are also legally empowered to issue official statements to donors verifying the amount they gave to them. This is a substantial incentive for many potential donors, because they can claim a tax deduction against the amount they've given.

Very recently a hybrid of the nonprofit and for-profit corporation has been created in certain states: the *low-profit, limited-liability company* (L3C). The L3C is designed for for-profits with a social purpose — groups for which profit is a secondary goal. Profits can be distributed to shareholders, but L3Cs pay income taxes, and contributions to them are not tax deductible.

Weighing the Pros and Cons of Incorporation

We can't tell you whether to incorporate. But we can fill you in on the pros and cons, so that you know your options. Your decision will depend on a variety of conditions, including the nature of governmental regulations on incorporation, the need for external funding, the amount of help you can expect from other leaders, and the necessity of insuring against risk faced by members working in service of the enterprise's mission. Your personal preferences will also enter into your decision.

If, after reading this section, you want still more information about the pros and cons of incorporation, visit the Web site of Score, Counselors to America's Small Business (www.score.org). And don't forget the Internal Revenue Service (www.irs.gov), which offers many details on incorporation for charities that will also help you decide for or against taking this step.

A brief history of the corporation

According to Lee Drutman, an expert on the history of the corporation, the origin of the modern form may be traced to 1601. This was when Queen Elizabeth I established the East India Trading Company. At the time, the idea of the corporation bore little resemblance to the modern conception. The typical corporation was linked with the British government, which granted it a charter to undertake a particular project. The goal was to attract investors eager to finance large commercial projects, many of them involving geographic exploration.

Drutman says that in post-revolutionary America, corporations continued to be small organizations commonly chartered by one of the states for pursuing particular projects. They operated in such relatively restricted areas as banking and seafaring. They had a limited life, could make no political contributions, and couldn't hold stock in other companies. Their owners were responsible for any criminal acts committed by the owners or employees when working in the name of the corporation. Moreover, there was no principle of *limited liability,* which states that investors are exempted from any responsibility for harm and loss brought about by their corporation.

There have been many changes since then, leading to the present day, in which the corporation has become an ascendant institution in many modern societies. Nowadays we're highly dependent on the products and services the corporation typically provides. Many corporations, using advertising, public relations, and the mass media, have the capacity to influence the ways we see the world and each other. We often entrust our finances and healthcare to corporations, and they're often a central link in our communication with other people. What's more, most people work for a corporation. In some countries — mostly in the West — corporations greatly influence the legislative process, sometimes more than any branch of government. These days they're the source of many of our essential services such as water and electricity. In the United States, corporations have constitutional rights, can be of unlimited size, and can live forever.

Informal social enterprises have undoubtedly existed since mankind first faced social problems, and someone took the initiative to solve them — with or without someone else's help. But formal incorporation could have been possible only with development of the arrangements just described. Thus, in 1869, Florence Nightingale, with Dr. Elizabeth Blackwell, was able to open the Women's Medical College, an incorporated entity. This was the world's first school of nursing.

The pros

The main advantage of incorporating is that doing so usually makes it easier to bring in money. Only incorporated social enterprises

- ✔ Are eligible for official charitable status (but only if they're nonprofit).
- ✔ Are eligible for special advantageous tax rates, if they're taxable at all.
- ✔ May invest in venture philanthropy (see Chapter 8).

- ✔ Are eligible to receive donations from either traditional or venture-philanthropic foundations (see Chapter 8).

- ✔ May enter into partnerships with private companies for the purpose of creating profit and social value.

- ✔ May issue shares to members who buy them at a specified rate. This arrangement gives the enterprise needed cash with which to operate.

- ✔ Can enter into legal contracts and other long-term agreements with other organizations.

- ✔ Are eligible for full banking privileges.

- ✔ May own real property.

- ✔ May insure members against the risks that may be incurred while working for the enterprise.

- ✔ Can protect their officials against having to use their personal possessions to pay off the debts of the enterprise in the event of liquidation.

- ✔ Can protect their individual members against lawsuits lodged against the organization.

- ✔ Can ensure that all members have, in the event of liquidation, equal access to the proceeds from the sale of all organizational assets.

You can see from this list — which is just a *sample* of the advantages of incorporating — that if you're the leader of a large-scale social enterprise, you probably do want to incorporate. Your organization's visibility, scope of operations, size of membership, financial needs, and other attributes are likely pushing your toward becoming a corporation.

Many of the advantages of incorporation have to do with particular legal conditions, which vary from state to state. For this reason, you should seek professional advice to ensure that you properly navigate the inevitable maze of rules and regulations that will come to bear on your social enterprise in the state where you live. The terrain is legal, but good advice and much of the paperwork need not necessarily come through a lawyer. (We come back to this subject in the "Incorporating Your Social Enterprise" section, later in this chapter.)

The cons

For some social enterprises, many, if not all, of the advantages listed in the preceding section don't have much appeal. These organizations have no money to invest, no interest in pursuing profit, and no assets of any significance to liquidate. Sure, they'd be thrilled if a foundation gave them a hefty donation, but maybe not at the expense of the time it would take to do the paperwork that accompanies such largesse. Some social enterprises may also have an aversion to some or all of the conditions restricting use of the money they receive when they're incorporated.

Many social entrepreneurs can recite a litany of the disadvantages of incorporation. Here are some examples:

- ✔ Incorporation requires considerable initial legal paperwork as well as more of the same over the lifetime of the corporation. This requirement cuts into time that could be devoted to realizing the enterprise's mission.

- ✔ There are often legal restrictions on the activities legally established charitable organizations may engage in. In general, their activities must relate to the basis on which they've been incorporated as a charity.

- ✔ With incorporation, the enterprise may tend to become too big and too bureaucratic. As a result, many of participants may be alienated from its mission. (See Chapter 13 for more on the perils of bureaucracy.)

- ✔ Incorporation, because of additional responsibilities toward government and members of the enterprise, often requires hiring special full- or part-time personnel to do such things as the accounting and examining and establishing various legal arrangements.

- ✔ In some countries, incorporated groups can be held liable for certain risks such as medical risks of members carrying out the mission, a kind of liability that unincorporated groups escape. Of course, the risks are there for unincorporated groups, but they would be, in this situation, borne by individual members who may be required to sign waivers freeing the enterprise from such responsibility. Note, too, that U.S. corporations operating in foreign countries must abide by the laws regulating these risks that have been established in those countries.

- ✔ Incorporation often calls for formalizing certain operating procedures. For example, meetings may have to be run using, say, *Robert's Rules of Order,* and it may be required that minutes be taken. In formal procedures, these minutes are subject to approval and official signature at the next official gathering of the group.

- ✔ Incorporation for nonprofits requires that a board of directors or trustees be established, and, in the case of for-profit enterprises, this may necessitate recruiting a group of shareholders.

- ✔ Incorporation may set in motion forces that eventually stifle your ingenuity and drive. It can lead to increased bureaucratization of your efforts to manage and sustain.

Incorporating Your Social Enterprise

Incorporation is a series of steps. First up is the process of registering the name of your enterprise. Then you have the matter of identifying its directors, or trustees. After that, you have to consider your enterprise's constitution or, if a for-profit group, its articles of incorporation. Finally, your social enterprise will need bylaws.

Of course, we can't in one chapter tell you everything you need to know to incorporate your social enterprise. If you want to go further in your research, we recommend *Incorporating Your Business For Dummies,* by The Company Corporation (Wiley), as well as Anthony Mancuso's *How to Form a Nonprofit Corporation* (NOLO Press).

Registering your enterprise's name

The process of incorporation begins with choosing a name (discussed in detail in Chapter 10) and then doing the paperwork to legally establish the name you've selected. Although the paperwork of incorporation can be annoying, choosing a name is usually very much the opposite. You and others close to you can have a great time brainstorming over the best possible designation for your enterprise.

You need to choose a name that's not the same as, or even similar to, the other legal names on file with the governmental office where you're registering. Most governments require you to follow their formal procedure for determining whether your proposed name is sufficiently distinctive.

If your proposed name is similar to the name of another organization, and you still want to use it, the government will probably require you to get formal assurance from the other organization that it won't challenge your proposal. If you don't follow this advice, you may face all kinds of legal repercussions.

A good place to start your name search is by searching your state government's Web site for the branch that deals with corporate registration. Instructions for corporate registration are likely available online at the Web site of the state office dealing with incorporation. You can find this office by Googling "incorporating in *the name of your state.*"

If you're setting up a for-profit social enterprise, you'll also have to decide on the kind of for-profit legal entity it will be. Will it be a nonprofit corporation, a general corporation, a close corporation, or a limited liability company (see "Introducing Corporations: Nonprofit versus For-Profit," earlier in this chapter)? Will it be, for example, XYZ Incorporated or XYZ Limited?

The typical procedure is to send your chosen name to the appropriate governmental office in the state in which you intend to incorporate your enterprise, which will then check its database of all corporations within its jurisdiction. If there are no red flags — no identical or similar names in the jurisdiction — you'll be free to seek incorporation under your proposed name. If the government office sends you a list of names identical and similar to the one you've proposed, you'll have to go back to the drawing board.

There may be a time limit on how long you have to submit another choice; if you go beyond it, you'll have to reapply.

Identifying and recruiting directors and trustees

We use the terms *director* and *trustee* interchangeably to refer to the members of a board of directors or board of trustees. These are the people who set organizational goals and policies, see to financial need, establish budgets, and report on the organization to its stakeholders, among other functions. The number of directors/trustees required for an incorporated nonprofit social enterprise varies somewhat by political jurisdiction: Some require only one; others require two, three, or four. Whatever the number of directors required, that number will have to be stated either in your constitution or in your bylaws (keep reading to find out about these).

Though you aren't obligated to be a director, you probably want to be one. After all, the directors in an organization have the greatest power in it — especially the president. Only as a director can you participate in the processes discussed in the preceding paragraph. If you're required to have other directors, it's up to you to find people who are passionate about the mission of your enterprise and can give the time needed to help realize it.

Finding directors/trustees may prove to be difficult. Start by checking with the appropriate governmental office to see whether it stipulates that a specified number of directors must be centrally interested in the mission. The regulations may allow for one or more directors whose role is only to serve as volunteers to help run the organization on a routine basis, and who don't also have to meet the requirement of being passionate about its goals.

A good director will be as passionate as anyone on the board about the goals and mission of your enterprise. Ideally, a director will also have had experience on other boards and show a capacity for working with others on the board. In the democratic give-and-take at board meetings, patience is often a virtue. Plus, a good director is seldom absent from board meetings, arrives on time at each one, and doesn't leave early.

Directors may also have to meet a residency requirement, such as a specified proportion of the board must live within the jurisdiction of the governmental office. There may also be an age requirement as well as rules about whether close relatives of directors may join their ranks. Finally, in for-profits, rules may exist about people who get paid for services rendered to the enterprise and whether they may also be directors. That such people do get paid for services is, however, an uncommon arrangement. If they're allowed, there may be an additional regulation stating the proportion of paid personnel who may serve on a board of directors.

Knowing in advance about all contingencies is a good idea. It would be awkward if, in your enthusiasm for incorporating your enterprise, you invited someone to be a director only to find out later that the governmental office didn't allow that category of person to participate. Again, you'll find much of the information you need on the Web site for your appropriate state governmental office.

Research in nonprofit studies has revealed three common approaches to recruiting directors to the boards of nonprofit organizations. One conclusion from these studies is that some form of democracy is the best way to choose a new director, even though other methods can also be effective. The following are all democratic approaches because directors in nonprofit boards must, by constitutional fiat, either eventually stand for election at an annual general meeting (discussed later in this chapter) or, more immediately, be approved by a vote by the board itself.

- ✔ **The active approach:** You advertise for your directors, choosing the best from among the candidates who present themselves. You might do this, for example, in your monthly bulletin, on your Web site, in the bulletins of kindred organizations, or in local print media.

- ✔ **The passive approach:** You wait for suitable candidates to emerge by whatever route is available (for example, they offer their candidacy to you or to a member of your enterprise).

- ✔ **The co-option approach:** You may want to co-opt one or more people you're convinced will make fine directors. In other words, you and your board members invite such people to join the board, commonly with the provision that, at the next annual general meeting or board meeting, they have to be voted in.

Which method you choose may depend on advertising costs, how much time you have, the urgency of filling the post, and the availability of suitable candidates.

Except where governmental regulations allow otherwise, the board of directors of your social enterprise must be staffed with people who are highly dedicated to its mission. These people must also be clear of any personal conflict of interest with that mission. You may also want to have members on the board who are also members of the target of benefits.

For enterprises that serve a membership group, such as a profession or a trade union, board members are usually elected from among the larger membership for a limited term. In this case, directors, by dint of their voluntary involvement with the enterprise, automatically espouse its goals and mission.

Many people who volunteer their time for a social enterprise do so with a commercial interest — although the work may be personally fulfilling, they also enjoy the networking and résumé benefits of being on the board. This is not a problem unless it hampers the operation of the organization. For example, a board member may push for the organization to hire a company to perform a service that the board member would stand to financially gain from.

Don't allow members on boards who have commercial interests in your enterprise or other personal goals that are incompatible with or marginal to it. Do your research and vet your candidates thoroughly. For example, you might think it's a good idea to recruit John Doe to your board, until a member of the board observes that, some years back, Doe started an organization whose mission clashes with yours.

Staffing boards of directors in social enterprises and other nonprofit groups remains a difficult endeavor. You're probably caught up with the details of reaching your mission and goals, so you may find yourself giving short shrift to recruiting members to your board of directors. Even when you find people, you may be slack about educating them so that they participate in the board effectively. You should always be looking to build and identify potentially good board members. Set aside considerable time to find your candidates and fill them in on what's required. You'll be glad you did.

Drafting your constitution

We use the term *constitution* to refer to the body of written rules prescribing the major elements of the structure of an organization and its principal activities, either for nonprofit or for-profit groups. (In your readings and discussions you may occasionally run into other terms. Sometimes the term *articles of organization* is used to refer to the constitutions of incorporated nonprofit groups, whereas *articles of incorporation* is reserved for the constitutions of incorporated for-profit groups.) A *constitution* is a democratic document that defines and protects the rights of members of the collectivity, whether it be a country, corporation, or social enterprise.

In your readings and discussions, you may occasionally run into other terms. Sometimes *articles of organization* is used to refer to the constitutions of incorporated nonprofit groups, whereas *articles of incorporation* is reserved for the constitutions of incorporated for-profit groups.

What do corporate constitutions typically contain? The following list of articles will suffice in most cases, though you may certainly add others you believe are necessary (for example, a clause about signing authority for checks, procedures for grant applications, or a clause about non-remuneration of volunteer members). The main idea in forming the constitution of a nonprofit is to establish its identity and basic operating procedures using principles that are unlikely to change. Changing your constitution (depending on its clauses pertaining to changing it) may be done through a formal amendment procedure, which is unwieldy and may provoke dissent, or done through a formal vote during a board meeting.

Your constitution should cover the items in the following sections.

Name

Be sure to include any official acronym designating your enterprise's name, the official shortened versions of the name, and, with for-profits, the legal commercial designation (such as Ltd., Co., and Inc.). For more information on choosing your name, see "Registering your enterprise's name," earlier in this chapter, as well as Chapter 10.

Mission statement

The mission statement proclaims the purpose of your enterprise — in other words, what you're doing for your target of benefits. (See Chapter 7 for more information.)

Mission orientation is the basic distinguishing characteristic of nonprofit groups.

Goals or objectives

Goals and objectives are what your enterprise is trying to achieve by following its mission. In social entrepreneurship, the goal is generally to change society to benefit a human, animal, or environmental target.

Membership

Here you define who may become a *member* of your social enterprise. That person could simply be anyone who pays the annual dues, with the amount set out in the bylaws. But you may also want to specify additional criteria such as age, commitment to your goals, and other identifiers related to your mission. But be sure that your country or state does not prohibit excluding people based on the criteria you choose. For example, if your enterprise centers on women helping women, then you may want to limit membership to women — just make sure such exclusion is legal. If it organizes people against crime in a certain neighborhood, then membership might be restricted to those who live there.

In addition, you may want to consider a category of *lifetime membership* (criteria and dues to be set out in the bylaws). Finally, you may want to allow for *honorary members* (who would pay no dues) and *corporate members* (who would pay dues, sometimes quite substantial). You can set out in your bylaws whether honorary and corporate members will have the right to vote

Officers

An *officer* in the nonprofit sector is someone who holds an office and, by dint of that position, participates in the management or direction of a nonprofit group. Here are the most common officers of such groups and their minimum responsibilities:

- ✔ President: The president sets the agendas for and presides at meetings of the board and those of the executive committee, oversees all board functions as well as the responsibilities of the executive director (if there is one), and may be the person who represents the organization to the outside world.

- ✔ Secretary: The secretary takes notes at board and executive committee meetings and writes them up as minutes for approval of the board.

- ✔ Treasurer: The treasurer monitors the flow of money in and out of the organization, keeps books related to these processes, and works with an accountant to prepare the annual audited financial report. In small organizations, the posts of secretary and treasurer are sometimes filled by the same person.

Some nonprofits and social enterprises name a vice president, and some don't. Even if you see no need for this position when framing your constitution, we still recommend that you include it there. A vice president, apart from substituting for the president (which might happen only rarely), is also a director as well as part of the executive committee (see later in this list). In some organizations, the vice president, after serving a specified term, will become the president and then, possibly, the *past president.*

Once your organization is up and running, all officers are elected, whether by the membership as a whole or by a committee elected by the membership. Still, organizations starting out don't have a membership, so the founders must appoint the initial board.

Board of directors/trustees

The *board of directors,* or *board of trustees,* consists of the officers of the enterprise along with a specified number of other members. Everyone on this committee is a director or trustee. In many nonprofit groups, the board is the highest policymaking and administrative unit.

Experts in nonprofit research consider boards of directors to be central to nonprofit effectiveness. Nonetheless, expanded boards tend to be unwieldy in small enterprises, which can usually be managed by a handful of officers.

Directors at large — members who are not officers — are also commonly subject to election in the same way as the officers.

Every constitution should contain a clause for provisionally appointing directors when a vacancy occurs mid-term, a process usually carried out by the board itself. Appointed directors are then officially accepted or rejected by an election held at the next annual general meeting.

Executive committee

Your enterprise's executive committee is a subcommittee of your board of directors. The typical executive committee is composed of the officers: the president, vice president, secretary, and treasurer. It acts between board meetings, being charged with implementing policy set by the board. Executive committees are common, especially in large boards of directors (those with 15 or more members).

Fiscal year

The *fiscal year* is your enterprise's financial year. By and large, modern governments and organizations conduct their financial business according to fiscal years. As soon as you have a budget, you need to account to members and funders for the ways it's spent. That accounting is commonly reckoned according to the fixed 12-month period.

You may want your fiscal year to coincide with that of the federal government, from whom you may receive some funding — in the United States the fiscal year runs from October 1 through September 30 the next year. Or you may find it more convenient to set year fiscal year with the calendar, starting in January. Maybe it makes sense to harmonize it with that of your principal corporate or foundational source of funding. In short, determining your fiscal year should be carefully thought out.

Annual general meeting

Holding an annual general meeting (AGM) to which all members are invited is traditional. Constitutions usually specify the month in which such a meeting must occur, which tends to be coordinated with the group's fiscal year. The AGM is where

- Officers and other directors stand for election.

- Treasurers make their reports.

- Members may question all their directors on matters of financial concern.

- Chairs of committees (set out in the bylaws) report on what they've accomplished since the previous AGM.

Amendment procedures

Constitutions are supposed to have a sort of permanency about them. But the world changes, members of the enterprise develop new perspectives, and as a result, constitutions must occasionally be modified. You may need to add a director to the board, change the fiscal year, or redefine membership criteria. Typically, in nonprofit groups, the board of directors develops proposals for such changes. These proposals are then presented to the membership for their ratification at the next AGM.

Constitutions must also allow for proposals for amendments that emanate from the general membership. Such a clause serves as an additional democratic check on the board. If the amendments are ratified, the constitution is then rewritten accordingly.

Because your constitution contains your legal articles of incorporation, changes made to it through amendments must ordinarily be filed with the governmental agency enabling your incorporation. The steps to be followed for doing this are usually available on the Internet, though you'll have to send in signed paper copies of the changes.

Laying down the bylaws

A *bylaw* is a rule created for and adopted by a nonprofit group, primarily for governance of its members and regulation of its routine affairs. A set of bylaws consists of all the formal internal rules and procedures for operating and governing a nonprofit corporation.

In some governmental jurisdictions, a set of bylaws is known as a *code of regulations*.

There are no set criteria for bylaw content. Nevertheless, the Citizens Media Law Project (www.citmedialaw.org) has set out some general areas of nonprofit life where bylaws are commonly written:

- Responsibilities of nonprofit corporate officers and directors
- Board size and how they're elected
- The timing and methods of board meetings
- Methods of functioning for the board of directors
- Distribution of grant monies

Drafting bylaws can be a complicated and, hence, intimidating undertaking. But strategies exist for writing satisfactory bylaws without need to hire a lawyer. We recommend Anthony Mancuso's book *How to Form a Nonprofit Corporation* (NOLO Press). Mancuso, a lawyer, guides you through the process of creating bylaws appropriate to nonprofits, including nonprofit social enterprises.

Unlike constitutional amendments, changes in an organization's bylaws don't have to be filed with any governmental agency, so bylaws are much more easily changed than constitutions are. Still, you have to keep a record of your original bylaws and all changes you make to them. In the United States, the people responsible for incorporating a nonprofit and/or its initial directors (if named in the articles of incorporation) typically have the authority to set and adopt that group's original bylaws at its initial organizational meeting. Though not a legal requirement, some organizations require that this original document be ratified at the first AGM (see the preceding section for more on AGMs).

Sets of bylaws are typically quite lengthy, as well as highly detailed and specific. You can find samples of them on the Internet. We recommend that you start by visiting the Web site of the Foundation Center at `http://foundationcenter.org/getstarted/faqs/html/samplebylaws.html`, which features links to several samples. Additionally, you can use your favorite search engine to search for "sample nonprofit bylaws." Keep in mind that bylaws are, of necessity, highly particular documents, setting out rules and procedures peculiar to the organization to which they pertain.

Cutting through the red tape

You may feel that all this detail about constitutions and bylaws is leading to a life of red tape and the need to adhere excessively to bureaucratic procedures and formalities. Plus, don't we argue in Chapter 13 that you should avoid over-bureaucratization and bureaucratic bloat? Aren't we contradicting ourselves in promoting the need for a constitution and set of bylaws for your social enterprise?

Over-bureaucratization comes from adding more organizational functions than *required* or more people to carry them out than *needed*. Creating a constitution and a complementary set of bylaws is in no way excessive or superfluous. Instead they serve as the very organizational foundation of your nonprofit. Constitutions and bylaws also help ensure that your enterprise functions democratically.

Nonetheless, bits of over-bureaucratization might creep into the framing of your bylaws or the bylaws themselves. Bylaws, among other things, regulate routine behavior in the organization, and it's common for the organization to try to control member behavior that might be harmful to its goals and mission. This could happen, for example, when setting the number of directors or the number of signatures (usually those of directors) required on checks issued by the enterprise. The treasurer and president normally do the signing, but a third person might be appointed as a substitute when one of the first two is unavailable. Over-bureaucratization may occur when a super-cautious director insists on requiring, say, a fourth signature.

Authors of bylaws sometimes want to set more rules than necessary for effectively running board meetings. The best antidote we know of to enacting unnecessary rules or rules that are too constraining is for you and board members to constantly ask yourselves whether your enterprise can do without the rule being considered. Another way of living by this precaution is to always try to find the simplest way of achieving the purpose of the proposed rule.

Part IV
Keeping Your Organization Running for the Long Haul

The 5th Wave   By Rich Tennant

"Remember when Bruce wanted to 'rally the troops,' we all just got a memo in e-mail?"

In this part . . .

A social enterprise is like any other ongoing endeavor — it needs to be nurtured and tended in order to survive. This part focuses on the best ways of doing that.

Chapter 15 offers insight into the business end of social business — how to use capitalism to your advantage. In Chapter 16, we explore the concept and application of leadership, a key aspect of the success of any organization. In Chapter 17, we go over the critical concepts of management. The part finishes up with Chapter 18, which is about the power of collaboration and the wisdom of teams.

Chapter 15

Putting the Entrepreneur in Social Entrepreneurship

In This Chapter

▶ Figuring out what an entrepreneur is

▶ Discovering what makes social entrepreneurs different

▶ Cultivating pragmatic creativity

*W*e may be about to land in hot water with some people. Problems sometimes crop up when we try to define the term *entrepreneur*. There's a very popular misconception that an entrepreneur can only be a special form of capitalist, one who tries to set up a new business — or perhaps save and revive a failing one — with the ultimate goal, of course, of pursuing a profit.

We don't exactly *argue* with that position — it's correct as far as it goes. We just think it's insufficient and incomplete, especially for our purposes. Business entrepreneurs are certainly one kind of entrepreneur. But they're not the only kind. In this chapter, we tell you our definition of an entrepreneur. Then we explain how social entrepreneurs are different from the rest. Finally, we cover the important social entrepreneurial principles of creativity and pragmatism.

Defining What an Entrepreneur Is

What's fundamental about entrepreneurs is that they embody and exhibit an entrepreneurial *mindset* or *spirit*. This mindset can be applied within four large domains of human activity — not only to general economic and business (that is, for-profit) concerns but also to solving social and cultural problems (as is the case with social and political entrepreneurs), contributing to scientific knowledge, and improving the ways in which information is shared across the other domains. These different entrepreneurial domains are shown in Figure 15-1.

Domains of Entrepreneurial Practice

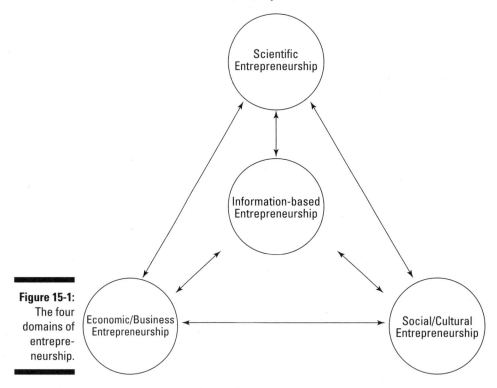

Figure 15-1:
The four domains of entrepreneurship.

But even more than that, the entrepreneurial mindset can range freely *across* all the domains. You can be *mostly* a social entrepreneur whose work is primarily nonprofit, while at the same time find ways to generate a profit that can sustain your efforts. (We talk about this possibility in Chapter 8.)

Social entrepreneurs may also, for example, find themselves practicing *political* (another form of social/cultural entrepreneurship) and *knowledge* entrepreneurship along the way. All these possibilities and more are suggested in Figure 15-1. In short, entrepreneurship can express itself widely and creatively in many areas of human activity.

A tremendously important example of a hybrid entrepreneur — in this case, working across scientific and social/cultural domains — is Dr. Norman Borlaug, winner of the 1970 Nobel Peace Prize. Dr. Borlaug is credited with saving the lives of at least *a billion people.* A key figure in the green revolution, Borlaug, a microbiologist, worked tirelessly until his death in 2009 to bring the world spectacularly successful new strains of high-yielding, disease-resistant wheat. Today, revolutionary yields are now harvested in Latin American countries including Mexico, the Middle East, and Africa, though plenty more places could benefit from Dr. Borlaug's ideas.

Doing more than minding the gap

So, what are the characteristics of an entrepreneurial mindset?

Things start off with a gap between what *is* and what *ought to be* — between reality and imagination. The world seems out of whack, and not what it could or should be. To the entrepreneur, this gap often causes a powerful emotional response — sometimes even anxiety and frustration. The solution can't be to simply "mind the gap," as the British say about stepping between a subway car and platform. In the entrepreneur's view, the gap has to be *repaired*.

You may be thinking, "But isn't that just discontent? After all, aren't our lives filled with unlimited needs, wants, and desires that we struggle daily to satisfy? We're hungry, we're homeless, we're lonely, we want to have kids, we want the joys of family and community, we want spiritual rewards, and on and on. . . . And we're constantly trying to find ways to gratify all these urges. So, are we all entrepreneurs then?"

No, and here's why: Although we all feel the initial discontent that motivates entrepreneurs, entrepreneurs organize to do something about it. Entrepreneurs seem to be cut from a different cloth. Many people, if they sense that can't get from Point A (what is) to Point B (what ought to be), *downgrade* their expectations so that getting to somewhere short of Point B becomes doable and acceptable.

And that isn't necessarily a bad move. The problem, of course, is that it means settling for less, which isn't what they really wanted in the first place. So they're still left with a gnawing, half-empty feeling. And that emptiness still irritates them and can cause more dissatisfaction.

Identifying the characteristics of the entrepreneurial mindset

Entrepreneurs see challenges differently from most folks. Coping has its place, but not here and not for them. If a problem is important to them, for whatever reasons, entrepreneurs don't cope. They won't settle for less. Lowering their expectations in order to work with limited ability and resources is not an option for entrepreneurs. Instead, entrepreneurs fix firmly on their ideals and vision and work on *upgrading* their own abilities, those of others, and the resources around them, in order to *repair* the gap. That's hard work — the entrepreneur's vision may be quite lofty, and the abilities and resources, at least initially, meager.

But hard work is not a deterrent to entrepreneurs. They stubbornly cling to their vision and are resilient and enthusiastic in believing, perhaps beyond apparent reason, that they can materialize it. They believe they can improve themselves and others and marshal the resources they need in order to realize their dreams.

When Thomas Edison was working on a prototype of the electric light bulb, he remarked after one success, "If it will burn that number of hours [4 ½] now, I know I can make it burn 100!" This self-assurance was not really a sudden result of his success with that particular bulb. The self-assurance, the conviction, the integrity, all existed long before — even before the electric light bulb was nothing more than a glimmer of an idea in a notebook.

In psychological terms, entrepreneurs have a tremendous *internal locus of control.* This means they believe that, in the end, success or failure depends on their own efforts. Very simply, they believe in themselves and don't give up at the first sign of trouble.

Entrepreneurs are also simultaneously creative and pragmatic. It can't be any other way. If they're going to realize their ambitions, they must creatively overcome the limitations of their current abilities and resources by rethinking what they have at hand and what they need in order to succeed — and they must do so in practical, down-to-earth ways. This stuff is off-road, and there are no maps.

In a nutshell, the entrepreneurial mindset can be summarized as follows:

✔ The sense of a lack between *is* and *ought to be* and the motivation to repair that gap.

✔ The conviction that lowering expectations solves nothing; instead, the answer is to change and improve the world to conform to one's vision.

✔ The acceptance that changing the world is awfully hard work because abilities and resources are inevitably in need of great development.

✔ The internal locus of control to develop deficient abilities and resources through constant, creative, and pragmatic innovation.

The qualities discussed in this section are the qualities you should cultivate in yourself from now on if you want to be the best entrepreneur you can be.

Knowing What Makes a Social Entrepreneur Different

So, how is the social entrepreneurial mindset different from the general entrepreneurial mindset we cover in the preceding section? We spell it out in this section.

Focusing on what is and what ought to be

One difference is the specific type of *is* versus *ought to be* troubles that motivate a response from social entrepreneurs. Social entrepreneurs are deeply concerned with the social problems and issues of the world, such as poverty, equitable distribution of food, shelter, health, education, human rights, and so forth. They are, in short, *humanitarians* who envision a far better, kinder, more tolerant, and cooperative world. This is not necessarily so for the general entrepreneurial mindset, or for other types of entrepreneurs (refer to Figure 15-1).

Feeling people's pain

At the same time, social entrepreneurs tend to be deeply distressed, perhaps more so than other entrepreneurs, by the lack of their own and others' abilities and external resources to meet the desperate and visceral needs of others. People's lives, or quality of life, are at stake, and this is more than just an abstract problem, as it might be for a business entrepreneur seeking profit for profit's sake. Put it another way: Helping someone escape poverty, for example, is a heavier, more serious burden to bear than helping someone light her home or office, as Edison was concerned with.

Facing trying conditions

After you leave the Western democratic umbrella, the work to be done in social entrepreneurship is, in many cases, beset by difficult political and economic environments. Business entrepreneurs, in contrast, generally operate under the good graces of democracy and generally supportive political and economic agreements. That's not necessarily the case for social entrepreneurs who may be operating in extremely hostile or unfavorable conditions.

Lingana Foundation (www.lingana.org) and its supporters are trying to assist Darfurian refugees just inside the border of eastern Chad. Doctors Without Borders often intercedes in areas where violence and displacement are widespread and where other humanitarian organizations have failed to meet massive and extremely urgent needs. This kind of risk is not normally borne by business entrepreneurs (though there are exceptions).

Being inventive out of necessity

In social entrepreneurship, the level of creative and pragmatic innovation involved, thanks to the heroic efforts required, can be nothing short of astonishing. If necessity is the mother of invention, you can see that played out remarkably in some of the emerging technologies being developed by initially small-scale eco-entrepreneurs to mitigate the effects of climate change and other forms of ecological degradation.

Take, for example, the work of a former engineer for the oil industry, now known as China's "Solar King," Huang Ming. Thanks to Ming's life-changing decision to leave the oil industry and concentrate on building a clean-air legacy for his newborn daughter, Dezhou City in the province of Shandong, China, is now 70 percent solar powered. It's popularly known as Solar Valley. Ming changed his thinking from oil to solar power, which resulted in staggering technological change. He employs 60,000 people at Himin Solar Energy Group, where the corporate headquarters is the world's largest solar-powered building. Ming's mission is nothing less than to promote a global cultural and environmental revolution that will energize China and the world through solar power.

Thinking local, no matter where

Social entrepreneurship is definitely not always the same thing as familiar high-profile international aid programs. Far-reaching social entrepreneurship has to always place a value on entrepreneurship at the local level. The nearby sidebar "Is creative capitalism social entrepreneurship?" mentions the difference between entrepreneurship and the history of Western attempts to aid poorer nations. Daniel Lavin, director of the Community Initiative Program (CIP; http://cipsierraleone.blogspot.com), and his partners Manfred Musa in Sierra Leone and the Fig Tree Foundation (www.figtreefoundation.org), show how "real development" must favor all forms of local entrepreneurship over everything else. Their own brand of social entrepreneurship, through CIP, lends a hand to local entrepreneurs who typically have a business focus (though this, in theory, need not always be the case) and who always look to strengthen local community projects.

Lavin has developed five keys to determining whether local entrepreneurship is really being benefited when Western organizations and companies arrive with their solutions (restated here with his kind permission):

- **Local:** Who's driving the priority? The donor, the organization, or the individual, group, or community? Are materials locally available or imported? Are methods appropriate for the local environment? External funding organizations love to erect buildings, which look great in pamphlets but later leave locals responsible for their maintenance and repair, even though there are no means for upkeep.

- **Ownership:** Does the individual, group, or community you're working with have an investment at stake? Does the project create an unfair advantage? When external donor agencies approach locals, money seems to be no object, and so recipients have no stake in the resources that flow their way. Irresponsible use can result. Local business plans fail in practicality, profitability, and accountability.

- ✔ **Repeatability:** When the project is over, could the individual, group, or community replicate what was done? Could others, and surrounding communities, without additional support, replicate the "development"? If rebuilding is necessary, is the knowledge available locally to do that? Can other local entities emulate the success of the project elsewhere without assistance? True development comes from projects completed autonomously.

- ✔ **Profitability:** Does the project generate a sustaining profit? Does it actually cover true costs? (Ignoring capital costs paid for by outsiders is unrealistic and can lead to disaster.) If profitability occurs only with outside influence and contributions, when that support stops, the project will fail.

- ✔ **Sustainability:** If outside supporters walk away, what happens to the project? Only when funding organizations or donors are *absent* can true development happen. Real development happens over the long term when everyone but the recipient of support has walked away.

Fostering Pragmatic Creativity

In the "Being inventive out of necessity" section, earlier in this chapter, we tell you that a primary characteristic of social entrepreneurs is their creative and yet down-to-earth, practical ability to innovate, brought on by the enormous real-life challenges they face. In this section, we look at ways in which your pragmatic creativity can be fostered.

Recognizing the power of story

The first, most important step to take in developing your pragmatic creativity is to get your story in order. That is, weave your passion and drive into a compelling narrative that engages people. Your story should be clear and true and authentic to the core.

As we've pointed out, entrepreneurship lives in the wide uncertainties between *is* and *ought to be*. Entrepreneurship embraces the unknown, chaos, and out-of-the-box thinking. As anthropology tells us, whenever humanity crosses the threshold from the comforts of everyday life into uncertain territory, our finely honed ability to take seemingly disconnected events and weave them into our life stories sustains us through the journey.

In one of his songs, Emmanuel Jal, child soldier, survivor of horrific genocide, internationally renowned rap artist, social entrepreneur, and founder of GUA Africa (www.gua-africa.org) sings, "I believe I've survived for a reason, to tell my story to touch lives."

In the case of entrepreneurs, their unyielding vision, acknowledgment of inadequate capacities, and paradoxical sense of potential lead to a practical urgency that is woven into the fabric of their stories — which they're happy to tell over and over to themselves and anyone else who will listen. In that telling, the power of the story to sustain the enterprise thrives and grows.

Is "creative capitalism" social entrepreneurship?

Microsoft founder and philanthropist Bill Gates recently argued that a hybrid form of business and social or ecological entrepreneurship in pursuit of a double or triple bottom line (profit plus social and environmental good) is a viable approach to meeting some of the world's most pressing problems. He calls this approach *creative capitalism*.

Bill Gates is a big deal and commands a lot of respect, so his notion of creative capitalism has sparked a lot of interest. Creative capitalism suggests that many Western multinational corporations, by tapping into their tremendous pools of human and other resources, can meet the challenges of our day and still turn a profit. Although this sounds extremely attractive, it may not be, by definition, particularly *entrepreneurial* — especially at the local level where it counts the most.

Why not? Because the approach basically calls for re-allocation of already existing talents and resources, instead of the promotion of local entrepreneurial activity that demands the best creative and pragmatic responses from those directly affected. The entrepreneurial mindset at the heart of dignity, integrity, adaptability, and social development could be seriously compromised. Unhealthy dependencies could result from the hopes that some corporate-backed cavalry will be riding in to save the day. A lot of

research bears out our criticism here. The history of corporate interventions is littered with failures that lacked local entrepreneurial "fit." The documentary *What Are We Doing Here?* provides an eyewitness account of the failures of Western intervention in Africa, in particular.

We don't mean to denigrate the possibilities for large corporations, universities, and governments to help. But if that help is to move from just a new form of charity to real development of broken societies, it must move from being another fancy form of *handout* to being a legitimate *hand up*. Tied aid — aid with strings attached — or Western investments with expectations of financial return are not social entrepreneurship. In our opinion, fostering local and autonomous entrepreneurship is the way to go.

Local entrepreneurs may be looking for assistance as they innovate. They're not looking, however, to have things done for them by distant, faceless institutions, whether for or not for profit. This is where the poor "fit" comes in. Western corporations know little if anything of local cultures, experiences, or dreams. The gap between *is* and *ought to be*, which is what must be dealt with after all, is the entrepreneur's, often embodied and storied in his own life and culture.

Boosting confidence with the Thomas theorem

The most important thing you can do to boost your confidence is *expect to succeed*. Too often, expectations are either of mediocrity, indifference, or helplessness. Clearly, if anyone has to avoid these negative expectations, it's you because you must succeed where there is little but a history of indifference or failure.

According to a classic little theorem called the Thomas theorem, devised by the American sociologist W. I. Thomas, situations that are defined as real are real in their consequences. The classic example is when a rumor of a bank failure starts a stampede to withdraw money from the bank — the crisis has become real, even though it was just a rumor. So, expecting to succeed means defining your success as *really real*, not as if it merely *could* be real. When you consistently treat your eventual success as real, real consequences will flow from

that, which might not otherwise. One reason for that is because other people will be far more apt to take you seriously and treat your success as real if you do. Treasure the support of those who, like you, see the reality of your success. They may be able to provide you with critical resources when you most need them.

When you're not succeeding, however — and these times will occur — you must not give up, but instead should seek out the best possible help. So-called *help-seeking behavior* is a sign of confidence and self-esteem. Those who don't seek help, or don't know how to seek help when they're in trouble, are in very deep trouble.

When you're succeeding, expect *more* success — this is the basis of any winning streak.

Someone who calls herself an entrepreneur but who doesn't develop a practically urgent story to tell is probably an armchair moralist, not a true entrepreneur.

In telling a practical and urgent story to others, the entrepreneur now has the potential to galvanize a community and organize and mobilize them to action. With a single narrative stroke, the whole becomes greater than the sum of its parts.

Looking at whether creativity can be learned

The classic view of creativity is that it's really the stuff of solitary genius. It comes naturally — or not — and can't be taught. People believe they're not creative, and so they aren't. However, recent thinking on the subject of creativity seems to disagree. Increasingly, researchers are telling us that creativity is contextual and emerges from within the four entrepreneurial domains mentioned in the "Defining What an Entrepreneur Is" section, earlier in this chapter. In other words, creativity is cultural, learnable, and socializable.

Plus, the more *interdependent* these domains are, the greater the possibilities become as practical creativity flows from one domain to another.

Finally, you can only really measure creativity against the value it has in specific social contexts. This is why some people argue that the best way to promote creativity is in environments that are playful and trusting and that promote freedom of action, application across a wide range of contexts, interactive exchange, and a concentration on real-world applications. More and more, this seems to be the direction that the promotion of creativity has to take.

In short, most people are potentially creative, given the right kind of nourishing cultural soil.

Ah, but where is this soil? The soil can be found in the idea of *shared creative literacy*. Everyone associated with entrepreneurial efforts should be "literate" with respect to creativity. That means being familiar with the lifestyles and practices associated with creativity, including developing the communication skills to inject out-of-the-box thinking into the conversation.

How can you do that? The old-fashioned way is a good start: Read lots, discuss lots, collaborate lots. The new-fashioned way — in the age of *Web 2.0,* or collaborative communities and social networking — only adds possibilities: Set up collaborative *wikis* (people-powered collaborative knowledge centers) and get onboard with Google Wave (http://wave.google.com), harness the power of face-to-face social networking to solve problems, visually map complex ideas and their relationships in teams (see, for example, www.mind meister.com or www.xmind.net), and so on. Robin Good's Collaborative Map of Best Online Collaboration Tools for 2009 provides an exciting overview of the possibilities (http://is.gd/5ESAm).

You can promote creative literacy and overall public awareness even more widely through the idea of *social looping.* This is where you demonstrate the positive impact of your efforts to financial, social, and political supporters and give those folks the tools to inspire others to do likewise. For example, charity: water (www.charitywater.org) encourages supporters to send e-cards to friends and loved ones while also giving a person or a family clean water for 20 years. All in all, the opportunities for Web 2.0 techniques in social entrepreneurship are mushrooming. (See Chapter 11 for more on Web 2.0 and social media.)

Here are some practical ideas for fostering your own creativity:

  ✓ **Juggle multiple projects.** Keeping your plate full of variety allows you to think from many different angles and provides opportunities to *cross-pollinate* — apply what you're learning in one setting to others.

✔ **Borrow from giants.** Because the materials you use to solve problems have a huge impact on the quality of your eventual solution, working with the best available materials is always a good idea. Don't reinvent the wheel when you don't have to. If someone has thought about problems like yours in a different domain, seek him out and learn from his successes and failures. Imitation, to borrow from something author Stephen King wrote a long time ago, precedes creation.

✔ **Maintain your enthusiasm and focus.** Realize that your creative entrepreneurial efforts will result in practical value to others. By being of service to others, you realize the importance of your work, and that helps to maintain your enthusiasm and focus. Thomas Edison's personal credo reflects this: "My philosophy of life is work — bringing out the secrets of nature and applying them for the happiness of man. I know of no better service to render during the short time we are in this world."

✔ **Stay confident.** Cling to your moral convictions and sense of urgency. You know things are not what they ought to be. If your confidence in that basic starting point is shaken, the strength and solidity of your entrepreneurial identity will melt away. At the same time, nobody wants to be Chicken Little ("The sky is falling, the sky is falling!"), so be sure your position is rock solid and unassailable by every fair-minded skeptic.

✔ **Shrug off setbacks.** There will be trials and tribulations, as well as failures (yes, realistically, most projects and ventures inevitably face failure or extinction). Don't get caught in the dumps, or even on emotional roller coasters. Lean on your friends. Celebrate and piggyback accomplishments, learn from failures, and then stay ahead of the great tsunami of uncertainty that threatens to sweep everyone away by constantly focusing on the process of your next practical creation.

✔ **Be open to serendipity.** It's long been accepted by creative folks of all kinds that serendipity can yield far more important results for the best-laid plans, so it's always good practice to make yourself available to serendipity. So, what's serendipity? *Serendipity* is artfully profiting from something accidental. It's unexpected, practical (in that the accident is profitable or useful) and artful (while the positive end result can't be thoroughly planned, that doesn't reduce it to "dumb luck" either). No, we're talking about chance favoring the *ready* mind.

How can you make yourself ready for serendipity?

✔ **In a world of probabilities, pay attention to *exceptions*.** They may have a great deal to tell you. Where you might expect commonalities, watch out for differences. And conversely, where you'd expect differences, be sensitive to hidden commonalities.

✔ Practice *free association,* **which is simply allowing ideas in the form of words or images to suggest other words or images, and letting those new ideas suggest even more, and on and on.** You can productively let your mind drift and wander in wonder, connecting one thing to another in an almost "sacred" time of leisure and reverie. Going for unhurried walks or listening to relaxing music might help to induce this creative drift. Or you can connect to other people's ideas which can, in turn, spark all kinds of serendipitous associations.

✔ **Look for occasional opportunities to just get things done, initially, as best you can.** This approach isn't about settling for less — at least not over the long run. It's about getting your feet set. That's the pragmatic part.

Be realistic when you have to. You may have to do things in less-than-optimal ways, not always in terms of best practices — but at least things are getting *done.* At least you're showing that you're responsive, reliable, and compassionate. This is how being pragmatic attracts more support, which is useful in terms of your enterprise's big picture. You may not get things quite right and hit the bull's-eye the first time, or the second time, or even the third time. But the feedback you get along the way is invaluable in terms of constantly innovating and improving what you do.

Similarly, don't wait for perfection before you bring these learning experiences back to those who share your creative literacy. Your quick, regular, and perhaps more modest contributions will add up to far more for everyone concerned than any single brilliant insight.

Be sure to demonstrate your improvements to all your supporters. Some form of social looping, discussed earlier in the section "Looking at whether creativity can be learned" would be an ideal way to go about this, whether that involved face-to-face networking or the use of social media.

Managing your entrepreneurial knowledge

All the practical creativity in the world won't amount to a plugged nickel if you lose track of its products. You shouldn't ever have to reinvent the wheel. Whatever new ways you develop to tackle social and environmental issues becomes your intellectual capital that will form part of your legacy. Record and keep all such innovations so that you're always in the position of building on your practical creativity.

All information associated with your social entrepreneurial efforts should be archived, stored, and backed up safely, on- and off-site, in multiple locations, on CD-ROMs, and in extra hard drives. If you keep handwritten journals, get yourself a digital camera or scanner and capture those pages in digital form so that they're also more useful and mobile.

Chapter 16

Leading Indicators: Leadership and Your Organization

Social entrepreneurs like you often share a particular and commendable mindset that challenges the status quo and strives for extraordinary change. But as valuable as that mindset may be for drawing up the blueprints for social or environmental change, no one can do it alone. Those blueprints won't amount to much if others are unwilling to help you make something extraordinary happen. If you want to build houses for the homeless and everybody else wants to go hot-air ballooning, your plans are in trouble.

How do you coax other people's priorities to line up with your own? That, in a nutshell, is the problem of *leadership*, and it's what distinguishes leadership from management (the subject of Chapter 17). Leadership determines *what* we ought to do — the ends we should be striving for — and *why*. Management is about *how* we get there.

When it comes to promoting social change, you have to establish, through leadership, the goals that people will work collectively toward before dealing with how, through management, you're going to get where you're going. Of course, in a real world of rapidly changing and competing interests, lining up purposes and priorities with your own can be a very difficult task. Leadership is hard — but it must be done.

In this chapter, we look at how social entrepreneurs, as leaders, can bring potential helpers together under one banner. In particular, we focus on two types of leaders — charismatic and servant leaders — and then we look at the promise of a third kind, called distributed leadership.

Building a Leadership Model for Social Change

Given the strength and virtue of your entrepreneurial mindset, the process of aligning the priorities of your potential helpers with your own priorities usually demands that they follow your lead, at least in the broadest forms, and not the other way around. Otherwise, the whole idea of your social entrepreneurship will be in jeopardy.

To understand how to get other people to change their priorities, you need to know something about how social change becomes possible. For that, we draw loosely on the work of the great social psychologist Kurt Lewin. Bear with us as we try to gently apply some unavoidable theory here.

Balancing driving and restraining forces

Achieving social change, even just changes in priorities, is a lot like walking. Forces that drive us toward what *ought to be* are what compel us to move forward. But these driving forces clash with rival restraining forces — the tendency to stick with the status quo — which try to take us in other directions (see Figure 16-1). You have to manage both forward momentum and upright balance while you walk. Similarly, moving forward for social change requires a delicate balance between driving and restraining forces. Too much driving force and you pitch forward and fall on your face. Too much restraining force and you don't get anywhere.

The very important and unusual lesson in this is that resistance to change is an enduring, expected, and necessary feature of any effort toward social change.

Change is difficult to achieve. It requires constant communication and negotiation — and it takes time. Simply ramming through driving forces to bully restraining forces into submission is next to impossible, regardless of the power or virtue behind the driving forces. The difficulty of actually addressing the global climate change issue, which would seem to be a no-brainer, is a good illustration. Too many entrenched industrial, energy, and transportation interests have too much on the line to simply abandon their long-term goals (which may be in conflict with a more sustainable world) simply because scientists are convincing politicians that they should. That's resistance, and it's entirely natural and to be expected.

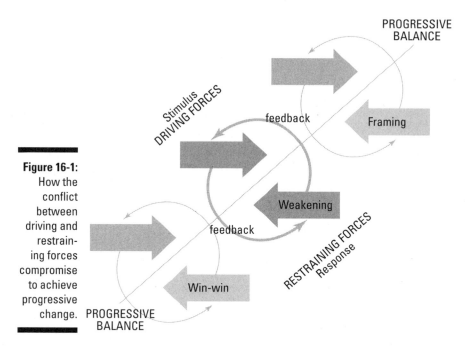

Figure 16-1:
How the conflict between driving and restraining forces compromise to achieve progressive change.

For every push forward instigated by driving forces, you can expect a corresponding push back from restraining forces. The important takeaway idea here is that where a more traditional view of social change might see conflict as destructive and unnecessary, this more contemporary view not only sees conflict as inevitable and central to positive social change but also claims that it also produces better-quality results.

Making sure driving forces win

In every case, changing priorities become possible through continual communication between the opposing forces. But the driving forces (that's you!) still have to win in the end. Change becomes possible as driving forces become stronger while the hardened and crystallized structures of restraining forces

- ✔ *Reframe,* or become seen in a new light so that they're now understood to conform to or support driving forces

- ✔ *Unfreeze,* or become weaker

- ✔ Become part of a negotiated "win-win" solution (in which both sides appear to have gained)

We explore each of these possibilities as we consider the question of leadership in this chapter.

Social Change and Charismatic Leadership

Charismatic leaders are leaders whose personal qualities include a certain magnetism that allows them to light the way for others. These types of leaders are often the first and most direct expression of driving forces. They seek mainly to unfreeze or weaken restraining forces, but they're also active in reframing and transforming them and possibly in negotiating win-win outcomes. (See the preceding section if you're not sure what these terms mean.)

Rarely seen or heard from during good times, charismatic leaders leap to the forefront during times of uncertainty and crisis, when the promise — the *ought to be* — of addressing human needs through existing social institutions is broken too much. Frustrated populations often start to oppose the status quo by abandoning or, in fancy talk, *disconfirming* the status quo and finding charismatic leaders to begin charting new directions.

This process is powerful feedback to the status quo restraining forces. The rational aspects of the disconfirming feedback are "coolly" logical and self-evident — so they're seen as trustworthy and effective. But charisma itself is not "cool" in the sense of cold and logical. Charisma is a form of *hot cognition*, or passionate thought, as are its social origins. Heated by broken promises of human betterment and compassion, the growing critiques begin attacking complacency and setting new priorities and directions.

When restraining forces resist, driving forces can use the "heat" of that resistance to strengthen the charismatic message.

Don't think you can pull off tricks or shortcuts: Trying to create a *false* sense of urgency is a sure way to waste your social change efforts. This can happen when the charismatic leader is not selected by the upset population but is only self-proclaimed — in other words, when the leader lacks credibility among those demanding change.

The basis for driving forces' sense of urgency comes out of those forces' internal discussions. That is, the charismatic leader's legitimate social selection is often thought to rest on an inspired, sometimes even divine, mandate. This results not in a pharaoh (anymore), but in a powerfully felt "calling" on the part of the supporters and the leader. This mutual support — "we call you" and "I honor your call" — energizes and unifies the group to the advantage of the driving forces because the restraining forces are typically less driven and organized. This slow process is more or less why progress, even though it seems glacial, *does* in fact happen throughout history.

You as a social entrepreneur may well be a charismatic leader, even if that talent is latent. Your ability to express and share your vision and to exercise sound practical and ethical judgment every step of the way will be critical to realizing that talent. However, beyond that, your success will depend on your *legitimate* and freely chosen social "selection" by at least the people you want to assist — your target of benefits. If and when you're selected, you'll experience the double commitment of your own compassionate response (as in, "How could I *not* respond to this need?") and the strong social expectation that goes with the calling.

Switching allegiances and reframing

Due to their social backing, charismatic leaders may weaken resistance by bringing out feelings of shame and guilt in members of the restraining forces. Though causing this kind of shame and guilt may not be the goal, it doesn't hurt. In trying to rid themselves of those negative and conflicting emotions, the guilt-ridden and shamed parties may switch allegiances, align themselves with the charismatics and their supporters, and endorse the driving forces. This is what we mean by *reframing* — a self-perceived weakness among restraining forces is suddenly seen, by them, as evidence of their character and integrity (or lack thereof).

One classic example comes from the civil rights movement, which reached its peak in Nashville, Tennessee, in 1959 and 1960. Driving forces included the African American boycott of Nashville businesses and a deluge of negative publicity surrounding segregation itself. The weakened restraining forces were revealed in the futile backlash of mass arrests and the shocking bombing of a prominent African American lawyer's house. This struggle motivated black students to join the driving forces by marching on city hall and confronting Nashville's mayor, Ben West (a conservative symbol of restraining forces). Charismatic student leaders vehemently argued with West against the validity of the racist status quo. The mayor — likely shamed and guilt-ridden in the face of so much opposition (not only among the assembled protesters but also across Nashville's black community and the United States as a whole) — conceded that segregation is wrong. Shortly thereafter, Nashville began to desegregate — though not without resistance, which was anticipated by civil rights organizers, who went to great lengths to help formerly whites-only businesses save face in the transition.

Restraining force denial and resistance shouldn't be surprising to anyone. After all, those whose priorities are being challenged want to protect their years of investment in self-identity, their fragile egos (which cringe at admitting to errors in judgment), and the group norms themselves — traditions and rituals that mark shared membership in social life. There will *always* be resistance to driving forces because of the learning curves associated with investing in change. As a result, inducing guilt alone may produce short-term gains, but probably little in the long run, as defensive mechanisms kick in to protect the priorities that are under siege.

The other-attentive and the self-absorbed

Charismatic leaders have a purpose that makes their lives important, coherent, and worthwhile. Their lives make emotional sense, and they meet the demands and challenges of their lives with energy and commitment. These characteristics are tremendously attractive to others. Charismatic leaders typically have substantial and widely recognized interpersonal skills such as charm, magnetism, and powers of persuasion. History tells of two main kinds of charismatic leaders, and they have funny names:

- **Other-attentive (OA):** Other-attentive charismatic leaders are inclined to social inclusivity (they don't reject anyone), full participation, and the flourishing of others. Examples include Jesus, Mohammed, Buddha, and more recently Mahatma Gandhi, Mother Teresa, Martin Luther King, Jr., and Nelson Mandela.

- **Self-absorbed (SA):** Self-absorbed leaders are inclined to social exclusion (they reject some people), elitism, domination, and subjugation (they oppress people). This is the dark side of charisma. Think Hitler, Mussolini, Pol Pot, Joseph Stalin, Kim Jong-Il, and even "small-timers" like David Koresh and Jim Jones. You get the picture.

Frequently, charismatic leaders of either stripe (OA or SA) manage to get restraining forces to reframe their resistance into benefiting driving forces. When restraining forces have been weakened by the urgency of the charismatic, some people on the restraining side feel their resistance weakening. Combining that development with the basic human attractions that charismatic leaders offer — their meaningfulness and life purpose, their easy social skills and ability to promote a sense of fellowship — creates an inviting form of leadership that is hard to resist (given the human need for *affiliation* — see Chapter 2). These same qualities can be used to build adoration and unity among driving forces.

So what's the difference between the two types of charismatic leaders? The crucial difference between OA and SA charismatic leadership types revolves around respect for what the experts call *boundaries of identity* (the outlines and limits of who people understand themselves to be), both for individuals and groups. OA charismatic leaders respect boundaries and build bridges across them, valuing the differences among people while promoting core commonalities. SA charismatic leaders do not tolerate such boundaries; they're colonizers — boundaries are threats to be attacked, not unique features to be celebrated.

With OA charismatic leaders, everyone is born acceptable, and from such a safe position it's easy to admire charismatic leaders and voluntarily join with them and the driving forces they represent. The same cannot be said for the SA charismatic. Some of the best and worst leaders in human history illustrate this distinction.

Social Change and Servant Leadership

In their social origins, selection, and sense of calling, all charismatic leaders are leaders who, in some broad sense, serve communities. With those who display OA charisma, though, there is a special inclination toward what leadership scholars today call *servant leadership.* Simply put, *servant leaders* are leaders whose main purpose for leading is to serve others. Their leadership is an investment in the development, well-being, and good of others. There seems to be a strong relation between a servant leader's "other focus" and the inclusiveness of the OA charismatic.

Distinguishing servant leaders and charismatic leaders

Where servant leaders differ from OA charismatics is in the way they serve others. Other-attentive charismatic leaders motivate, inspire, galvanize driving forces, and passionately critique restraining forces, creating doubt among them. They may lead protest marches, for example, or give public speeches and communicate through popular media. When OA leaders retire from public view or die, they leave behind a legacy for others to continue.

Martin Luther King, Jr., challenged a set of restraining forces in 1968 when, in collaboration with the Southern Christian Leadership Conference, he organized the Poor People's Campaign. The campaign strove to achieve economic justice for African Americans, starting with sanitation workers who were, at the time, making $1.70 an hour. Proper economic justice called for a much higher minimum wage, which the organizers suggested should be $9 per hour. The campaign took the form of a cross-country march, ending in Washington, D.C., with a demand made to Congress to establish a bill of rights for poor people and to grant aid to the most impoverished communities in the United States. As the march progressed from its starting point in Marks, Mississippi, it gathered more and more participants, coalescing into what Dr. King called "a multiracial army of the poor."

The Poor People's Campaign strove to help the destitute segments of every minority. Poor Mexicans, Puerto Ricans, Native Americans, and even poor whites were targeted in the campaign. King described it as the "second phase" of the civil rights movement (the first phase having focused on ending racial segregation). Dr. King intended this campaign to be the largest, most widespread manifestation of the civil rights movement. And though Dr. King was assassinated on April 4, 1968, the campaign continued. Less than a month after his death, demonstrators reached Washington, D.C., where they engaged in two weeks of lobbying at various federal agencies.

Servant leaders, on the other hand, are more engaged in the daily lives of those they serve. They're capacity and skill builders, as well as educators, who help create priority-setting growth among both driving and restraining forces. If OA charismatic leaders can be said to till the soil, servant leaders sow the seeds. They tend to work far more personally, in more intimate, interactive, and face-to-face settings such as classrooms and workshops, and they may sustain their efforts over multiple encounters.

That isn't to say that OA charismatics *can't* be servant leaders. Certainly, the two roles can be combined in one person, so that a lot of switching hats may go on. Mahatma Gandhi and Mother Teresa are excellent examples of leaders who exhibited both OA charismatic and servant leader traits. Both worked diligently and in very practical and prolonged ways to educate others about the goals and objectives of their compassionate ways of life.

Charismatic leaders tend to be "home grown" — committed members native to the populations they want to help — whereas the quieter, more hands-on servant leaders, although they *can* be home grown as well, can also be "parachuted in" to serve, or may accidentally arrive on the scene and end up helping. An enormous amount of development work being done by Western organizations in economically disadvantaged countries is being done by parachuted servant leaders. This situation requires sensitivity because of cross-cultural differences, and so in those cases it's best if servant leaders work in support of local OA charismatic leadership.

Can parachuted-in or accidental servant leaders become OA charismatics? Possibly, but not without legitimate social selection, which usually takes quite a while to come to fulfillment. Gandhi's work in South Africa was definitely of the accidental kind, because he arrived there at only 24 years of age and then experienced firsthand a racism that he felt compelled to serve against.

Nothing is more embarrassing than aid workers/servant leaders who believe and act as if they've been called as OA charismatics when they're virtually unknown, are not yet trusted, and lack legitimacy. The same mistake can happen on a larger scale, in the case of Western nations who mistake servant leadership for OA charisma. These situations often lead to enormous animosity and end up actually strengthening restraining forces.

The nuts and bolts of servant leadership

Although servant leaders help strengthen the membership of driving forces, perhaps their most important work is with those who represent restraining forces and yet may be waffling or fence-sitting as a result of charismatic messages.

Four general areas of involvement for servant leaders are key:

- ✔ Educating and communicating
- ✔ Enhancing participation and involvement
- ✔ Facilitating and supporting
- ✔ Negotiating and moving toward agreement

Servant leaders are often involved in starting conversations, perhaps for the first time, about goals of cooperation, fair play, appreciation of diversity, tolerance, and so on. They may be restating similar OA charisma points, but it's more likely to be in an intimate office setting across a table than before thousands of people.

Servant leaders also engage in simple cost-benefit conversations with resistors in an attempt to show the rewards of changed priorities. Servant leaders may also broker win-win agreements or they may work with mature individuals who are perhaps more set in their ways, in order to reduce anxiety over adjusting to and embracing new priorities. Ideally, through reframing, servant leaders can demonstrate that much of the fear of change is unfounded or exaggerated.

Servant leader "interventions" can also be done with solidified social institutions, such as *patriarchies* (male-dominated societies), which have formalized rules and procedures or highly structured organizations, including bureaucracies. Finally, servant leaders often deal with the "smaller stuff," such as misunderstandings, entrenched self-interest, lack of trust, and so on, helping those mired in restraining forces to see, in nonthreatening ways, that change is possible while maintaining integrity and dignity.

Social Change and Distributed Leadership

Distributed leadership is an increasingly popular alternative to other current understandings of leadership. *Distributed leadership* says that leadership and influence don't come from individuals so much as from within the holistic qualities of groups. In other words, in this view, leadership emerges from a whole that is greater than the sum of its parts — from a general culture or lifestyle that is shared, practiced, and achieved by entire organizations or communities of people.

Leadership, then, is a latent potential in any social organization, and leaders emerge from that potential.

Distributed leadership is an extension of the close relationship that communities have with leadership, and that we discuss earlier in terms of charismatic and servant leaders. However, researcher Nigel Bennett reminds us that, unlike the case of charismatic and servant leaders, with distributed leadership the boundaries of leadership become *permeable* — that is, who plays which leadership role in promoting changes in priorities is not fixed. Proponents of distributed leadership emphasize that leadership is involved in small-scale daily activities and interactions, as well as the large-scale plans of many people.

In an educational setting, the question of school leadership is often flexible as ideas on direction are set by parents, students, and the surrounding community, as well as by teachers and administrators. In these ways, the leadership becomes a full, inclusive, culturally sensitive, and democratic social construction.

When applied to driving forces, distributed leadership has the potential to strengthen those forces through continuing conversations that enhance collaborative learning and shared understandings. As a result, leadership is returned to social organization where it properly belongs.

Extending distributed leadership to involvement with restraining forces reveals many possibilities for reframing, weakening, or negotiating win-win outcomes. With reframing, for example, driving forces leaders might invite restraining forces to help them combat "group think" among those promoting change by offering up new information and understanding. This invitation might serve as a powerful incentive to weaken or resistance to driving forces. With that incentive, the likelihood of bringing others to your side increases dramatically.

Developing Your Own Leadership

Both charismatic and servant leaders need to work toward creating a culture of distributed leadership, but make no mistake: Developing that culture is never a simple task. In fact, leadership development is an area that could benefit from the efforts of social entrepreneurs all around the world. Nobody in all of history has had a patent on how to practice leadership — yet it always desperately needs to be done.

Leadership is constantly reinvented by everyone who engages in it. That includes you.

We have two modest suggestions that might help to piece some of the puzzle of leadership development together. The best leadership development efforts will do both of the following:

✓ **Promote public compassion, social inclusion, attachment, the discerning use of culture, and social insight at every turn (see Chapter 2).** Remember that asking people of any age to change and grow as leaders involves dynamic challenges and tensions that must be dealt with sensitively.

✓ **Intentionally incorporate child, youth, and adult learning theory into any curriculum (see Chapter 4).** Leaders in training need to earn their stripes in deeply embedded, contextual, and practical circumstances. What they do should not be pie-in-the-sky but rather social entrepreneurial — in other words, aimed at making real, concrete change — and feedback and evaluation should, at the very least, come from those most affected by their leadership efforts.

Natural relationships exist among the three types of leadership we discuss in this chapter, especially in their attempts to bring positive and extraordinary social change on behalf of any community that might be in need.

Our model suggests that out of frustrated community needs and crises, charismatic leaders emerge who contribute to the driving forces of change and deal with restraining forces in particular ways. These leaders, in turn, work with servant leaders who strategically promote a culture of distributed leadership that makes its way deep into the heart of the community in need and strengthens it to the core. In Figure 16-2, that progression runs in sequence from 1 to 4.

However, the connections among the leadership forms and the frustrated community can be varied. Community frustrations don't necessarily have to be the only point of departure. For example, distributed leadership (4) could give rise to servant leadership (3), which could heighten awareness and frustration in a community (1). From that could emerge charismatic leadership (2), which — well, you get the picture.

Working to change priorities is complicated and dynamic stuff, but in the end, these components and their interrelations are central, especially as they deal with the dynamics of driving and restraining forces.

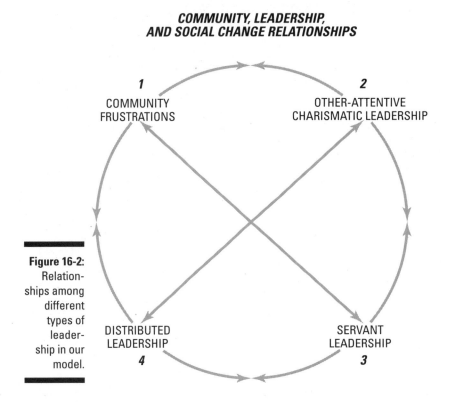

COMMUNITY, LEADERSHIP,
AND SOCIAL CHANGE RELATIONSHIPS

1
COMMUNITY
FRUSTRATIONS

2
OTHER-ATTENTIVE
CHARISMATIC LEADERSHIP

Figure 16-2: Relation-ships among different types of leader-ship in our model.

DISTRIBUTED
LEADERSHIP
4

SERVANT
LEADERSHIP
3

Chapter 17

Managing a Social Enterprise

*I*t's one thing to start a social enterprise, but it's quite another to manage one well enough to successfully fulfill its mission.

In this chapter, we look at several issues that tend to spring up when managing both for-profit and nonprofit social entrepreneurial organizations. Even small social enterprises can develop managerial problems, so we encourage you to read this chapter if you're serious about achieving your goals — regardless of the size of your enterprise.

Recruiting Paid Staff

When it comes to recruitment of paid staff, your goal, quite simply, is to find the best person for the job at a level of pay that both you and that person can accept. Many times, you can find candidates through word of mouth and networking (see Chapter 11). But if networking doesn't work, you'll also want to take the steps we outline in this section.

Writing a job description

When you're recruiting new paid staff, your first step is to identify and write down the tasks of the job. The time you spend doing this will be time well spent. Make sure to

- ✔ Describe, as precisely as possible, what the candidate will be expected to do.
- ✔ State the skills, knowledge, and experience required.

For example, don't just say you want a secretary. You want one who will type all letters, copy material for board meetings, make appointments for the top leaders, handle telephone calls, and so on. The candidate must have two years of formal clerical training and three years of experience.

The more specific you can be, the better. These details can help eliminate unhappy surprises later on. Candidates who've been selected for interviewing must read this job description, which should also be used later in reviewing the employee's job performance and determining his role and responsibilities in the organization.

After you've written a full description of the job, come up with a summary of that job description. Your summary should be as short as possible — the length is commonly determined by the word limit set by the media in which you intend to publish. Still this summary must be informative and clear. Be sure to indicate how long the recruitment phase will last, including when you'll end your search and start interviewing applicants.

When you're coming up with your job description, it may help to browse other job posting boards for ideas, such as Monster.com, craigslist (www.craigslist.org), IdeaList (www.idealist.org), and CareerBuilder (http://nonprofit.careerbuilder.com). Look for nonprofit job listings.

Make the post specific in your requirements to avoid having to wade through hundreds of applicants to find the right one. Don't be afraid to put the feel and personality of the organization into the ad to help attract like-minded people. And if the job has special criteria, state them in the notice as well. For example, people suffering from allergies to animals should be advised that the advertised post requires them to work with animals or work in spaces where animals live.

The following is a sample of a typical job notice that may be used in recruiting paid staff to a social enterprise:

> Receptionist/secretary: Competitive salary; starting date: December 1, 2010; minimal qualifications: two years post-secondary education, two-years experience; bilingual English/Spanish preferred. Send résumé and two references to *name of social enterprise* by e-mail at *e-mail address* or by ordinary mail at *mailing address*. Deadline: November 1, 2010.

Notices should be short and to the point. Traditional media charges by the word, which reinforced the short and sweetness, but in the Age of the

Internet, you don't really pay by word anymore. Instead, you pay for featured ads and bold headlines.

Really think more about using the best, most accurate search terms, bearing in mind that prospective job seekers will type in certain words to pull up results. Choose the proper wording in the ad to make sure your ad comes up in the proper results. Also, be clear in the ad how you want to be contacted. If you leave a fax number, be sure to keep the machine stocked with paper. If you hate being bothered by phone calls, be sure to specify "No calls, please." Crafty and competitive job seekers will even show up unannounced at your location after Googling your office address.

Posting a want ad

Circulate the want ad, or job notice, wherever you think it might attract qualified candidates. The Internet is the obvious place to start these days. Here are a few of the better-regarded job boards on the Internet:

- ✔ **Career.com:** www.career.com
- ✔ **CareerBuilder:** www.careerbuilder.com
- ✔ **craigslist:** www.craigslist.org
- ✔ **Hound:** www.hound.com
- ✔ **Jobs at Change.org:** http://jobs.change.org
- ✔ **Job Central:** www.jobcentral.com
- ✔ **Monster:** www.monster.com
- ✔ **Opportunity Knocks:** www.oppotunityknocks.org
- ✔ **Yahoo! Hot Jobs:** hotjobs.yahoo.com

Be sure to put all job notices on your own Web site and link to these job openings from your site's home page. If you have a newsletter, you might want to list your job openings there.

Consider the various employment services in your community, whether private or governmental. Contact related or compatible enterprises and organizations and see if they'll allow you to list your job openings in their newsletters. Depending on the vacancy to be filled and the appropriateness of the location, good old-fashioned bulletin boards can also be an effective showplace for job notices.

In a down economy, it's a good idea to contact other organizations that may be downsizing. When you're faced with having to lay off good people, it may help them for you to come along and provide a job opportunity. This method is especially good for finding short-term (per-project) positions — to help other orgs keep good staff members busy in slow times.

Creating a job application

You'll probably want to state in your ad certain criteria that candidates must speak to when applying. For example, you might want to ask them to indicate their

- ✔ Educational background
- ✔ Languages spoken, written, and read
- ✔ Citizenship and country of origin
- ✔ Any other information you believe is relevant to the mission and goals of your enterprise and is legally permissible to ask for

Many countries and states prohibit asking the age or sex of applicants.

If you want to use a prepared application form or develop your own, check out the samples and free forms online at www.entrepreneur.com/formnet.

Interviewing candidates

After you have some applications trickling — or flooding — in, you need to review résumés and cover letters. Separate out the ones that aren't qualified so you can focus on those who are. You're looking for people who can do the job and who also have demonstrated a commitment to social and community causes, especially yours. You may also be looking for people who stand out in some way from the crowd. Narrow your choices to three candidates and call them in for interviews.

Try to bunch the interviews together as much as possible — see if you can do them all in one week, or over two weeks at most. The closer the interviews are together in time, the better — you want the interviewers to note everything that's important about every candidate, so memory is critical.

Don't do it all yourself. Ask at least one or two colleagues to be present at each interview session. Two heads are better than one when it comes to forming impressions about people in the interview process.

Hold the job interviews at the work site where the candidate, if hired, will be employed. Dress well for the occasion out of respect for the candidate and for your enterprise. You want to impress the candidate in every way possible with the importance of both the job opening and the mission of your organization. Make notes directly on each résumé to help you in your evaluation. Some interviewers even take simple photographs of qualified candidates to help keep track of each meeting (but be sensitive — some people dislike having their photo taken).

Good candidates are often in demand, so use the interview to sell *them* on why they want to work for you. If the job is on the low end of the salary spectrum, make a point of explaining the other perks or benefits to working for your organization. Some people place as much value on quality of the work environment as they do on the salary amount, so be sure to tell them about your casual-Friday dress code or the monthly cookie party you hold for the staff. They're interviewing you as much as you're interviewing them.

Create a short list of acceptable candidates, review it with any staff who were involved in the interviews, and offer the job to the top person immediately.

Drafting an employment contract

Develop a contract that sets out, at minimum:

- ✔ Conditions of employment and its termination
- ✔ Conditions of leaves (sick, maternity, personal development), advancement, and similar matters as they relate to working in your enterprise

You may also want to include the full job description in the contract. If you do, be sure to also give your new hires copies of their job descriptions separate from their contracts — employees are likely to refer to their job descriptions more often than they will their contracts, so a separate copy of the job description will come in handy.

The contents of the contract should be discussed during the hiring interview, and the new hire should receive a copy and be given a chance to discuss it further. Both you (the employer) and the new employee should sign two copies of the contract; give one copy to the employee and keep the other in your files.

LawDepot (`www.lawdepot.com`) offers free detailed advice on preparing contracts as well as samples of contracts that you might want to create. It also provides sample employment offers, employment termination letters, and many other helpful samples of business documents.

Managing and Training Paid Staff

Managing staff is a huge subject — people get MBAs and PhDs in this stuff — so we can't tell you all there is to know about management in this chapter. Hundreds of books have been written on the topic. So, after you read this chapter, we recommend you check out *Managing For Dummies,* 2nd Edition, by Bob Nelson, PhD, and Peter Economy (Wiley).

The five fundamental areas of management that are especially germane to social enterprises are planning, organizing, directing, monitoring, and training paid staff — and we cover these in the following sections.

Planning

Planning is so important and complex that we devote an entire chapter to the subject (Chapter 7). There we make the point that good planning in social enterprises revolves around their mission and goals. But after you've determined your official goals, remember to consider the following as you manage your employees:

- ✔ Who in the enterprise is assigned to do what to bring each goal to fruition?

- ✔ What kind of person or persons should be asked to reach each goal?

- ✔ How should these people work with your target of your benefits to achieve each goal?

In the course of managing your employees, you also want to consider how far your enterprise has come in realizing its goals. Ask yourself how your employees' performance figures into your answers to these three questions:

- ✔ How long has it taken you to reach this point, and is that faster or slower than you had planned?

- ✔ How much more time will be needed to achieve those goals?

- ✔ Are there any ways of speeding up achievement of your goals?

Organizing

The good organization of work tasks is what will help you and your group meet your goals. Organization also leads to worker satisfaction and minimizes employee burnout. Good, everyday organizing involves

- ✔ **Identifying and assigning workable tasks for members of your enterprise to carry out:** *Workable tasks* are those that a worker can accomplish with the skills and knowledge brought to the job, doing so in a time frame that allows the tasks to be carried out effectively and without stress.

✓ **Finding and mobilizing the best people to do so.**

Over-bureaucratization and bureaucratic bloat come from adding more organizational functions than required and/or more people to carry them out than needed. In other words, as you organize your tasks, don't forget the merits of flat bureaucracy (see Chapter 13).

Directing

After you've organized your people, you need to give them some direction. People who've been mobilized to carry out a particular task — whether as individuals, members of a team, or part of a work group — must be told how to do it. In some cases, you can achieve this kind of direction through written instructions (for example, a manual), but face-to-face explanation is the way it's typically done — especially for tasks that are somewhat complex.

Be sure to provide all the information your employees need to complete the tasks they've been assigned. Share with your workers your hard-earned tricks of the trade and talk about effective shortcuts, ways to work smarter, and tried-and-true ways of meeting deadlines. Be sure to tell them where the tasks they're working on fit in the larger picture of how the enterprise functions and pursues its goals. Give constructive criticism of people's performance at those tasks and don't forget to pile on the praise when they do a good job.

Monitoring

When the individual, group, or team gets to work on the assigned task as directed, you (or someone you assign) must monitor the progress toward the task's completion. We're not saying you should be an overbearing *micromanager* (someone who obsesses over every detail of the work of others). Your monitoring doesn't even have to be intense, especially if you have confidence in the workers you're managing.

Part of the art of management is deciding how much looking-over-the-shoulders-of-workers is necessary. Too little monitoring, and you risk losing control. Too much, and you can annoy your workers and maybe even shake their self-confidence, both of which can reduce their motivation to perform well.

Annual performance reviews of work performance are probably the most formal kind of monitoring. You or other managers should review the performance of all employees at least once a year. Create written evaluations to be filed away, but be sure to talk with each employee face to face about his performance review. Make sure the employee agrees with everything in the review, and both of you should sign it. Performance reviews can become the basis for promotion and pay raise decisions, as well as the difficult task of terminating employees.

Use the reviews as a chance to get feedback on the management of the organization as well. Reviews are two-way streets — they're more than just a chance for you to tell employees everything they did wrong this past year. Use the review to show employees how their work helped the organization achieve a larger success, but also be constructive in your criticism of things they could do to improve in the future.

Schedule and honor the dates for reviews. Some employees get tense and nervous when the date of a much-anticipated review passes by silently. Be proactive in scheduling the reviews and make it a fun and worthwhile experience for everyone involved.

For much more information on conducting these kinds of reviews, check out *Performance Appraisals & Phrases For Dummies,* by Ken Lloyd, PhD (Wiley).

Training paid staff

Training paid staff is another important managerial function. Most people have some formal training — through a university, trade school, or special high school program. They may have undergone on-the-job training in another organization or taken one or more courses through a continuing education program. The job with your enterprise has unique features, though, so you'll need to do at least some training.

You might require the workers to take a formal course or program of courses, work with a mentor or coach, or engage in some self-education through reading manuals or books, to mention a few possibilities. You may have to give the needed training yourself.

Depending on your organization's function, the staff may be required to undergo formal training from an outside education provider. Plan for these expenses in your annual budget and ask staff members to take notes. Over lunch or a staff meeting, staff members can return and give brief overviews of the items covered and learned in the training.

Recruiting Volunteers

Volunteers work for social enterprises out of different motives than paid staff (see Chapter 3 for more on volunteers) and must be managed differently (see the next section for more on this). But recruitment procedures often start out similarly for both categories of workers. As described earlier, you need to start by describing your volunteers' roles — the tasks they're supposed to carry out.

Create detailed volunteer "job" descriptions in summary form that you can disseminate through various media to attract potential recruits. Instead of a job announcement, this is known as your *call for volunteers*. As with paid positions, the Internet is the obvious place to start.

Put the call for volunteers on your own Web site.

You want to circulate your call for volunteers wherever you think it might pay off, but because most if not all of your volunteers will be local people, you should also place notices of volunteer positions with local (or regional) volunteer centers. A *volunteer center* is a local nonprofit organization whose goals include promoting volunteerism as well as coordinating, recruiting, placing, and recognizing volunteers. A modern volunteer center almost certainly has a Web site as well as a physical location where hard-copy lists and descriptions of volunteer work are available for walk-in inquiries.

Dealing with unions

Many if not most social enterprises have little or no direct contact with organized labor. That's because the majority of social enterprises are nonprofit groups employing so few paid employees that unionization would result in scant benefit for either party.

Large social enterprises with many paid employees, however, may become unionized. For example, the Red Cross in the United States must work with the unions who represent its front-line blood-drive event workers. If you're managing a large social enterprise, you have to strive, through negotiations with unions, to harmonize unionized-employee interests with the enterprise's goals.

Look ahead and try to avoid generating worker dissatisfaction so that unionization is not seen by employees as the only remedy to their grievances.

Remember: When you're running a socially conscious business, you have to be more sensitive to union concerns than other types of businesses have to be. Your organization's goal probably has something to do with alleviating human difficulties, so you need to be especially alert to difficulties that crop up within your own confines.

VolunteerMatch.com is a Web site that helps organizations meet potential volunteers.

Look for volunteers who fit, so as to avoid burnout (see the "Avoiding burnout" section, later in this chapter). Ask trusted members of your enterprise about possible recruits to volunteer posts, and then have them help you screen for the best candidates.

Unlike in paid employment, contracts are uncommon for volunteers. If you were to put a contract in front of your volunteers, you'd give the impression that the commitment (on their part and on yours) was greater than it really is. When contracts *are* signed by the volunteer and the organization, they usually amount to no more than a list of responsibilities formally agreed to by both parties.

Managing Volunteers

Organizations that engage volunteers commonly treat them as if they were paid staff. But managing volunteers is an entirely different job. Here are several critical reasons why you need to manage your volunteers as volunteers rather than as paid staff:

- **Volunteers can much more easily say "I quit" than paid staff can, because they aren't dependent on the money they earn from the position.** Volunteers are pursuing a *leisure activity* (see Chapter 3) — they're doing something they want to do because they like it. If a volunteer in your enterprise starts to find the work disagreeable, she'll be inclined to look for leisure activities elsewhere.

- **Because they receive no pay, volunteers expect some nonmonetary rewards.** The rewards experienced by serious leisure participants include the following:

  - Personal enrichment from cherished experiences

  - Self-actualization through the development of skills, abilities, and knowledge

  - Self-expression using the skills, abilities, and knowledge they've already developed

  - Enhanced self-image by becoming known to others as a particular kind of serious leisure participant

  - Self-gratification via a combination of enjoyment and satisfaction — also known as *fun* or, for the slightly more hip, *flow*

  - Re-creation or regeneration of oneself, often especially gratifying after an obligatory workday

- Social attraction by associating with other serious leisure participants and in the social world of the activity

- Group accomplishment derived from a sense of helping with a group effort in accomplishing a serious leisure project

- Contribution to the community, including senses of helping, being needed, and being altruistic

Some people volunteer for less than purely altruistic reasons. One such reason is to gain experience in an area that will lead eventually to a paying job. They may be hoping to put their volunteer work at your enterprise on their résumé and may later even ask you for a letter of reference. Although their motives differ from those volunteers who are serving for more purely altruistic reasons, their contributions can still be valuable.

Paid staff would like to experience these rewards, too, but that's uncommon in the modern workplace because the typical job today fails to meet the six criteria of *occupational devotion* (see Chapter 3). Paid staff stay on, by and large, because they're attracted by the money they make, and equivalent work may be hard to find elsewhere.

✔ **Because they're substantially motivated by altruism, compassion, and urgency, volunteers are more inclined to persevere when the going gets tough than paid employees are.** As we note in Chapter 3, such perseverance is a distinctive characteristic of their serious leisure. By contrast, some employees may be interviewing for jobs at competitors while having learned how to avoid work difficulties that demand perseverance. (Volunteers may even agree to do the work for the very opportunity to work directly with the founder, especially if that founder has a bold vision.)

In smaller social enterprises, managing volunteers commonly falls to the founding entrepreneur and later, possibly, to another senior leader. In larger enterprises this function is usually assumed by *volunteer coordinators,* who may themselves be volunteers or full- or part-time paid staff members. The volunteer coordinator's job is to develop and run the organization's volunteer program as well as supervise the volunteers working within it.

The role of the volunteer coordinator: Knowing what makes volunteers tick

In common with managers of paid staff, volunteer coordinators must consider the four principles of planning, organizing, directing, and monitoring. But some additional features of volunteer management make it unique.

In organizations with lots of paid staff, the post of volunteer coordinator tends to be unsung and, at times, nearly invisible. The emphasis in such environments is on work and career, with volunteering commonly seen as a sort of adjunct or afterthought. One of your roles as the leader of a social enterprise is to prevent your coordinator from being marginalized in this way. If your group depends heavily, perhaps even exclusively, on volunteers, because they're so central to its mission they must be managed in the best way possible.

The job of volunteer coordinator must, like the volunteer roles to be filled, be carefully defined.

Volunteers have their own personal needs that have to be addressed in their task descriptions, and your organization has needs as well. Because volunteers have the freedom to quit without financial consequence, you want to make sure to give them assignments that don't conflict with their family life, their other serious leisure interests, or their moral principles. Serious leisure volunteers want to develop themselves, and they see their volunteer roles as a major route to this goal. Time and flexibility of duties, for example, are as important to a volunteer as they are to a paid employee, and that importance should never be offhandedly disregarded or dismissed by a volunteer administrator.

Volunteer coordinators need top-notch interpersonal skills. They have to get to know the volunteers in their charge in order to avoid tensions and disappointments.

One main reward of volunteering is its social side: Volunteers enjoy the contact they have with other people while they're volunteering — and that includes the volunteer coordinator.

Believe it or not, we've known some volunteer coordinators who were insulting, sarcastic, distant, angry, and underhanded when dealing with volunteers. If your volunteer coordinator exhibits any of these traits, he'll definitely spoil the social side of volunteering — and you'll lose plenty of good volunteers as a result.

Because of the altruistic component in volunteering, volunteers are significantly more likely to be motivated by the enterprise's mission than paid staff are. So, volunteer coordinators must be sure that volunteers are always kept informed of the mission, its associated goals, and any changes made to them. Accomplishing a group goal is a valued achievement for volunteers. The volunteer coordinator needs to do everything possible to help volunteers feel part of achieving the group's goals.

What happens when your volunteers are tasked with doing things that fall under the jurisdiction of your paid staff? Should the volunteer coordinator manage them in these situations? In this case, no. Always let your paid staff supervise the work of volunteers whose activities fall within their jurisdiction. Paid staff working in the same area as the volunteers tend to understand best the challenges of reaching organizational goals that they both face and the rewards that come from successfully meeting them. (See the nearby sidebar for more on helping your paid staff and volunteers work well together.)

As with the management of paid staff, the management of volunteers has been the subject of a great deal of writing. If you want to go deeper into this subject than we have the space for here, we suggest the book *The (Help!) I-Don't-Have-Enough-Time Guide to Volunteer Management* by Catherine Campbell and Susan Ellis (Energize, Inc.). The authors have considerable experience in this area, and as its title suggests, the book is especially helpful for volunteer coordinators who also have other responsibilities in the enterprise — the lot of many entrepreneurs trying to run small or medium enterprises. Indeed, almost every entrepreneur faces this situation during the startup period.

Training volunteers

Your serious leisure volunteers will require the most substantial training. That means you can assign casual and even project-based volunteers much simpler tasks that take comparatively little time to learn. (See Chapter 3 for more on the different kinds of volunteers.)

Serious leisure means the systematic pursuit of an amateur, hobbyist, or volunteer activity that people find so interesting and fulfilling that they launch themselves on a (leisure) career.

One of the rewards for the serious-leisure volunteer is *self-development* (the acquisition of new skills, knowledge, and experience). In social enterprises, training is one of the main ways this development occurs. Even before training begins, however, new volunteers need to be inducted into your enterprise, and the enterprise needs to be prepared for their arrival.

Create a code of conduct, or code of ethics, for volunteers in your enterprise and make sure volunteers learn it. This code may include statements about confidentiality, honesty, punctuality, taking breaks, and giving notice of intent to leave the volunteer post.

Can't we all get along? Helping your staff and volunteers work together

A major area of potential friction in social enterprises with large groups of paid staff and volunteers are the relations between the two. And a major managerial concern in nonprofit groups and volunteer programs is to develop smooth working ties and mutual respect between paid staff of the larger organization and participants in the volunteer program. Friction between the two groups can arise on occasion. When it does, the volunteer coordinator and management as a whole should stamp it out as quickly as possible.

Reward staff who work well with volunteers. It may not always be possible to do this with money (as in a bonus), but good work should be prominently noted on the employee's annual performance review, acknowledging her special value to the enterprise.

Volunteers can't be disciplined as paid staff sometimes must be. You can fire them, but short of that, it's impossible to force them to work extra hours or dock their pay. With volunteers you have to handle disciplinary problems more informally, such as through discussion, negotiation, compromise, and similar accommodations.

Frequently, volunteers in trouble in these ways are unaware that they're in the wrong, which can often be traced to inadequate training or supervision.

Because volunteers tend to not follow a regular or full-time schedule, be mindful when assigning a volunteer a time-dependent task. Be clear with them that this needs to be done by a certain date in case they aren't able to finish it within the time allotted.

Some problems rest on a personal incompatibility with the volunteer activities to which the individual has been assigned — which was your job as manager to avoid, right? For example, it's possible that a volunteer has little taste for certain activities, finds them boring, lacks the required skills or knowledge, or is unable to do them at a level that meets her expectations.

College students may be able to earn college credit for their volunteer work with you. Embrace this option, and contact your local university and colleges for possible volunteer/college-credit programs. These programs could become a perennial source of good volunteers.

You can see a good example of a volunteer code of conduct on the Special Olympics Web site: www.area3specialolympicsva.org/files/volunteer%20code%20of%20conduct.pdf.

Make sure your volunteers get a sense of the history of not just your enterprise and its range of services for your target of benefits. Don't be afraid to go into the strengths and weaknesses of your enterprise. Obviously the volunteers are already interested, or they wouldn't be volunteering.

Bring in some of your staff to share with the volunteers their own perspectives on the enterprise and its mission.

Let staff who will be working with the volunteers help design volunteer training programs. Ensure that all staff know how to properly and effectively use the volunteers with whom they'll be working, and that volunteers know the staff have received these instructions. If you have one, you should ask your volunteer coordinator to look after such training. Otherwise, you or a manager must do it. In general, this involves familiarizing staff with their volunteers' strengths and weaknesses (such as education, background experience, and time limitations) and with the points on morale we cover in the next section.

Volunteers should understand that they can ask questions of and challenge the staff about the volunteer work. Likewise, you should inform new volunteers about the basic responsibilities of the staff they'll be dealing with. Managing volunteers is an opportunity for a staff member to demonstrate managerial skills and potentially move on to a formal management role.

Be sure to tell new volunteers, where relevant, about the volunteer program's policies concerning liability and management of risk. Some volunteer roles may be hazardous — for example, if they're working in a disease-infested or violent environment, or if they're subject to extreme weather. You and your board of directors (if you have one) must formulate policies of this sort. Regularly update the policies in light of new information bearing on organizational and personal risk and liability.

Serious leisure volunteers are usually subject to routine evaluation, something they should be made aware of. Let them know how those evaluations will be conducted. It doesn't have to be as formal as the employee performance reviews we mention earlier in this chapter, but you can use those as a springboard for considering volunteer performance.

Whipping Up Morale

Part of managing a team — whether paid staff, volunteers, or a mix of the two — is generating and maintaining high *morale* (the positive sense of optimism and achievement). You can do this by keeping your organizational and team goals visible, giving constructive feedback on performance, recognizing and rewarding people when they do a good job, and avoiding burnout. In this section, we show you how.

One easy way to get the ball rolling on raising morale is to encourage everyone to express new ideas for running the enterprise and reaching its goals, as well as to give feedback on how they the feel present arrangements are working. A suggestion box is one classic way to accomplish this. But if relations are warm among staff and volunteers, face-to-face discussion is the more effective and personally rewarding way.

Keeping goals visible

Getting lost in the minutiae of the everyday running of a social enterprise is all too easy. There are countless details associated with keeping it going: the demands of immediate events, the effects of external forces, and the navigation of interpersonal exchanges all day long. In the midst of day-to-day activities, your enterprise's goals may get pushed aside — at least in the minds of your staff and volunteers.

What can you do to keep the mission clear at all times? Here are a few ideas:

- ✔ **Create and hang posters that spell out the mission and goals of your enterprise throughout the work space.** They should be unobtrusive and attractive, but visible from almost anywhere. The idea is to ingrain these words into the workday, into the very environment in which people work, so no matter what's happening, the enterprise's main purpose is never forgotten.

- ✔ **Talk about the mission and goals frequently in one-on-one and group meetings of staff and volunteers.** Don't worry about repeating yourself — you need to. Incorporate the mission and goals into broader discussions about, say, recruitment practices, media policies, or choices of funding sources. This repetition not only reminds your staff and volunteers of the importance of your mission and goals, but it also places the mission and goals in different contexts that are readily graspable and real.

- ✔ **Bring up the mission and goals even during informal interactions with staff and volunteers.** You can easily slip in a reference or two to one or more goals while engaging in light shoptalk at an organizational picnic, holiday party, or after-hours get-together with them at a nearby bar or restaurant.

- ✔ **Ask individual paid staff and volunteers to review, however briefly, the enterprise's goals every day.** Printing up and distributing small cards entitled something like "What are we here for?" with the goals listed below can serve as a quick reminder of what the social enterprise is trying to accomplish. Conspicuously placed in offices or work spaces, this notice can work wonders in keeping all personnel pointed in the direction of your mission.

Giving constructive feedback

Don't forget that your serious leisure volunteers and paid staff are all striving to improve themselves through their assignments in your social enterprise. In effect, both groups are looking for personal enrichment, self-actualization, and self-expression (see Chapter 3). Giving them constructive feedback on how well they're doing in their assignments helps them realize these rewards.

Constructive feedback consists of two main components:

✔ **Content:** The pointers and helpful criticism you give to employees or volunteers must be useful — they have to be able to use this feedback to actually improve. That means your feedback should be clear, detailed, and logically presented. You don't want to say, for example, "You must do this task better." Instead, set out clearly what the person has to do, step by step if necessary, to perform the task better.

✔ **Style:** Your feedback should be delivered in a friendly, well-meaning tone, whether it's written or oral or both. The spirit of the feedback suggests that you care about both the enterprise and the volunteer or employee. If you're angry or indifferent in your delivery of feedback, volunteers and staff may come away from such exchanges knowing more about your mood than they do about the deficiencies in their own performance.

Recognizing and rewarding people for a job well done

So, some variables are beyond your control. One thing that is within your control is the way you recognize and reward your paid staff and volunteers. Recognition and reward are both motivating, and both encourage personnel to perform well and stay with your enterprise.

Recognizing achievements

Recognition hinges on the fact that your volunteers and paid staff want to feel that they're contributing to the enterprise and its mission. Recognizing people for their contributions is critical.

Here are some ways you can give this recognition to your staff and volunteers:

✔ **Present individuals with certificates, plaques, or letters acknowledging their contributions over a certain period of time.**

✔ **Hold an across-the-board recognition in the form of a dinner for all personnel who have served for one, three, five years or however long is appropriate to your situation.** *Note:* Although this approach expresses appreciation and recognition, it doesn't address *individual* contributions, which you still need to do in some way.

✔ **Call good personnel into the office individually to tell them how well they're performing and how valuable they are for your enterprise.** You don't have to give this informal pat on the back in the formal environment of the office — you can do it at any time and any place.

Of course, the formal annual review may well contain what amounts to pats on the back (see "Monitoring," earlier in this chapter for more on performance appraisals). But positive feedback where merited should come far more often than once or twice a year. You should give it whenever people are doing a great job.

✔ **Pay compliments for a particular job well done.** You can do this anytime that seems appropriate — in an office, while alone together, in a team or general meeting. It doesn't have to be long-winded. "Mary's fine work on the fundraising project has enabled us to . . ." (spoken during a meeting) would be great. The point is to be sure to compliment where compliments are due. They're greatly appreciated.

Rewarding people for a job well done

Rewarding means giving people something of monetary value. Recognition is great, but money talks.

How can you reward the paid staff and volunteers in your enterprise? Here are some suggestions:

✔ **For paid staff, a raise in pay is the ultimate reward.**

✔ **Reward paid staff with bonuses at the end of the year.** Don't feel like you have to give bonuses every year. Do what you can — even small bonuses are appreciated.

✔ **Give gifts of significant monetary value, such as artwork, gift certificates, tickets to a play or a game, books, or a free trip somewhere.** Make sure it has real value — a plate of home-baked cookies, however delicious, doesn't quite cut it. This reward works for paid staff and volunteers.

Volunteers are, by definition, eligible only for the third type of reward. They aren't in it for the money, anyway. The most rewarding of all, for them, is a good volunteer experience as they define it. Gifts can never equal this.

Avoiding burnout

No matter what kind of organization you're running, it's common for people to get burned out — they're physically and emotionally exhausted because of the long-term stress, frustration, and excessive obligation they face at their jobs or volunteer roles.

For volunteers, the leisure character of the volunteering undergoes a meta-morphosis — it slowly becomes an overbearing obligation and takes on a work-like quality instead of pleasure or fulfilment. In social enterprises, burn-out invariably also leads to a substantial reduction in a person's compassion for the target group — which is the biggest loss of all.

Burnout among paid staff commonly stems from being given more respon-sibilities than the exhausted worker can effectively handle in the time avail-able. Often, when burnout is an issue, the increase in responsibilities is not accompanied by a raise in pay, even though more hours of work may be demanded by the employer. But the burnout of paid staff is not usually the compassion burnout of volunteers. Most staff work for social enterprises because they need and like the job.

Whether with paid staff or volunteers, you want to do everything possible to avoid burnout. The good news is that wise management can go a long way toward controlling the conditions that lead to burnout. Here are some sugges-tions you can try to keep your volunteers and paid staff from burning out:

- **Know your personnel.** Learn as much as you can about each employee and volunteer, and write it down. The more you know about a person's skills, knowledge, and experience, the better you'll be able to find the best fit between that person and his role in the enterprise, lessening the chance of burnout.

- **Be realistic about expectations.** Assignments for employees and vol-unteers need to be manageable. Ones that are too difficult, too compli-cated, or too large risks burning someone out.

- **Use committees to spread out responsibilities and involve different people in everyday operations.** Committees are a good testing ground to see how much work is involved for a volunteer assigned to a committee.

- **Be clear in what you ask for.** Your paid staff and volunteers should know what you think they can do and what you think they're good at. There shouldn't be any ambiguity. Write it down and talk about it face-to-face with new employees and volunteers to get their buy-in.

- **Issue plenty of reminders about when things are due, and check in often.** Whether by phone or e-mail or face-to-face, make sure you know if someone has fallen behind in time to catch up and help that person get back on track. Give constructive feedback that will remedy the situation. Or, better yet, get someone help before he fails.

- **Highlight the importance of any project you've assigned.** Everyone wants to be valued.

- **Be a role model.** For example, demonstrate through your own work habits a reasonable pace for meeting responsibilities and an ability to maintain a cool head while doing so.

Managing the Finances

Financial management (administering income and expenses) is very complex in large, paid-staff nonprofit and for-profit organizations alike. In small enterprises, financial management can be very simple, primarily because there is seldom much money to manage.

Regardless of the size of your enterprise, you need a treasurer, even if (in extremely small groups) it's someone who informally fills that function.

Putting your treasurer to work

Treasurers are appointed or elected (depending on the system of governance at work in the enterprise) to administer the funds. In practice, treasurers receive revenues and donations sent to the group and then use them to pay, for example, wages and bills.

In smaller enterprises, the treasurer also keeps the enterprise's accounts: a monthly list of the money, goods, and services received; its expenditures; and other payments made to outside receivers. The treasurer balances the credits and debits on the two sides of the financial ledger.

In larger organizations, the income and outflow of money, goods, and services is so complicated that an accountant is usually hired to keep track of them. Smaller organizations often use accountants to verify the treasurer's work, typically at the end of the fiscal year.

Being closer than anyone in your enterprise to the flow of cash in and out, the treasurer is likely to become a sort of financial advisor as well. Treasurers can say, "Wait a minute, we can't afford that." They can say, "We can afford this because at the end of next month, certain large bills will have been paid." In other words, before spending money, consult your treasurer. Definitely consult your treasurer if you're having thoughts of giving pay raises and bonuses to paid staff and gifts of significant monetary value to volunteers.

Managing finances and people are intimately entwined. If the treasurer advises effectively about the use of money, there may be enough for raises, bonuses, or gifts, thereby easing some managerial concerns about motivation. There may even be enough to hire more paid staff or engage more volunteers, heading off possible burnout among present personnel.

Needless to say, there are limits to what a treasurer can do. Treasurers have little control over revenues — they just record what comes in and goes out.

Attempts at generating new revenue and keeping current sources from deteriorating usually fall to someone else in your enterprise, most commonly the board of directors (see Chapter 14). Treasurers only advise — their advice can be ignored by others who have the power to authorize expenditures. If this happens, the treasurer is forced to duly note those expenditures, even though he'd rather not.

Cutting costs

The treasurer is at the center of your enterprise when it comes to advising on how to reduce costs and on how to make your money go as far as possible. The treasurer knows better than anyone else how much money the group has, how much will probably be received, and how much will have to be spent paying bills and financing projects. But unless your treasurer is somehow intimately involved with every operation in your enterprise (an impossible requirement in large organizations), she likely doesn't know where costs can be cut while still retaining optimal effectiveness in reaching the enterprise's goals. The people who know best what could be cut are the ones routinely working in a particular operation.

For example, in an enterprise whose mission is to interest children in the fine arts, the person responsible for the media-based publicity of its programs may have a good idea where money could be saved without seriously reducing the effect of the publicity. Maybe publicity expenditures in a certain newspaper could be cut, because few parents or teachers who are interested in the fine arts actually read that paper. Or maybe Internet advertising is now more effective than TV advertising, and a savings could be found by switching to the former. These details aren't the kind that treasurers are normally familiar with.

Try to schedule regular meetings between your treasurer and various leaders in your enterprise. Doing so raises the chances of finding great ways of cutting costs, and also integrates your treasurer better in the organization.

Try to keep the goal of reducing costs in perspective. Cost-cutting should not be the end-all and be-all of your organization. A good rule to follow is to reduce costs where the reduction would save money that could be used to pursue other organizational goals — but not where the reduction would weaken pursuit of one or more of those goals. Budget cutting sometimes becomes a goal in itself. Your enterprise has important social goals to accomplish, and too little money available for this purpose will eventually spell failure.

Taking a Hard Look at Your Managerial Ethics

As a manager, you need to set some ground rules for yourself about what you will and won't do — for fairness and consistency's sake if nothing else.

Ethics are a set of moral principles that serve as a guide to acceptable behavior — in this case, behavior related to social entrepreneurship and the management of people who work in your enterprise. Being ethical means doing the right thing according to ethical principles.

Business ethics is a huge topic we don't have room to cover in much detail here. For a good read on the subject, see *Managing Business Ethics: Straight Talk about How to Do It Right*, by Linda K. Trevino and Katherine A. Nelson (Wiley), or *Essentials of Business Ethics: Creating an Organization of High Integrity and Superior Performance,* by Denis Collins (Wiley).

In this section, we briefly touch on three ethical issues around which problems frequently emerge in social enterprises: honesty, fairness, and avoiding exploitation of volunteers.

Talking the talk: Being honest with your team

Lying, cheating, stealing, and similar morally reprehensible behaviors are looked askance at in nearly all walks of life. But their presence in a social enterprise is *especially* disturbing. After all, your enterprise has come into existence based on its goal of correcting imperfect conditions, some of which may be morally wrong themselves. Dishonesty, especially by a social enterprise's leaders, is extremely unsettling. It undermines the group's mission by revealing that its leadership is hypocritical and two-faced, and it undermines morale among those who work for the enterprise.

Moral problems can occur in organizations of all kinds. Of course, many white lies are told sometimes to avoid, for example, hurting someone's feelings or provoking discussion of a trivial matter. Sometimes a white lie is useful and justified; other times it's useful but not justified, and still other times it's neither useful nor justified. Because such minor dishonesty revolves around particular situations, all we can advise in general is to be sure that your own white lies are both useful and justified. Otherwise, here too, honesty is the best policy.

It may seem obvious that organizational leaders should be honest. But it's also obvious if you've even glanced at headlines through the years that a number of leaders — including some high-profile people — choose the opposite ethical position.

Who's the fairest of them all: Treating your team members fairly

Fairness is probably a more elusive goal than honesty because what's considered fair is often a matter of interpretation. In theory, people act fairly when they treat others impartially or equitably according to commonly held rules or standards. A main problem in applying rules or standards of fairness is that some people may feel that they've been applied inconsistently or out of ignorance of certain critical information. The manager accused of unfairness may disagree, arguing that she *is* consistent or *is* aware of the information.

The best advice we can offer is that you recognize that, as a leader in your enterprise, you may at times be called unfair. Do your utmost to avoid this charge, of course, but having made the effort, you may still arrive at an impasse with an employee or volunteer claiming that unfairness has occurred. At the same time, catering to any particular person because he's crying foul may smack of favoritism. If a belief that favoritism has occurred gets around, it can undermine the larger organization.

Usually when one employee cries "unfair" about a policy or other employee, it's because she wasn't told about how she would be judged. For example, in giving a promotion to a recent but hardworking employee, a more tenured employee may complain or cry foul, thinking that the promotion should go to whoever had been there the longest. The problem in such a case is that the staff wasn't told the criteria for how promotions would be given.

Watch out for your own communication failures in not explaining (or even realizing you need to explain) something to the team. Don't assume everyone holds the same virtues and values as you do. Be clear with everyone about your expectations, which should be set out in the contract and job description (see "Drafting an employment contract," earlier in this chapter).

Favoritism can cause no end of resentment among the employees of an enterprise. It can spawn the poisonous feeling that however well a person does his job, it makes no difference — instead it is the person's "connections" that count. The perception that some people have ties to the people in management (such as you) who can elevate their chances for promotion and reward, and some don't, must never be allowed to exist. Morale can slip, and the next area to be hit could be employee productivity as members of the enterprise give up striving for excellence.

When all is said and done, if you've done your best to show fairness to everyone who works under you, then you can, with a clear conscience, stick to your position.

Making sure you're not exploiting your volunteers

By *exploitation* of volunteers, we mean taking undue advantage of their altruism and their willingness to serve the enterprise. Many volunteer coordinators or managers have erred in thinking that the cheery cooperation of a particular volunteer signals that she has unbounded enthusiasm for the volunteer role. The coordinator then piles on more responsibilities, which volunteers often accept because they're altruistic and want to serve. But that can't go on forever.

All volunteers have other things to do in life, even if they're retired from their careers and even if they truly love working in your enterprise. Many volunteers also volunteer elsewhere and engage in other serious leisure activities. Some have families, who make demands on their time. An all-too-common outcome of this situation is burnout among those volunteers who find it hard to say no. Don't push volunteers too far or exploit their good will toward the enterprise.

Check in once a month with your volunteers to make sure that they see their responsibilities as manageable. Doing so shows not only that you're concerned about keeping them from burning out, but also that you want to maintain the leisure quality of their volunteer experience (see Chapter 3 for more on leisure). Checking on stuff like this with your volunteers is particularly important during the first year or so that a person spends with your enterprise.

Chapter 18

No Man Is an Island: Teamwork

*T*eamwork is one of today's buzzwords and a highly prized one at that. Like motherhood and apple pie, teamwork seems to have no negative associations. It's often viewed, especially in sports and management circles, as an unalloyed good.

Fair enough. For the most part in this chapter, we agree and consider teamwork in this positive light. But we also note those cases in which teamwork can become problematic.

A *team* is a small number of people (from two to a couple dozen) formed to work, often temporarily, in a joint effort to achieve an end. *Teamwork* refers to acting as a team, which means that many of the members must have complementary skills.

Whether members of the team work *independently* or *interdependently* (through *collaboration,* discussed later in this chapter) to help the team reach its goal is one teamwork variable in social entrepreneurship. Most teams in social entrepreneurial organizations work independently — that is, the members pretty much do their own thing as they work on their parts of the project — although they're dependent on each other for the overall success of the project they're working on.

Is that a team or a committee?

Some may use the term *committee* for their teams. Independent teams could be considered committees, though the idea of a team implies that it's generally a more temporary group than many committees are. A steering committee or hiring committee, however, would be temporary. We don't think it matters much what you call your groups. If calling a working group a team instead of a committee gives it a certain cachet, go ahead. The idea is to inspire further its members to carry out the group's assignments and be proud of this involvement with your enterprise.

Three people working independently might make up a publicity team for their social enterprise. One of them contacts print and online media, another deals with radio and TV media, and the third sees to the design and printing of flyers and other promotional materials. Most, if not almost all, teamwork in social enterprises appears to be of this kind. Rarely is there the sort of teamwork typified by rigorous, interdependent roles, observed in sports teams.

Being a Team Player

Given that social enterprise teams around the world are overwhelmingly of the independent variety, being a *team player* boils down to carrying out as well as possible each individual role. Breaking it down a bit, being a team player means that the participant

✔ Has the required skill, knowledge, or experience to fill his or her role

✔ Is willing to do his or her best for the group

✔ Is willing to do so in a cooperative, pleasant manner

When such participation is a part of volunteering — when it's leisure-based (see Chapter 3) — the desire to be a team player follows logically from the participant's involvement.

When a person's participation is obligatory — not leisure — then you can't assume that the team member is naturally inclined to be a team player. It becomes necessary to monitor that person's contributions to the group.

Playing on a school sports team is often a person's first experience of being a team player. Trevor Dudley, a panelist on the African Economic Forum Panel (AEFP), once joked that he didn't realize he was a social entrepreneur until a few years ago when he was given a grant by the Ashoka Foundation (www.ashoka.org) for *being* a social entrepreneur. Dudley's entrepreneurial mission is called the Kids League, in which he uses sports to generate confidence and life skills in the children of Uganda. Many of these children live in poverty — often with the psychological consequences of prolonged civil hostilities. Dudley became concerned that, because Ugandan schools face considerable pressure to better the academic performance of their students, they've been cutting back on sports as part of their curricula. Dudley believes that if students don't learn to be effective team players, they may not grow up to work with others cooperatively or become as competent at setting goals and acting as leaders.

Being a Coach: Managing Teams

Teams don't exist in a void. They're given their goals by someone, report back to someone, and have their results assessed by someone. In other words, teams must be managed. Most of what we have to say about the broader aspects of managing social enterprises is covered in Chapter 18. This section focuses on managing teams.

The basics of team management

Because individual team members sometimes tend to stray off in their own direction, you as the leader of the social enterprise may find it necessary to coordinate your teams. One way to do this is to assign a team leader or captain; this person may be you or someone else, and she may or may not be a member of the team. A team leader must, of course, be able to work well with others and have a decent understanding of the team's purpose.

To assess how the work of the team is going, you want the team to meet regularly. Use agendas to track items and updates. There is an old saying, "You can't manage what you can't measure." So, critical items, tasks, and to-do's should be measured, and regular meetings help you do that. Holding regular meetings also helps with setting goals and deadlines and coordinating fundraising campaigns.

If used sparingly — not so many meetings that they become a burden — team meetings can be motivating in and of themselves. In the meetings, members learn not only what teammates have accomplished toward the team's purpose, but also about problems encountered and the effectiveness of the solutions invented to meet them. Team meetings are social gatherings and they're often occasions for storytelling, in which members recount interesting experiences in carrying out team goals. This camaraderie helps to develop a sense of progress toward realizing the team's purpose.

Team progress should be documented, but the documentation doesn't always have to be formal. Teams and their members must be accountable for what they do in the name of the team, but often reviewing the accomplishments of each member suffices as a record of the team's work (as in the publicity team we gave as an example in the introduction to this chapter).

For some teams, documentation is more critical. For example, a team formed to examine the financial records of the enterprise should at least produce a report; indeed, some nonprofits are permitted by law to use such an informal audit procedure. Also, a team that's sent into the community of the target of benefits to investigate their situation as it relates to the mission of the enterprise should keep a record of daily efforts and accomplishments, as well as write a report on their visit.

Daily records and final reports can be motivating, and anything that's motivating makes team management easier. Records and reports are a kind of stock taking, giving feedback to players about how well they're doing. Research on volunteers indicates that keeping records and reports plays a major role in whether volunteers remain interested in their assignments.

Firing up teams

When people talk about social entrepreneurs, they often say that social entrepreneurs must have a "passion" for what they're doing. The passion you share with those working with you may well be the key driving force needed to see the enterprise through to success, over the many hurdles along the way. How do you communicate passion and fire up your teams?

What fires up teamwork is often a combination of

- Passion for the mission of the enterprise
- Compassion or sympathy for its target of benefits
- A sense of urgency about your goals

The advantage of teams is that they bring teammates together face to face, where they can share these feelings to spur each other on. Small social enterprises may be able to act as one team.

Large-scale social enterprises — especially those whose membership includes participants in a social movement, which can draw thousands of members — usually lack this interpersonal intimacy. Here, members are at best able to interact directly with only a small number of like-minded enthusiasts. Becoming a member of a team in this situation helps counteract the estrangement inevitably felt in vast entrepreneurial projects. Remaining fired up with passion and urgency for a cause is a lot easier if you're routinely brought face to face with others of the same persuasion.

Sharing passion and urgency

Aseem K. Chauhan, chief executive of the Amity Innovation Incubator (www.amity.edu/aii), places passion and making money in for-profit social enterprises in perspective. He believes that social entrepreneurship has to do with making money. Nonetheless, he says the best entrepreneurs are those who pursue *passion* over money. The money will follow if they follow their ideals. Chauhan holds that such people develop remarkable businesses and, of course, make money while doing so. Because of the depressed economy, many are searching for a business that they can quickly get underway through private investment or releasing an initial public offering (IPO), which is when a company issues common stock or shares to the public for the first time to generate capital. Not all these businesses will succeed in the long run. To succeed, Chauhan maintains that they must have not just passion but long-term vision.

Habitat for Humanity (www.habitat.org) is a social enterprise whose mission is to build decent, affordable housing for low-income families throughout the world. Each house is built by a team of volunteer builders and finishers, including the family whose application for housing has been accepted by Habitat. Along with this family, the volunteers contribute to the project according to their skills. Those lacking skills in construction who nevertheless want to help are trained by Habitat to, for example, frame walls, install roofing, or sand and paint interior surfaces. All people recruited to build a house function in a coordinated manner as a team — that is, they perform their skills at the appropriate time, when the structure being built by their teammates has reached the stage where they can use it (for example, when the structure is now ready for the plumbing to be installed, the drywall to be painted, and the carpet to be laid).

All team missions are urgent in some degree. Otherwise, there'd be no need to establish them. Nevertheless, the urgency of a team's work may not always be evident to its newest members. Sure, in social enterprises formed to deal with natural disasters, health epidemics, and urban violence, for example, the urgency of the cause is obvious to all. But not so obvious is the urgency surrounding, say, improving reading skills, cleaning polluted air whose impurities can't be sensed without technical aid, or controlling largely invisible political corruption.

Sometimes you have to create, as much as possible, a sense of urgency for your teams. A high degree of urgency can galvanize a team into action, generating a corresponding level of excitement. New members have to be informed of the urgency of the team's work, so that they're inspired. Team leaders shouldn't take for granted that all team members understand and share a sense of urgency. It's up to the team leader to

- ✔ Present relevant facts and statistics on the urgent matter
- ✔ Show what might happen if the problem isn't promptly solved
- ✔ Identify who or what conditions have created the critical problem
- ✔ Identify the team's allies and resources and indicate how they can help deal with the problem
- ✔ Present a plan for solving the urgent problem in a timely way

Both passion and urgency can be contagious, spreading from team member to team member. Light a fire, and it'll spread!

Using the Power of Persuasion

How do you get your teams to do what you want them to do? When working with volunteers, using persuasion and influence are generally more effective than using your power of authority. Sure, you could lay down the law and try to force them to do what you want. But you'll get a lot farther if you convince them to see things your way.

When volunteers are persuaded by the reasoning of their leader that the course of action he wants them to take is effective and justified, volunteers become fired up. When colleagues are equals, influence is the only way of getting others to act in a certain way. But even where there are differences in power, you're often better off trying to persuade the less powerful to do something than you are trying to force them with threatening consequences.

In Chapter 16, we examine the nature of charisma and the role of the charismatic leader in social entrepreneurship. *Charisma* — the exceptional powers and qualities of a leader, beyond those of an ordinary person — where it exists, can be a potent basis for influence and persuasion on teams, especially in the early stages of an enterprise. Unfortunately, we're not all charismatic. And what works to persuade and influence during one stage of development of your enterprise may not necessarily work in other stages.

The Social Enterprise Knowledge Network (SEKN; www.sekn.org) studied team leadership and concluded that every leader develops his or her own style to carry out the roles for each stage of an enterprise's development. Mandatory formulas don't exist. Different leadership styles respond more effectively than others to management needs as the organization grows. Start-up processes are helped along by charismatic leaders exerting personal influence. During a later stage, social ventures benefit from managerial leadership (see Chapter 17 for a discussion of managerial leadership).

Power is hierarchical authority to demand actions from others. It can be a mighty handy resource because it allows you to get people to do something they would prefer not to do, but that you want them to do anyway. When you use power — and you should use it only as a last resort — try to avoid its more caustic applications. Don't insult, demean, or manipulate your team members. Refrain from sarcasm.

Collaborating with Your Team Members to Work toward a Common Goal

When you *collaborate* with other people, you work with them on a task or project. Teamwork is, by definition, collaboration. Collaboration happens through two types of teamwork:

- ✔ **Independent teamwork:** Independent teamwork involves team members working more or less on their own and coming together regularly to share what they're doing.

- ✔ **Interdependent teamwork:** Interdependent teamwork involves routine coordination and, depending on circumstances, timing of individual actions. Sports like hockey and basketball are examples of interdependent teamwork.

More than the sum of its parts

A main hurdle faced by teams in the United States, and possibly some other countries, is bias toward individual performance in groups instead of toward true teamwork. A glance at how Americans, for example, honor the superior performance of certain star players on sports teams demonstrates this attitude.

The message in this for you is to try to commend teamwork wherever it occurs, but also to recognize outstanding individual effort and accomplishment.

The special power of teams: Team idioculture

The social psychologist Gary Alan Fine once observed that small groups, including teams, whatever their size, generate their own *idiocultures* (distinctive sets of shared ideas that emerge in small groups).

Because idioculture is local culture, developed within and as an expression of a small group such as a team, it consists of a system of knowledge, beliefs, behaviors, experiences, and customs peculiar to that group of people and shared by them. Members use this idioculture system when interacting with one another, expecting that they will be understood by other members. As a social entrepreneur, you should encourage and develop the power of team idioculture.

Independent teamwork is — not surprisingly, given its name — less collaborative than interdependent teamwork. However, even in independent teamwork, individual contributions to the team's goal are collaborative, in the sense that they result in an overall group accomplishment. In the publicity team example mentioned earlier in this chapter, a sense of collaboration is shared by everyone on the team when it becomes evident that, throughout the community, the enterprise's visibility has risen noticeably thanks to the team's efforts.

To undertake some team building in your social enterprise, try organizing a session of staff lunchtime slideshows where you show images of people benefiting from your efforts. If you have a monthly newsletter, feature a different staffer every month describing his or her reasons for working for your organization. For a list of game and other activities designed to build teamwork, go to www.wilderdom.com, click "Index to Group Activities and Games," and then select the team-building category.

Collaboration often involves team members sharing practical tidbits about how to accomplish the team's goals. Useful tips, gained from experience, are passed along to others in team meetings to enhance their effectiveness.

Joining a team is one way to become empowered within a social enterprise. People become *empowered* by acquiring the power, authority, or license to do something. In teams, empowerment is limited by the need to collaborate with teammates in carrying out the team's business. But just being part of a team, having a role in achieving its goals, can be empowering.

Online tools, both the free kind and ones that cost money, are available for the social entrepreneur. Check out the free online wiki site PBworks (www.pbworks.com), Huddle.net, Google Documents (http://docs.google.com), ProjectSpaces (www.projectspaces.com), and especially Basecamp (www.basecamphq.com) for some terrific online collaboration action.

As an entrepreneur, you're automatically the boss. Therefore, you're empowered (by yourself) to make decisions and proceed toward the goals of your enterprise. You're also empowered to empower others, and a good way to do this is to form teams and give them goals to achieve.

Empowering the target of benefits

One of the goals of your enterprise may be to empower your target of benefits, as in the example of Principia (see the sidebar, "Principia's mutual healthcare," at the end of this chapter). Professor Marie Lisa M. Dacanay is Program Director of Social and Development Entrepreneurship at the Asian Institute of Management (AIM) Asian Center for Entrepreneurship. One of the goals of AIM is to encourage practitioner-oriented research that produces practical and easily applicable results.

Dacanay's work at AIM concentrates on empowering the poor and other marginalized people to benefit from their own social enterprises. She works with them to help them start and successfully run these organizations. Dacanay points out that the communities where the enterprises operate often experience positive social change, stemming from the fact of created jobs and an increased sense of well-being among employers and employees.

As always, at their best, social enterprises become a catalyst for broader changes in the community. For more information about the goals and accomplishments of AIM, go to www.aim.edu.ph.

What does empowering the target of benefits have to do with teams in social enterprises? Well, the goal of teams is often just that — to produce results that empower those targets. The Principia example shows how this can be done in the field of healthcare. But empowering a target doesn't always need to be reached by way of a team in a social enterprise. Dacanay's work suggests that her enterprises foster empowerment of their targets through efforts of the entire entrepreneurial group.

Principia's mutual healthcare

In 2005, following publication of a report by the National Health Service in Britain, a group of physicians formed a nonprofit social enterprise called Principia. Principia's mission was to try to solve the critical problem of optimal delivery of local primary-care services. The services in place at the time were judged inadequate for the job. Something had to be done.

Early on, a member of Principia came up with the idea of *mutual healthcare.* In this model, patients — one target of benefits — would be empowered by the opportunity to say how services affecting them should be planned and delivered. The other target, the physicians attending these patients, would become empowered to give more effective care and to perform their jobs with greater success. Principia formed a team to develop a workable response to existing government policy. This team strove to find ways that would enable fruitful collaborations between physicians, other healthcare professionals, and patients and their families.

Principia has been highly successful. It has since applied its model to dental practices, optometric and pharmaceutical care, and several other services established to promote healthy living.

Part V
The Part of Tens

The 5th Wave   By Rich Tennant

I'm gonna need help changing this tire. Do I have any volunteers?

VOLUNTEER CORP.

In this part . . .

Every *For Dummies* book concludes with a few short chapters that provide helpful information in list form, and this book is no exception. Here we offer a rich overview of areas ripe for social action — which we expect you'll find extremely helpful in the months and years ahead. We also tell you how to avoid many of the common mistakes inherent in social entrepreneurship. Other people have made the mistakes so you don't have to!

Chapter 19

Ten Great Areas for Social Entrepreneurial Action

In This Chapter

▶ Solving cultural and environmental problems

▶ Improving family, community living, health, and immigrant living standards

▶ Changing lifestyles and making a living

▶ Working on peace and reconciliation, community development, and urban issues

Maybe you're coming to this book because you know you want to help, but you're just not sure how or where. You want your life to matter. You want to make a difference. You're just having trouble focusing on one problem when you see so many worthwhile causes competing for attention. We don't blame you. In fact, we applaud you! You're coming to this subject with your heart in the right place. But before you can start your enterprise, you need to get focused on one problem, one cause, one issue that you'll work on.

In this chapter, we help you focus on ten key areas that are worthy of attention. We can't tell you what kind of business you should run, but we can give you some background information on areas you may not have considered. Read this chapter and see if any of these areas catches your attention. Then use this as a springboard to find out more information on those subjects, until you find the one area that's right for you.

You'll find occasional overlap between the areas, which means that your enterprise could kill two or more problems with one stone.

Culture Clash: Solving Cultural Problems in Your Community

You can focus your enterprise's efforts on your community's culture — either on matters that are philosophical or that have to do with language, literature, history, or the arts.

A social enterprise aimed at addressing an ethical issue in, say health (the abortion question), education (teaching evolution), or politics (corruption) would be tackling a philosophical question. Trying to facilitate retention and use of a foreign language in your community and establishing an enterprise to reach this goal, for example, is a linguistic concern; the goal may be to preserve competence in and use of the mother tongue of immigrants living in a society dominated by English speakers. You may even set up a group to promote a genre of literature, underappreciated events in history, or the love of certain kinds of little-known music. The problem to be solved by these enterprises is to correct what you see as a critical lack of understanding of an important art or field of knowledge.

Think about what's going on in your local culture. Do certain cultural problems keep cropping up in your community? Don't be afraid to think outside the box. Each local culture is different. Maybe yours has a unique challenge that no social enterprise has addressed yet.

It's Not Easy Being Green: Tackling Environmental Problems Head-on

Social problems emerge around our use — or misuse — of the natural environment: air, water, land, ice and snow, flora, and fauna. Climate change is also a growing environmental problem. Polluted air, water, and soil have long caused resource troubles and misery around the world, and numerous social enterprises have sprung up to help remedy those concerns. But there is plenty of room for more action on this front. Pollution alone remains a vital area for entrepreneurial action, as does the conservation of natural resources.

For example, erosion is an important, if relatively unsexy conservational issue. It's not the same process as pollution, but its results have a similar effect: depletion of the amount and quality of usable soil, especially for agriculture.

Water conservation, primarily for drinking, cooking, and industrial needs (including agriculture), is a growing challenge in many parts of the world. The need to conserve water goes beyond human supplies, extending to the supplies available in nature so that animals, plants, and trees may thrive. Even where water is plentiful, drawing it from lakes and rivers and providing it to people and industries that rely on it is often fraught with problems.

Questions of water purity and its additives (such as fluoride and chlorine) are also important ones we have to answer, and many social entrepreneurs are doing just that.

Protecting certain flora and fauna is ever more challenging due to the misuse of the environment, encroaching human habitation into previously wild areas, and the emerging effects of climate change. Efforts to identify and protect specific endangered species of fish, birds, and animals continue. Despite the good work done by big social entrepreneurial organizations like Greenpeace and the Sierra Club, we aren't winning the battle on many of these issues, which means much work remains to be done. Greenpeace uses nonviolent, but confrontational, methods to expose global environmental problems. The Sierra Club mounts major national campaigns to generate change in several problems areas — among them health and the environment, protection of biodiversity, and transition to a sustainable economy.

But more work remains to be done in all these areas. You could be the one to do it!

Providing the Comforts of Home: Food, Clothing, and Shelter

What can you do as a social entrepreneur to make family and community life better in your part of the world (or elsewhere)? For example, you may want to raise the quality of life of a target group by providing improved lighting, heating, water, heating, housing, clothing, or food.

Many social enterprises are already at work in these areas. Some of the biggest ones include

- **Habitat for Humanity,** which provides housing to families in need. Habitat volunteers work alongside the future homeowners to build their new homes, and in turn for their sweat equity (working not only on their own homes but on the homes of others), the future homeowners receive the homes at a greatly reduced cost. They still have to provide a down payment and make monthly mortgage payments to Habitat, and Habitat uses those mortgage payments to build houses for other families.

✔ **Oxfam,** which works with people to secure their basic human rights. It believes that citizens of the world can end poverty and injustice by working together in solidarity to assert their basic human rights. People blocked from opportunity often need to change laws, customs, and policies. Without these changes, real progress against poverty can't be achieved. Oxfam's economic and political analyses help change the minds of powerful decision makers.

✔ **The Salvation Army,** which seeks to bring Christian salvation to the poor, destitute, and hungry by meeting both their physical and spiritual needs. It has a semi-military structure that operates to extend a religious ministry to all people, regardless of ages, gender, color, or creed. A main part of its mission is to advance the Christian religion. Although the Salvation Army started as a mission to alleviate poverty, it now has other charitable objects that are beneficial to society or to mankind as a whole.

✔ **The Light up the World Foundation,** which believes that economic and sustainable light and energy solutions can offer significant opportunities to impoverished individuals and their communities. Sustainable light and energy lead to advances in education, household safety, cleaner indoor living, and significant economic savings. For local distributors, sustainable light and energy products translate into livelihood and family support. Globally, these products contribute to reduced greenhouse gases and other kinds of pollution.

Although these organizations are doing great work, they can't do it all themselves. A lot remains to be done in the area of basic living standards. After all, if the big organizations had solved the problems, they wouldn't be needed anymore, right?

You can use the successes of the big guys as a model for your own enterprise. You may start up an enterprise to solve problems in standard of living that they have yet to tackle. For example, water quality, which is both an environmental issue and one of comfort at home, must always be tackled locally (because water quality differs from one community to the next), and it's one problem crying out for entrepreneurial action. Another entrepreneurial area that may be ripe for consideration is controlling dangerous insects, plants, and animals where they threaten people. Perhaps there is more to do in your local area than a big organization could hope to tackle.

Heal Thyself: Tackling Health Problems

It's no secret that healthcare is a major problem. Many Americans are uninsured and have limited access to quality care. If healthcare is your passion, you may want your social enterprise to hone in on this arena.

If you want to get involved in the healthcare field, you can focus your efforts in one of two main areas:

- ✔ **Injuries and the chronic and infectious diseases:** Here you might create an organization that fights cancer, heart disease, malaria, HIV, or various sexually transmitted diseases. Numerous social enterprises focus their efforts on this area of healthcare, but there's plenty of work left to go around.

  Social enterprises can also be established to foster change and solve problems in lesser-known fields. You might consider starting an organization to promote medical use of an alternative form of treatment, such as using traditional herbs, vitamin therapy, massage, or even spiritual healing. Or you might work for the betterment of patients' rights, closer physician-patient relations, or improvement in a particular community health facility.

- ✔ **Preventive medicine:** Here you would focus on ways to *prevent* people from getting sick in the first place. This area encompasses such diverse fields as personal and public sanitation, mental and physical fitness, nutrition, tobacco use, workplace health and safety, or other community health measures. Areas such as quality garbage collection, water quality, and safety in public transit could also be filed under this heading.

  Mothers Against Drunk Driving (MADD) as well as various anti-smoking and anti-fluoridation groups exemplify social enterprises in preventive medicine.

Movement of the People: Migration and Immigration

The movement of people within and between countries has never been greater than it is today.

Migrants move within their society or country, whereas *immigrants* and refugees move between countries. *Refugees* are distinguished from immigrants by the fact that they're forced to move, typically through threats of death, torture, starvation, disease, and the like. People *emigrate* (become immigrants in another country) for less life-threatening reasons, though they're still driven to find, for example, employment, live under a more acceptable political system, or join relatives who have already emigrated.

All these folks can use help wherever they can get it. Social enterprises are often established to help immigrants and refugees integrate themselves into their host societies, to try to alleviate racial and ethnic tensions that may arise there, and, in some countries, to promote multiculturalism as a way of reducing these tensions. Many such enterprises operate locally, working directly with the newcomers. The United States is a land of immigrants, many of whom don't always get fair treatment, which means plenty of opportunity is there for your social enterprise to target them.

Migrants, in part because they're presumed to know their own country, are much less commonly targets of such help. The Welcome Wagon, a North American social enterprise that welcomes homeowners who are new to a community, has mostly served migrants. You might know of migrants in your community who could benefit from a social enterprise.

Ways of Living: Addressing Lifestyle Issues

Social enterprises have sprung up around a problem inherent in daily or routine living. Many social entrepreneurs hope to solve problems related to race, religion, birth control, consumption and consumer waste, the concerns of age groups such as youth and the elderly, and even leisure activities.

For example, you might organize to promote the importance of religion (or some aspect of a particular religion), to educate people on safe birth control and its methods, or to point out the wastefulness of our consumer ways.

Many social enterprises have been set up to help youth, people with disabilities, and the elderly; some of these groups try to steer their targets toward fulfilling leisure activities appropriate to their age.

Other groups exist to advance a particular kind of leisure, usually educational. Consider the Share the Universe project of the Astronomical Society of the Pacific, whose mission is to promote amateur astronomy.

What lifestyle issues do you see as problematic in your community?

Working for a Living: Helping Folks Find Work

Work is, directly or indirectly, vitally important for almost all the world's population. People need work for their livelihood, and, if they can't get it, they need social entrepreneurs like you to help provide the goods and services that make their living possible. Often you're dealing here with the question of *right livelihood:* What is a just wage and what are the proper working conditions for the employee on the job?

Social enterprises often spring up around the need for jobs. Small for-profit enterprises help provide job leads, and social entrepreneurial credit arrangements often help finance these for-profits. You may be able to help solve problems in the workplace, too — for example, worker exploitation, workplace health and safety, and worker health and pension plans.

Most labor unions started as social enterprises bent on solving such problems.

Blessed Are the Peacemakers: Working for Peace and Reconciliation

There is ample opportunity for entrepreneurial work intended to prevent or put an end to war, terrorist activity, torture, and the like. Amnesty International and the International Committee for the Red Cross famously serve in these areas.

Working in this area can be highly risky. Risk is something you have to consider very carefully. Only you can determine what level of potential danger you're comfortable with.

In general, you can probably have the greatest impact trying to promote peace and reconciliation by striving to eliminate the causes of conflict found in living standards, health, lifestyles, personal and community development, urban life, making a living, and the environment. Be aware, however, that enterprises in this area are often controversial. They may overlap political, spiritual, and social boundaries inside of which are some emotional differences in attitude and belief.

Back to School: Education and Personal and Community Development

Social entrepreneurs have created organizations that cover all types of formal education: primary through secondary, university, and technical. Many enterprises are devoted to adult and continuing education, as well as to civic education. Some organizations even teach people how to be good citizens.

Social enterprises may focus on less formal personal development as it relates to community development. For example, one area is encouraging civic engagement (as in meeting civic obligations). This might include getting out the vote in elections, keeping domestic property clean and neat, and beefing up lighting to make parking areas safe. Enterprises may be developed to stimulate community involvement or participation in any aspect of community life (such as singing in a community chorus, playing baseball in a city-wide league, and volunteering at a residence for the elderly). A social enterprise established to foster a certain kind of corporate social responsibility (see Chapter 8) constitutes yet another kind of community development.

Enterprises formed to solve governmental problems — for example, corruption, inadequate electoral representation, and weak representation of a political point of view — also fit in this category.

The Big City: Alleviating the Problems of Urban Life

Cities generate a variety of problems that often, in turn, give rise to social entrepreneurship. Groups have been formed to reduce theft or violence (such as block-watch programs and organizations such as Guardian Angels, which enlists unarmed volunteers to patrol neighborhoods), to build new urban housing or reduce existing housing density, and even to foster a greater sense of community in cities, so that people know their neighbors and look out for one another instead of being indifferent.

Public transit has its own set of problems — including violence, robbery, lack of hygiene and cleanliness, and scheduling — which are capable of generating entrepreneurial action. Other urban services that operate in the spheres of health, recycling, trash collection, and leisure and recreation can also become causes for social entrepreneurs to take up.

Chapter 20

Ten Common Mistakes to Avoid

In This Chapter

▶ Managing to avoid managerial mistakes

▶ Averting organizational mistakes

▶ Looking out for outlook mistakes

▶ Avoiding mistakes in personal relations

*U*nfortunately, the road to successful entrepreneurship has some sharp curves and big potholes, any of which are capable of seriously delaying you as you strive to reach your destination — which is fulfilling your mission. In this chapter, we put some orange cones up around these areas so you can steer clear and be on your way.

Overlooking Potential Leaders

You put yourself at a great disadvantage when you fail to recognize potential leaders in your enterprise.

Constantly be on the watch for individuals who show exceptional commitment to your mission, work well with others (especially the target of benefits), are able to take charge of a task or assignment, and show signs of leadership ability (see Chapter 16 for more on leadership). Manning such a "lookout" should be a routine procedure for you and other leaders in your enterprise; in fact, this senior group of leaders should regularly discuss which people may be admitted to their ranks.

Encouraging and promoting leadership from within your organization is key to building its future.

Mismanaging Volunteers

Ineffective management of volunteers is another serious mistake when running nonprofit social enterprises. If you're the one who personally manages volunteers, be sure to adhere as faithfully as possible to the principles set out in Chapter 17 — including carefully training, directing, and monitoring the efforts of your paid staff and volunteers in an ethical and honest manner.

If someone else manages your volunteers, you *must,* using these same principles, routinely monitor him to make sure he's managing the volunteers well.

Getting Too Bureaucratic

Over-bureaucratization is a common mistake that many entrepreneurs make, whether the enterprise is a nonprofit or a for-profit establishment. In Chapter 13, we describe the many problems that the subtle process of creeping bureaucratization can create.

You have no choice but to be aware of this unwanted tendency toward more and more bureaucracy and do everything you can to counteract it. Make sure that other leaders and administrators in the enterprise also remain conscious of the perils of over-bureaucratization.

Incorporating When You Don't Have To

Incorporating when incorporation is unnecessary is a more common mistake than many people realize. Why do businesses incorporate if they don't have to? Because there's something glamorous about having your own legally recognized enterprise, with its distinctive seal and, where possible and useful, its special charitable status expressed as a unique identification number. For-profit entrepreneurs have no choice but to seek such incorporation — but many nonprofit entrepreneurs do have a choice.

Small social enterprises, usually those driven by a local mission, can accomplish their goals without becoming legally established. They can, among other things, establish and adhere to their own democratic procedures, collect dues, develop a budget, hold annual general meetings, and still not be incorporated groups.

Before launching into the corporate form of organization, consider very carefully the advantages and disadvantages of incorporation that we set out in Chapter 14.

Failing to Spot Trends

You can easily get caught up in the routine operations of your enterprise — after all, they're what move you along toward your goals. However, if you keep your head down too much and ignore the broader trends and social context affecting your enterprise, you're likely setting yourself up for failure. In Chapter 5, we examine some of today's important trends, including women's issues, multiculturalism, and corporate social responsibility.

Important demographic changes may also be at work — for example, changes in age, sex, education, and ethnicity of your target population. You have to stay abreast of these changes and their effects on your enterprise.

Being Unrealistic about Funding

Research has shown that nonprofit groups are often unrealistic about funding. They're inclined to think that finding money to support their enterprise and its mission is easier than it really is. So, when you're seeking government or foundation grants, for example, go into it with a positive attitude, but don't count on success.

Competition for funding is typically fierce, and granting programs may be fickle — they may change their requirements on short notice. By all means apply for funding, but have alternatives in mind in case you get rejected, because you often will be. Even raffles, auctions, bake sales, and so forth can have disappointing results.

To avoid facing impossible financial commitments, be realistic about the outcome of any funding ventures.

Failing to Innovate

Failing to innovate is another grievous mistake — and a tricky one to boot. It's tricky because, though you can't really know it in advance, some innovations turn out to be duds. Our advice: Constantly look for and carefully consider new ways of running your enterprise and trying to reach your goals. In fact, you can never improve too much in seeking ways to innovate. On the other hand, don't make innovation your religion.

Change for change's sake alone — by which we mean change merely to have something new in your enterprise — could be harmful to its health and to its mission.

Choosing the Wrong Name

In Chapter 10, we cover the ins and outs of choosing a name for your enterprise, and we caution against selecting a name that's uninformative. Cutesy names that fail to quickly, clearly, and imaginatively reveal the nature and mission of their enterprises are all too common. What's worse is when such mis-names actually suggest quite *different* entities than their leaders are trying to develop. Don't follow examples of this sort (see Chapter 10).

Not Having a Good Web Site

In this digital day and age, being without a Web site can spell disaster for a social enterprise, no matter how small. More and more people are turning to the Internet in search of information, and they expect to learn about your organization online. True, some old-school enthusiasts who really want to track you down may persevere by turning to a phone book, social network, or other online resources that may mention you. But most would-be members won't be so motivated, which means you'll lose them. In Chapter 10, we cover the minimum features your Web site should have.

Not Using the Media to Your Advantage

If you don't take advantage of the media — and by *media* we include social media such as Twitter, Facebook, LinkedIn, and other similar services — you're making a potentially big strategic mistake. In Chapter 12, we set out in detail various strategies and ways of harnessing the media to your entrepreneurial advantage. Dealing with the media requires extra effort, to be sure, but it can also generate significant payoffs. Social enterprises and their missions require visibility. Media visibility brings the group to the attention of funding bodies and individual benefactors. It promotes the social cause of your organization and the need for change in a particular sphere of community life. Finally, it can inspire people to join you in your work toward betterment of the target.

Appendix

Resources

· ·

*M*ost of the resources we list in this appendix have either easily accessible books or Web pages. Some are also mentioned elsewhere in this book. We've compiled them all here to provide a quick reference for you.

Before we dive into more specific categories of resources, we start you off with some important direct supporters of social entrepreneurs, including foundations, alliances, resource centers, and more:

- ✔ **Ashoka** (www.ashoka.org) is a nonprofit organization devoted to developing social entrepreneurship as a profession. So far, it has elected and supported more than 2,000 Ashoka Fellows in 60 countries.

- ✔ **Authenticity Consulting's Social Entrepreneurship Toolbox** (www.authenticityconsulting.com/npbd/toolbox.pdf) is a rich compendium of many more social entrepreneurship resources, some of which are free, and some of which cost money. The site also lists several books and workbooks, consultants in the nonprofit area, and organizations on the Web.

- ✔ **Business Exchange**, an online service offered by *BusinessWeek* magazine (http://bx.businessweek.com/social-entrepreneurship) has an extensive section on for-profit social entrepreneurship. It covers a large range of subjects of interest to commercial social entrepreneurs.

- ✔ **Echoing Green** (www.echoinggreen.org) is another fellowship-oriented nonprofit that supports social entrepreneurs. Whereas Ashoka Fellows are often high-profile figures, Echoing Green supports undiscovered social entrepreneurs. The organization emphasizes seed funding for new organizations at their earliest stages.

- ✔ **The Schwab Foundation for Social Entrepreneurship** (www.schwabfound.org) does not give grants, but it supports social entrepreneurship through research, publications, media, and organized events. Professor Klaus Schwab and his wife, Hilde, created this nonprofit, independent organization in 1998 in order to promote social innovation.

- ✔ **Serious Leisure** (www.soci.ucalgary.ca/seriousleisure) has its own Web site at the University of Calgary. Here you can find out more about serious, casual, and project-based leisure. Articles 16, 17, and 21 in the "Leisure Reflections" series in the Digital Library contain especially useful information on volunteers and volunteering.

✔ **The Skoll Foundation** (www.skollfoundation.org) was created in 1999 by Jeff Skoll, the first president of eBay. The foundation supports social entrepreneurs and related researchers in an attempt to build social-sector capacity and infrastructure. The foundation makes grants in excess of $40 million per year.

✔ **Social Enterprise Alliance** (www.se-alliance.org) is a membership network that advocates for social entrepreneurs, acts as an information and education hub (see its online Knowledge Center, which is open to everyone), and hosts the large and popular Social Enterprise Summit.

✔ **Social Venture Network** (www.svn.org) is a membership network, but is designed for "leading social entrepreneurs," including CEOs and social investors. Its online Tools & Best Practices library is open to everyone.

The Foundation Center (www.foundationcenter.org) is another important, terrific resource, which we discuss later in this chapter.

Finding Funding

Gifts In Kind International (www.giftsinkind.org) in the United States and **In Kind Canada** (www.inkindcanada.ca) represent *in-kind funding*, in which an organization matches contributions made by others. This type of funding can be of great benefit to social enterprises. Both organizations are devoted to making in-kind gifts to other charities, and both are nationwide charities whose mission is to provide smaller charities and nonprofits with access to practical resources typically available only to larger organizations.

One of the trickiest aspects of funding is writing grant proposals. For a deeper look into this process than we can provide here, we recommend Beverly A. Browning's *Grant Writing For Dummies,* 2nd Edition (Wiley). We also urge you to explore **Nonprofit Guides: Grant Tools for Nonprofit Organizations** (http://npguides.org/guide), a set of Internet links to grant makers, grant-seeking resources, and glossaries.

Also consider the various "angel-investor" groups and networks, which are interested in the social entrepreneurial work that you do or want to do. Among them are **Investors' Circle** (www.investorscircle.net) and **Good Capital** (www.goodcap.net).

See Chapter 9 for many more ideas on funding nonprofit social enterprises.

Creating an Identity

In Chapter 10 we devote several pages to the process of creating an identity for your social enterprise. An important component of your identity is developing an attractive and effective home page for your Web site. There are plenty of free Web site templates on the Internet (try Googling **free web template**), but not all are appropriate or professional enough in appearance. If you're interested in shelling out a bit of cash for something better, try **Buy Templates** (www.buytemplates.net).

Advertising and marketing bureaus provide services such as designing logos and other aspects of branding — you can find them by searching the Internet and, if your community is large enough, in your local phone book as well.

Interbrand (www.interbrand.com), in business since 1974, maintains a collection of informative articles on many of the different facets of successful branding (www.interbrand.com/best_global_brands_intro.aspx).

Don't reinvent the wheel: Use the Internet to find inspiration when creating your identity. Try Googling **catchy slogans**. You'll find innumerable pithy mottos from a wide variety of areas of commercial life.

Incorporating Your Social Enterprise

If you're planning on incorporating as a for-profit social enterprise, we suggest you read *Incorporating Your Business For Dummies* by The Company Corporation (Wiley).

Also, check out the guide to corporate bylaws written by the **Citizens Media Law Project** (www.citmedialaw.org/legal-guide/bylaws-nonprofit-corporations). *Bylaws,* as we discuss in Chapter 14, are the rules and procedures for how corporations, including nonprofits, should be governed and operated. The Citizens Media Law Project says you can write satisfactory bylaws without hiring a lawyer.

We also recommend Anthony Mancuso's book *How to Form a Nonprofit Corporation*, 9th Edition (NOLO Press). Mancuso, a lawyer, guides you through the process of creating bylaws appropriate to nonprofit organizations, including nonprofit social enterprises.

Because bylaws are typically quite lengthy and detailed, we recommend that you look at some examples. **The Foundation Center** (http://foundationcenter.org/getstarted/faqs/html/samplebylaws.html) is a good source of links to several samples.

Managing Paid Staff and Volunteers

Resources dealing with many aspects of the management of small and medium-size enterprises of various kinds abound in print and online. We recommend starting with *Managing For Dummies,* 2nd Edition, by Bob Nelson and Peter Economy (Wiley).

As we point out in Chapter 17, there are differences between managing paid staff and managing volunteers. Most management books focus on paid staff — for details on managing volunteers, we recommend a book by Katherine Noyes Campbell and Susan J. Ellis called *The (Help!) I-Don't-Have-Enough-Time Guide to Volunteer Management* (Energize). This slim volume is especially helpful for administrators who have to tack volunteer management onto a long list of other tasks, which is the reality for many social entrepreneurs.

An excellent treatment of the problems related to volunteers is available in a free PDF from **Voluntary Works** called "Dealing with Volunteer Problems" (http://www.voluntaryworks.org.uk/action-southbeds/documents/DealingwithVolunteerProblems.pdf).

The Volunteer Development Agency (www.diycommitteeguide.org/category/tags/volunteers) provides several free documents that deal with many aspects of working with volunteers, including inducting, recruiting, and developing volunteers in your enterprise.

Burnout is a perennial problem for volunteers — and it's obviously a problem you want to avoid in your enterprise. The **Risk Management Association** (www.rmahq.org/RMA/Chapters/managing_volunteers.htm) presents a range of helpful suggestions for keeping volunteers busy, happy, and rewarded.

Pursuing an Education in Social Entrepreneurship

Major universities, especially through business schools, are now investing in research and teaching social entrepreneurship, especially from the for-profit side. The following are some of the more committed schools:

- **Canadian Centre for Social Entrepreneurship at the University of Alberta:** http://apps.business.ualberta.ca/ccse

- **Center for the Advancement of Social Entrepreneurship at Duke University's Fuqua School of Business:** www.caseatduke.org

✔ **Center for Social Innovation at Stanford Graduate School of Business:** http://csi.gsb.stanford.edu

✔ **Skoll Center for Social Entrepreneurship at Oxford University:** www. sbs.ox.ac.uk/centres/skoll

✔ **Social Enterprise Initiative at Harvard Business School:** www.hbs. edu/socialenterprise

✔ **Social Enterprise Program at Columbia University's Business School:** www4.gsb.columbia.edu/socialenterprise

There are at least two academically oriented networks — intent on developing social-enterprise intellectual capital through research, education, and networking — that are well worth visiting:

✔ **The Social Enterprise Knowledge Network:** www.sekn.org/en

✔ **The University Network for Social Entrepreneurship:** www. universitynetwork.org

Index

Business/Accounting & Bookkeeping

Bookkeeping For Dummies
978-0-7645-9848-7

eBay Business
All-in-One For Dummies,
2nd Edition
978-0-470-38536-4

Job Interviews
For Dummies,
3rd Edition
978-0-470-17748-8

Resumes For Dummies,
5th Edition
978-0-470-08037-5

Stock Investing
For Dummies,
3rd Edition
978-0-470-40114-9

Successful Time
Management
For Dummies
978-0-470-29034-7

Computer Hardware

BlackBerry For Dummies,
3rd Edition
978-0-470-45762-7

Computers For Seniors
For Dummies
978-0-470-24055-7

iPhone For Dummies,
2nd Edition
978-0-470-42342-4

Laptops For Dummies,
3rd Edition
978-0-470-27759-1

Macs For Dummies,
10th Edition
978-0-470-27817-8

Cooking & Entertaining

Cooking Basics
For Dummies,
3rd Edition
978-0-7645-7206-7

Wine For Dummies,
4th Edition
978-0-470-04579-4

Diet & Nutrition

Dieting For Dummies,
2nd Edition
978-0-7645-4149-0

Nutrition For Dummies,
4th Edition
978-0-471-79868-2

Weight Training
For Dummies,
3rd Edition
978-0-471-76845-6

Digital Photography

Digital Photography
For Dummies,
6th Edition
978-0-470-25074-7

Photoshop Elements 7
For Dummies
978-0-470-39700-8

Gardening

Gardening Basics
For Dummies
978-0-470-03749-2

Organic Gardening
For Dummies,
2nd Edition
978-0-470-43067-5

Green/Sustainable

Green Building
& Remodeling
For Dummies
978-0-470-17559-0

Green Cleaning
For Dummies
978-0-470-39106-8

Green IT For Dummies
978-0-470-38688-0

Health

Diabetes For Dummies,
3rd Edition
978-0-470-27086-8

Food Allergies
For Dummies
978-0-470-09584-3

Living Gluten-Free
For Dummies
978-0-471-77383-2

Hobbies/General

Chess For Dummies,
2nd Edition
978-0-7645-8404-6

Drawing For Dummies
978-0-7645-5476-6

Knitting For Dummies,
2nd Edition
978-0-470-28747-7

Organizing For Dummies
978-0-7645-5300-4

SuDoku For Dummies
978-0-470-01892-7

Home Improvement

Energy Efficient Homes
For Dummies
978-0-470-37602-7

Home Theater
For Dummies,
3rd Edition
978-0-470-41189-6

Living the Country Lifestyle
All-in-One For Dummies
978-0-470-43061-3

Solar Power Your Home
For Dummies
978-0-470-17569-9

Internet
Blogging For Dummies,
2nd Edition
978-0-470-23017-6

eBay For Dummies,
6th Edition
978-0-470-49741-8

Facebook For Dummies
978-0-470-26273-3

Google Blogger
For Dummies
978-0-470-40742-4

Web Marketing
For Dummies,
2nd Edition
978-0-470-37181-7

WordPress For Dummies,
2nd Edition
978-0-470-40296-2

Language & Foreign Language
French For Dummies
978-0-7645-5193-2

Italian Phrases
For Dummies
978-0-7645-7203-6

Spanish For Dummies
978-0-7645-5194-9

Spanish For Dummies,
Audio Set
978-0-470-09585-0

Macintosh
Mac OS X Snow Leopard
For Dummies
978-0-470-43543-4

Math & Science
Algebra I For Dummies,
2nd Edition
978-0-470-55964-2

Biology For Dummies
978-0-7645-5326-4

Calculus For Dummies
978-0-7645-2498-1

Chemistry For Dummies
978-0-7645-5430-8

Microsoft Office
Excel 2007 For Dummies
978-0-470-03737-9

Office 2007 All-in-One
Desk Reference
For Dummies
978-0-471-78279-7

Music
Guitar For Dummies,
2nd Edition
978-0-7645-9904-0

iPod & iTunes
For Dummies,
6th Edition
978-0-470-39062-7

Piano Exercises
For Dummies
978-0-470-38765-8

Parenting & Education
Parenting For Dummies,
2nd Edition
978-0-7645-5418-6

Type 1 Diabetes
For Dummies
978-0-470-17811-9

Pets
Cats For Dummies,
2nd Edition
978-0-7645-5275-5

Dog Training For Dummies,
2nd Edition
978-0-7645-8418-3

Puppies For Dummies,
2nd Edition
978-0-470-03717-1

Religion & Inspiration
The Bible For Dummies
978-0-7645-5296-0

Catholicism For Dummies
978-0-7645-5391-2

Women in the Bible
For Dummies
978-0-7645-8475-6

Self-Help & Relationship
Anger Management
For Dummies
978-0-470-03715-7

Overcoming Anxiety
For Dummies
978-0-7645-5447-6

Sports
Baseball For Dummies,
3rd Edition
978-0-7645-7537-2

Basketball For Dummies,
2nd Edition
978-0-7645-5248-9

Golf For Dummies,
3rd Edition
978-0-471-76871-5

Web Development
Web Design All-in-One
For Dummies
978-0-470-41796-6

Windows Vista
Windows Vista
For Dummies
978-0-471-75421-3

How-to?
How Easy.